VICTORIAN CONTEXTS

Victorian Contexts

Literature and the Visual Arts

Murray Roston

NEW YORK UNIVERSITY PRESS
Washington Square, New York

First published in the U.S.A. in 1996 by
NEW YORK UNIVERSITY PRESS
Washington Square
New York, N.Y. 10003

Library of Congress Cataloging-in-Publication Data
Roston, Murray.
Victorian contexts : literature and the visual arts / Murray
Roston.
p.   cm.
includes bibliographical references and index.
ISBN 0–8147–7485–7
1. English literature—19th century—History and criticism.
2. Art and literature—England—History—19th century.
3. Aesthetics, English—19th century.   I. Title.
PR468.A76R67   1996
820.9'008—dc20   96–3309
                                                      CIP

Printed in Great Britain

Contents

Contents

List of Illustrations

Illustrations 1, 3, 4, 5, 6, 17, 18, 22, 23, 24, and 30 were supplied by Art Resource, New York.

Acknowledgments

In the course of preparing this book, I have had the privilege of spending three separate years as a visitor at UCLA, and I should like to express my deep appreciation to the successive chairs of the English department, Professors Jonathan F.S. Post, Robert Watson, and Eric Sundquist, as well as to Professor Arnold Band, chair of the Comparative Literature programme, for the hospitality and friendship which they, together with their colleagues, extended to me. Apart from the pleasure of teaching there and of discussing ideas with scholars and students sharing my interests, the visits provided me with access to research libraries not available to me in Israel, and for that I am especially grateful.

A number of friends were kind enough to comment on various chapters while this book was in manuscript, among them Albert Boime, Menahem Fisch, Regenia Gagnier, G.B. Tennyson, and Alexander Welsh, and I am duly appreciative of their comments. Excerpts from this book have appeared as articles in *The Dickens Studies Annual* (1994) and in *Homes and Homelessness in the Victorian Imagination* (New York, 1995), and are incorporated here by permission of the editors. I would also like to express my warm gratitude to Mr Timothy Bartlett, Mr Tim Farmiloe, and Ms Charmian Hearne for their editorial encouragement and support.

Lastly, to my wife Faith I offer, as always, my affectionate thanks for her delightful company, as well as her valuable critical comments, during our frequent visits to art centres throughout the world.

Bar Ilan University　　　　　　　　　　　　　　　　MURRAY ROSTON
Ramat Gan, Israel

Acknowledgements

Introduction

The acceptance within contemporary criticism of the concept of 'intertextuality', of cultural interchange crossing the boundaries between the media, has provided fresh validation for interdisciplinary studies. Within the sphere of literature, post-modernists have come to acknowledge how authors inevitably bring to the process of composition minds steeped in previous reading, absorbing and transforming themes, images, phrases, and associations derived from the texts of others; and such recognition has been extended to include, as part of that creative process, the incorporation of elements drawn from the broader matrix of communicative experience prevalent in that generation. The 'I' which approaches the task of writing, as Roland Barthes has argued, is itself to be seen as a plurality of other texts and codes assimilated from outside sources, those sources not always literary.[1] As a result, current gender assumptions, power struggles in the political arena, shifts in class structure, and fluctuations in the economic sphere are now perceived as *con-texts* stimulating the author's inventiveness.

The implications of this critical change for interart studies are far-reaching. In the past, the academic world has often been suspicious of attempts to cross the barrier separating the verbal from the visual arts, arguing, in the tradition of Lessing's *Laocoön*, that such intrepid adventuring ignores fundamental differences divorcing the aims and procedures of the two media. But the new principle enunciated in our own time by such critics as Stephen Greenblatt, that there exists in each generation '. . . a shared code, a set of interlocking tropes and similitudes', has reversed the previous axiom, now making any segregation of literature from other forms of art appear both arbitrary and artificial.[2] It has, for example, become self-evident in recent years that current fears of social unrest, variations in class literacy, shifts in social *mores* and changes in commodity culture have a simultaneous effect upon all media, not only determining the marketability of books, paintings, furniture, and domestic architecture but to a considerable extent moulding their form, content, and style, as the creative artist adjusts to the new dispensation.[3]

1

And the effect is by no means one-directional, as the potential customer, eager to accommodate to the latest fashions, adapts his or
her taste to the innovative modes introduced by artist, craftsman,
or writer.[4]

The ways in which literature on the one hand and the plastic
arts of painting, architecture, and sculpture on the other react to
these contemporary contexts – sometimes independently, sometimes interacting across the media – can be fascinating to watch, and
enriching to the historian. That fascination holds especially true for
the Victorian era, when society was undergoing such fundamental
change, when tensions between moral conservatism and social
revolution, between a nostalgic longing for the past and an eagerness for industrial advancement, created a broader diversity of response than occurs in more settled times. To offer just one instance,
related to commodity change, Frederic Leighton's huge canvas of
1855, *Cimabue's Celebrated Madonna Carried in Procession through the
Streets of Florence*, which was to win him immediate fame, was more
than the chance evocation of a historical scene. It was of consciously
topical import, aimed at increasing the sale-value of art works by
elevating the status of the artist within society. The theme of the
canvas highlighted the profound respect in which the painter had
been held as Florence began its emergence into the Renaissance, the
reverence offered there to the creative artist, in contrast to Leighton's
own time. Cimabue, attired in the garb of the nobility and crowned
with a laurel wreath, is assigned there the place of honour, leading the solemn procession and preceding the holy painting itself,
with his pupil Giotto by his side to symbolize the responsibility of
transmitting art through the generations.[5] It was a message especially appropriate from the young, twenty-five-year-old Leighton,
whose brilliance as a scholar and linguist had seemed to mark him
out for a splendid career as a diplomat or member of parliament
but who chose instead the profession of painter. The success of this
canvas (purchased by Queen Victoria herself) opened all doors,
leading him eventually to the presidency of the Royal Academy
and to the first baronetcy ever to be conferred upon a painter. Its
popularity thus not only increased the value of the canvas itself but
also changed the contemporary situation, creating a demand for
further paintings of that kind and raising the prestige of the painter's
avocation. It was, however, a process closely paralleled in literature,
as, in the same year, Robert Browning introduced into his verse a
similar revivalist interest in Florentine history, this time in order to

enhance the standing of the poet. His 'Men and Women', published in 1855, dramatically revitalized for his generation the predicament of such Renaissance painters as Andrea Del Sarto and Fra Lippo Lippi as they strove to achieve true art while subjected to the whims of the public and their patrons. But by presenting their predicament in verse-form, Browning was depicting the dilemma of the Victorian poet too, chastising the public for its neglect of genius, urging upon them a refinement of their taste, and endeavouring thereby to cultivate a new respect and demand for his own art.

One of the primary objections among scholars to the search for parallels between literature and the visual arts has been the implied assumption in such studies that there exists a dominant spirit in each age, a *Zeitgeist* which imposes a fixed or monolithic pattern upon the artistic productions of the time, producing, as it were, a dull uniformity among its writers, artists, and thinkers. The principle adopted in this present study assumes the existence of a more subtle and, for the historian, more stimulating configuration. It recognizes the predominance in each generation of a central complex of inherited assumptions, of emergent ideas, of urgent contemporary concerns, to which each creative artist needs to respond individually. Poet, novelist, and painter may each choose to adopt those assumptions and priorities, they may question them, they may even vigorously deny them, but only at their peril may they ignore them. And even when the writer or artist resists them most forcefully, those impulses will, as matters of immediate pressure, continue to affect, often without conscious awareness on their part, aspects of their own art.

Moreover, in contrast to those historians adopting the more traditional diachronic method, tracing the sequential 'influence' of an artist's work upon a later writer, where such relationships must be historically proven before such deductions can be made, here, in the synchronic approach, the focus upon the simultaneous response of writer and artist to current problems makes such requirements superfluous. Few would argue in this present century, for example, that it is necessary to prove T.S. Eliot's familiarity with Picasso's canvases in order to perceive the filaments connecting their work, their concern with the fragmentation of the individual, with the collapse of traditional values, with the revelation of mythic substructures to culture which permeated the cultural configuration of their time. In examining earlier eras too, writer and artist should be seen as responding, each in his or her own way, to that central amalgam of contemporary concerns in a manner appropriate to the medium in which they work, often unaware of the innovations being effected in the kindred arts. What they share are the challenges specific to their time; and a close study of the techniques, themes, and symbols they employ to deal with those challenges can often prove mutually enriching to an analysis of the works produced.

One aspect of the shifting aesthetic concepts to which they must respond in each generation involves what I would term 'perspective' – perspective not in its narrower sense of mimetic fidelity, as in the attempt to transfer a three-dimensional scene onto a two-dimensional canvas or page, but in its original meaning of 'seeing through' one scene into another scene beyond. There has in the past few years been a renewal of interest in the concept of spatial and temporal form, whether in the illusionist sense of volumetric verisimilitude or as a metaphor applied to the morphology of language and to narrative sequence in literature. Earl Miner has suggested the connection of spatial metaphor to physiological factors in the brain, others have examined the tradition of seeing chronological progression in terms of linear movement, as in the use of *long* and *short* to describe intervals of time (with Wayne Booth musing whether the introduction of the digital clock will affect that usage).[6] My own interest, however, goes further than concern with the spatial measurement of actuality, whether in its literal or metaphorical forms, and even than the representational illusionism implicit in attempts to capture the concrete world realistically. For I would argue that the artists' and writers' view of the tactile world in which they live is itself profoundly affected at all times by their conception of the imagined world beyond, whether that has been the Christian eternity of afterlife, the semi-pagan Neoplatonic heaven of idealized forms, the redemptive dream-world of the Loyolan meditator distorted by the intensity of religious fervour, or the physically apprehended, rationalized infinity of the baroque cosmos. In each instance, as in subsequent eras, the entity beyond has constituted a projection of dissatisfactions and assertions, aspirations and fears implicit in man's mortal condition as conceived in that generation. It has both reflected and retroactively modulated areas of human experience, including the preference accorded in certain generations to rational proof as opposed to transcendental paradox, to social conformity as opposed to a cultivation of the inner life, to self-indulgence as opposed to asceticism and, not least, has moulded the current conception of the artist's and writer's task. The depiction of reality, whether in terms of the volumetric fidelity of Renaissance art or the deliberate distortions and elongations of time and space in the work of El Greco and Donne, is a function of the way the artist uses his or her earthly setting as a frame through which the hope of future, eternal existence can be asserted, implied, or at times bitterly denied.

The Victorian period provides an especially absorbing illustration of this 'perspective'. Overshadowed by the doubt cast upon the biblical account of Creation by the geological findings of Lyell and by the discovery of dinosaur fossils, each thinker had to find his or her own means of coping with it. The arts of the time produced deeply-felt responses, ranging from the cataclysmic visions of Carlyle and Turner to the nostalgical pietism of Pugin's neo-Gothic churches, from the 'muscular' Christianity of Charles Kingsley to the startling realism of Millais' *Christ in the House of his Parents*. That concern, not always perceptible on the surface, permeates all areas, even the apparently trivial. Lewis Carroll's 'Jabberwocky' may appear an amusing experiment with non-existent words, words which convey meaning only by verbal association. But a glance across the media at the drawing Sir John Tenniel provided for the poem (a drawing meticulously supervised by Lewis Carroll) reveals another element, as the monster has been endowed there with the pterodactyl wings, scaly neck, and sauropod tail associated with the fossils of dinosaurs. It suggests that, at a more profound level, the poem was psychologically liberating for Carroll, the unconscious wish-fulfilment of a deeply troubled Christian, offering a dream-vision of the younger generation overcoming with consummate ease, by the simple snicker-snack of its vorpal blade, the religious threats implicit in the dinosaur image:

> 'And hast thou slain the Jabberwock?
> Come to my arms my beamish boy!
> O frabjous day! Callooh! Callay!'
> He chortled in his joy.[7]

Such synchronic, cross-media exploration forms the co-ordinating theme of this present study, locating aspects of Victorian literature within the changing contexts of the painting, architecture, and decorative arts of the time, in order, by such comparison, to identify the contemporary impulses to which these media were reacting.[8]

In analysing the insights which the approach can offer for a study of nineteenth-century literature, I have attempted to offer a representative cross-section from the period, focusing upon three major novelists, two leading poets, an influential prose-writer, and an instance of thematic convergence. The latter, a gender theme constituting the symbolic projection of male concerns upon the female image, was a topic which emerged simultaneously in mid-century paintings and novels, indicating by that simultaneity the intimate relationship of the media in their response to the urgent, shared problems of their time.

1

Carlyle's 'Fire-Baptism'

The decline in Carlyle's reputation induced by the extremist views he espoused in his later years, and intensified by the appearance, soon after his death, of Froude's ungenerous and hastily written biography has left his image tarnished, and attempts by modern historians to restore him to his earlier eminence have achieved only limited success.[1] But the ethical stimulus Carlyle provided for his fellow Victorians by his thunderous attacks upon the cant of his times, as well as the high regard in which he was held during the zenith of his career in the years 1837–50, cannot be retrospectively expunged. Initially baffling readers by its stylistic idiosyncrasy and the unconventional thrust of its rhetoric, his was a voice soon to be revered, even idolized, as that of the authentic Sage of the era. George Eliot testified to the charismatic quality of the influence he had exerted over the leading thinkers of her generation, even over those least in agreement with his opinions, for whom, she averred, the reading of *Sartor Resartus* had proved 'an epoch in the history of their minds'.[2] It was a tribute repeatedly echoed by such distinguished contemporaries as Matthew Arnold, Dickens and John Stuart Mill.

The problem confronting the historian is less the clouding of his reputation in later years, which has absorbed so much critical attention in this century, than the unpredictability of his initial impact; for his emergence was greeted not as the culmination of some process embryonic within the Romantic era and developing out of it, but as an unheralded innovation. The sense of a break with the past which his works suggested was one he consciously cultivated, as he deliberately dissociated himself from the writings of his British antecedents, not least by the neologistic prose style he developed.[3] Hybrid compounds, unfamiliar to English-speakers and drawn from the German writers he so admired, irrupted unmodified and unassimilated into roughly-hewn sentences, the latter dominated by capitalized nouns, often personifications of universal ideas, which together conveyed by indirection rather than tangibly apprehensible statement the passionate commitment of the writer. It was a

7

communicative idiom foreign to his time yet strangely compelling,
in which, as Elizabeth Barrett described it, '... new words sprang
gauntly ... from savage derivatives, and rushed together in out-
landish combinations' to create what was essentially a new language.[4] Thackeray, acknowledging that it was a style of writing
initially repellent to him, noted how its alien grotesqueness gradually imposed its spell upon the reader: 'It is stiff, short, and rugged, it abounds with Germanisms and Latinisms, strange epithets,
and choking double words, astonishing to the admirers of simple
Addisonian English ... But those hardships become lighter as the
traveller grows accustomed to the road, and he speedily learns to
admire and sympathize, just as he would admire a Gothic cathedral in spite of the quaint carvings and hideous images on door and
buttress.'[5] Even in passages where the foreign elements were less
obtrusive, the rhetoric was bizarre in its sequential irregularities
and in the luminous abstractness of argument, qualities arising, as
he himself declared, from the precedence he granted to fantasy
over what he termed the duller impulses of reason. The paragraph
in which he expounds that principle offers in itself a paradigm of
his stylistic individualism of manner, the argument proceeding
not by smoothly logical progression but by a series of apparently
disjointed images, linked only by a subjective or emotional association which the reader is left to discern for himself:

> ... not our Logical, Mensurative faculty, but our Imaginative
> one is King over us; I might say, Priest and Prophet to lead us
> heavenward; or Magician and Wizard to lead us hellward. Nay,
> even for the basest Sensualist, what is Sense but the implement
> of Fantasy; the vessel it drinks out of? Ever in the dullest exist-
> ence there is a sheen either of Inspiration or of Madness (thou
> partly hast it in thy choice, which of the two) that gleams in
> from the circumambient Eternity, and colors with its own hues
> our little islet of Time.[6]

While style has always been seen by critics as integral to content,
recent theory has granted to rhetoric a more performative and
manipulative function than was previously accorded, regarding it,
as do Terry Eagleton and others, in terms of cultural relativism, stylistically reflecting and at times creating economic, philosophical,
and political assumptions. Epistemologically, Richard Rorty has
taken that view much further, denying altogether the existence of

transcendental absolutes, and interpreting the rhetorical strategies of texts as devices for creating substitute values in a world of shifting criteria. Truth, he argues, is not to be seen as a vertical relationship between representations and what is represented, but should be regarded

> ... horizontally – as the culminating reinterpretation of our predecessors' reinterpretation of their predecessors' reinterpretation ... It is the difference between regarding truth, goodness, and beauty as eternal objects which we try to locate and reveal, and regarding them as artifacts whose fundamental design we often have to alter.[7]

It is in that context that the rhetorical innovations and neologisms of Carlyle's prose should be examined, not as mere eccentricities but as essential ingredients of his philosophical perspective.

Sartor Resartus, from which the above passage is cited, proved indeed so eccentric and incomprehensible on its first publication that it was almost totally ignored, Carlyle claiming, with pardonable exaggeration, that it had been favoured with only two readers, an Irish priest and Ralph Waldo Emerson. Even the American publication of the serialized essays in book form, under the aegis of Emerson himself, did little to enhance his standing at home. It was only with the appearance of his *French Revolution* three years later in 1837 that the public discovered the prophet-poet within its midst, now avidly turning back to his *Sartor Resartus* (soon to be republished) with that reverence for his every word that was to characterize the enthusiasm of his disciples thereafter. While the new work discarded the fictive Professor Teufelsdröckh as supposed expositor, a literary contrivance which had further puzzled the earlier readers, it remained similar in its predilection, even within an avowedly historical study, to move away from the tactile into a visionary insubstantiality where amorphous images conjure up the writer's interpretation of the scene more convincingly than any particularized account could achieve. Of Mirabeau he wrote:

> In fiery rough figure, with black Samson-locks under the slouch-hat, he steps along there. A Fiery fuliginous mass, which could not be choked and smothered, but would fill all France with smoke. And now it has got air; it will burn its whole substance, its whole smoke-atmosphere too, and fill all France with flame.

Strange lot! Forty years of that smouldering, with foul fire-damp and vapor enough; then victory over that; – and like a burning mountain he blazes heaven-high; and for twenty-three resplendent months, pours out, in flame and molten fire-torrents, all that is in him, the Pharos and Wonder sign of an amazed Europe . . .[8]

The only literary forebear in any way comparable to Carlyle as visionary, moral castigator and political commentator combined was Blake; but there were fundamental differences separating them, quite apart from Carlyle's choice of prose as the vehicle for his message.[9] Blake, for all his concern with the social inequalities of his time, his anger at the oppression of the poor and his support for the struggle of the individual against tyranny, was ultimately committed to an other-worldly vision, part scriptural in origin and part self-generated. His thought was dominated by the dream of the apocalypse, as in his splendid watercolour of *The Last Judgement* with souls rising joyfully to take their place at the right hand of the divine, or as in the conclusion of his poem *Jerusalem*, where mankind is foreseen at the end of days '. . . awakening into His bosom in the Life of Immortality.' In contrast, Carlyle's focus was at all times on the human conditions upon this earth. His mind was oriented to cultural and social patterns, to events in national and world history which, while conceived indeed in the broadest perspective and *sub specie aeternitatis*, were evaluated within the parameters of terrestrial experience. Although hailed by many as a religious teacher, he was perceived, even by the most ardent of his admirers within the church, as only marginally Christian in his beliefs, applying the fervour as well as the vocabulary of religious experience to his crusade for social and national reform yet only vaguely relating his notions to traditional theological precepts. Hence Charles Kingsley's animadversion that the 'eternities' and 'abysses' of his rhetoric were only '. . . clouds and wind put in the place of a personal God.'[10] For Carlyle it was the individual will of man and woman, the heroic imagination alone that could, by the vigour of personal determination, transform the conditions of human existence; and even if that power was acknowledged as deriving from the divine, it was through the agency of man's personal endeavour that it was to be manifested. Such was the principle he asserted in the recently discovered manuscripts in the Forster Collection dating from 1841–2: 'For indeed the History of the Past is the real Bible . . . That is the true series of incarnations and avatars. The splendour of God shone thro' the huge incondite chaos of *our* being, so and then so; and by heroism after heroism, we have come to what you see.'[11] For many years, Blake too was regarded by historians as a strangely alien figure erupting incongruously upon the eighteenth-century scene. Only in this century has more thorough and detailed research revealed how integral he was to his time, serving in all his astonishing individuality as the poetic exponent of emerging cultural modes.[12] In what way, we may enquire, does Carlyle also represent, in his very innovativeness, a broader shift in aesthetic sensibility specific to his own time and discernible in related art forms?

Carlyle's reference in the latter passage, echoed repeatedly throughout his works, to the incondite *chaos* of the human condition has led Karl Kroeber to argue in a stimulating article that Carlyle was essentially a Romantic historian, belonging to a tradition conscious of the haphazardness prevailing in human affairs. In contrast to Gibbon and Hume, who had authoritatively recorded with the formality of scholarly hindsight the rise and fall of civilizations and cultures as rationally comprehensible processes, Carlyle asserted the essentially random condition of the world, revealing in his own reading of history the same awareness of impermanence and change in all things as had prevailed among the leading Romantic poets. This premise of historical incoherence Kroeber perceives as linking him both to his predecessors at the turn of the century and to writers in the decades ahead. On the one hand, he is seen as echoing Wordsworth's belief that it is not the major decisions that direct the life of the individual but the 'little, nameless, unremembered acts'; and, on the other hand, he is to be regarded as adumbrating the theme later dominating Tolstoy's *War and Peace* of 1862–5, where major battles and historic events are determined not by careful military planning or the political acumen of national leaders but by the most trivial and fortuitous occurrences. The game of war, as Tolstoy describes it, is entirely a matter of chance and coincidence, '. . . the outcome of the friction and shock of all the thousand wills and passions which are brought into play' during the inevitable medley and confusion of battle, producing a series of shifting contexts arbitrarily created by disconnected events, insignificant in themselves. That shared sense of universal turbulence or chaos is then interestingly connected by Kroeber with the vortex element dominant in so many of Turner's paintings, as in his *Snowstorm: Hannibal and his Army Crossing the Alps*, which employs

the meteorological turbulence there as a metaphor for military confusion. The crossing is presented not as a strategic triumph but in
terms of the stragglers at the rear, the abandoned and the dying
being callously stripped of their clothing by avaricious marauders
as part of the meaninglessness of the scene at large.[13]

Such positing of a nineteenth-century sense of the incoherence
of history, stretching from the early writings of Wordsworth to the
mature novels of Tolstoy, is liable, however, to obscure the most
original aspect of Carlyle's work; the change in conception discernible within that movement which gave his own writings their
marked individuality and was largely responsible for antagonizing
many of his early readers. For he represented, I would argue, a cultural response specific to the 1830s. As regards Tolstoy, for example,
whatever similarities may be drawn between Carlyle's sense of
universal chaos and Tolstoy's belief in the irrationality of historical
process as expressed some thirty years later, there is surely one
distinction which must not be overlooked – that Tolstoy's vehe-
ment rejection of charismatic leadership as a determining factor
in history is diametrically opposed to Carlyle's faith, derived from
Fichte, in the powerful will of heroes as the necessary directors and
moulders of national affairs. Tolstoy's denigration of Napoleon represented, indeed, a conscious rejection of the Romantic belief in
Promethean figures capable of altering the course of human history. He can scarcely be categorized as belonging within it. A more
valid parallel to Carlyle's sense of universal chaos can be found, as
Peter Conrad has persuasively suggested, closer to home as well as
closer in time in such novels of Dickens as *Oliver Twist* (1837–8) and,
even more obviously, *Barnaby Rudge* (1840–1), which are permeated
with a similar satiric sense of the contrariness, hubbub, and inco-
herent fortuity of city life. In such sprawling, densely populated
urban areas, sentimental spirituality and evil grotesquerie are
close neighbours, colliding and intertwining by the weird dictates
of chance; and the scenes of the city in turmoil attest to the utter
madness and purposelessness of mob frenzy. In the welter of the
wild, spontaneous rioting in London, a vintner's warehouse is set
afire, the inflammable alcohol from the vats streaming out into the
streets:

From the burning cellars, where they drank out of hats, pails,
buckets, tubs, and shoes, some men were drawn, alive, but all
alight from head to foot; who in their unendurable anguish and

suffering, making for anything that had the look of water, rolled, hissing in this hideous lake, and splashed up liquid fire which lapped in all it met with as it ran along the surface, and neither spared the living nor the dead. On this last night of the great riots – for last night it was – the wretched victims of a senseless outcry, became themselves the dust and ashes of the flames they had kindled, and strewed the public streets of London.[14]

Yet here too one must be wary in deducing synchronic similarities, as Dickens was a self-acknowledged disciple and admirer of Carlyle, drawing his inspiration for such chaotic scenes directly from him and not constituting an independent manifestation of a current mode.

If we must be cautious in identifying Carlyle with the later Tolstoy, there exists, in relating him to his predecessors, a similar danger of overlooking certain shifts in sensibility which the intervening years effected and which were incorporated in his work. For the conception of mutability and impermanence prevailing among the Romantic poets and connected by Kroeber to Carlyle had been based upon an assumption very different from that motivating the latter's *French Revolution*. Such ephemerality, including the transience of human life, so far from being chaotic and unpredictable, had been seen by the Romantics as functioning within the ordered framework of cyclical nature, seasonally bringing its spring buds, ripe fruits, falling leaves, and winter frosts. Constable, fascinated by the shifting forms of clouds as they move across the sky, strove, it is true, to depict within his landscapes the mobility and the variability of impermanent cumulus or nimbus forms; but, as the regular agricultural tasks being performed within those scenes confirm, reinforced by the overall tranquillity of his canvases, they are conceived with all their changeability as part of the settled climatic patterns of the British countryside. Shelley, more volatile in temperament, identified the cloud as a projection of his own capriciousness, yet, even so, as participating in the normal processes of nature:

> I wield the flail of the lashing hail,
> And whiten the green plains under,
> And then again I dissolve it in rain,
> And laugh as I pass in thunder.[15]

There is no such reassuring cyclical framework in Carlyle's view of the impermanence and purposelessness of history, erupting fortuitously out of disconnected and inconsequential occurrences. As

J. Hillis Miller has recently pointed out, there is a self-annihilating movement in *Sartor Resartus*, defying any comforting sense of order or pattern. Carlyle may argue that 'Facts are engraved Hierograms, for which the fewest have the key', yet at the same time he makes it clear to the reader through the figure of Professor Teufelsdröckh that those supposed facts are themselves obvious fictions. The work is thus constantly destroying itself and renewing itself, as figure follows figure.[16]

That distinction between the Romantic sense of cyclical history and Carlyle's conception of it as essentially amorphous holds true for the individual too. If Wordsworth contended that the character of each person was formed not by the major events in life but by the little unremembered acts that mould each person's moral values, he had never suggested that the influence of such acts was either random or indeterminate. He saw them rather as contributing to an organic process of development within the individual, a process which he was to record in his *Prelude* (begun in the same year as his comment on those unremembered acts), a poem recounting the 'growth' of a poet's mind. Mutability in that organic sense is far from Carlyle's conception of the fundamental unintelligibility and discontinuity of history, and of humanity's need in each generation for forceful leaders to impose some degree of order upon the inherent chaos. If, therefore, he does not belong intrinsically within this Romantic tradition, where are the filaments to be found that connect him, in his inventiveness and originality, to the developing modes of his time?

Carlyle's philosophy resulted, together with many other changes, in a basically new conception of the function of the 'poet', a term which he uses in its original Greek sense as comprehending all forms of artistic creativity; and the key to an understanding of that innovative idea is to be found in the image to which, in its varied forms, he instinctively resorts. The hallmark of Carlyle's writings is the metaphor of blazing light, of luminescence, of dazzling effulgence and conflagration. 'Behold the World-Phoenix, in fire-consummation and fire-creation', he proclaims. An autograph letter is for him '. . . all luminous as a burning beacon, every word of it a live coal'. Ancient towns and cities two thousand years ago received their first culinary fire, he recalls,

> . . . and there, burning more or less triumphantly, with such fuel
> as the region yielded, it has burnt, and still burns, and thou thyself

seest the very smoke thereof. Ah! and the far more mysterious live ember of Vital Fire was then also put down there; and still miraculously burns and spreads; and the smoke and ashes thereof ... and its bellow-engines ... thou still seest; and its flame, looking out from every kind countenance, and every hateful one, still warms thee or scorches thee.

There is the Mirabeau passage quoted above, describing that French leader as a '... Fiery fuliginous mass, which could not be choked and smothered, but would fill all France with smoke'.[17] This image, recurring throughout his writings, does so not through paucity of imagination on the part of Carlyle but from the intrinsic applicability of the figure to his mode of thought. For linked with each of the myriad instances of such imagery is his prophetic call for a passionate rebirth of the individual soul through the burning away of outmoded fears and allegiances; and inherent in that call is his conception of the poet-preacher as the cultural ignitor of the spark, offering a blazing imaginative vision which should in its turn inflame the hearts and minds of his readers.

It is here that a deeper link with Turner may be perceived, the shared idea of the vortex forming only one aspect of a profound cultural bond. Turner's contribution to British and continental art was as far-reaching as Carlyle's and, like his, as polarized in the reactions it evoked because of its radical departure from inherited modes. He remained until the end of his life an admirer of the classical landscapes by Claude Lorrain, being consciously imitative of them in his earlier and middle periods; but it was his break with that tradition that revolutionized the British scene, producing a sense of puzzlement or sheer animosity from many of his generation who were unable to comprehend his purpose. *Blackwood's Magazine*, following the lead of Sir George Beaumont, was implacably hostile to him during that period of his career, revealing by the very virulence of its attacks a recognition of his wide and allegedly pernicious influence upon younger artists; an essay in the *Tatler* in 1831, probably by Leigh Hunt, assumed scathingly that Turner must be suffering from some ocular disease '... (ophthalmic or calenture) which leads him into the most marvellous absurdities and audacities of colour that painter ever ventured on. This is very melancholy, but we feel that a timely application of blistering and phlebotomy may arrest the current of his disorder'; while in 1838 (the year that saw the British publication of Carlyle's *Sartor Resartus* in book form),

the prestigious *Athenaeum* summed up more generously the general
feeling towards Turner during that later period, expressing its sad
sense of abilities misguided and misapplied: 'It is grievous to us to
think of talent, so mighty and so poetical, running riot into such
frenzies'.[18]

The condemned 'frenzies' referred, of course, to his canvases
employing brilliant yellows in a manner unprecedented in art, inducing in many of the initial viewers a bafflement paralleling that
which greeted Carlyle's neologistic style, with its abstraction into
images of dazzling brilliance and conflagration in place of the sober
recounting of events normally expected from the historian. Turner
was, like Carlyle, fully aware of the hostile reaction, wrily enclosing
in a letter he wrote to Robert Balmanno a newspaper cutting with
a review of three paintings he had recently exhibited, of which the
central comment ran:

> In all, we find the same intolerable yellow hue pervading every
> thing; whether boats or buildings, water or water-men, houses or
> horses, all is yellow, yellow, nothing but yellow . . .[19]

But he continued unperturbed to produce such 'frenzies'.

Structuralist reinterpretation of myth – whether in Lévi-Strauss's
sense of it as a semiotic system of language repatterned by each
generation in its own image, in Roland Barthes' political conception
of it as a form of manipulative propaganda imposed by one class
upon another, or in Frank Kermode's idea that it is (unlike fiction)
a retrogressive, conservative element within society resisting change
– has focused new attention upon the solar myth which fascinated writers and artists in the late eighteenth and early nineteenth
centuries, as in the interesting collection of essays on that theme
produced under the editorship of J.B. Bullen.[20] During the period
they examine, despite a growing awareness, in the works of Jones,
Faber, and others, of the deeper significance of folkloristic tradition,
myth had not yet been endowed with the authoritative universality
with which it was to be assigned after the appearance of Frazer's
anthropological study *The Golden Bough* and Jung's theory of the
archetype. For that earlier period, the discovery of underlying
mythological patterns had functioned for the most part as a tool for
either corroborating or undermining Christian faith. Bryant's *A New
System, or, An Analysis of Antient Mythology* (1774–6), widely read in
England and influencing Blake among others, had suggested, on

the basis of the author's research into the history of sun-worship, that the pagan religions were merely perverted or degenerate forms of Hebraic monotheism; and Sir William Jones had strengthened their derogation by tracing back both the classical and Hindu divinities to forms of primitive nature worship: '... the whole crowd of gods and goddesses in ancient Rome and modern Varanes mean only the powers of nature and principally those of the SUN, expressed in a variety of ways, and by a multitude of fanciful names.'[21] Turner came into contact with those views early in his career, and his *Sun Rising Through Vapour* of 1807 no doubt resulted from the painter's friendship at that time with Richard Payne Knight who, as an ardent mythographer working in the anti-religious direction, had identified Priapus, the main theme of his somewhat daring research, as being a solar as well as a sexual symbol.[22] This interest in current mythological theory clearly directed Turner's attention to the Apollo themes which he began to introduce into his work; but it does not account for another aspect of his art which forms the link with Carlyle suggested here.

The excellent edition of Turner's works published by Yale University Press under the joint editorship of Martin Butlin and Evelyn Joll permits a chronological overview of his artistic development not readily available in any of the previous collections. From such an overview, it becomes manifest how marked was the revolution in his style that occurred not at the time of his contact with the new mythology but much later, around 1828. In contrast to many artists (Gauguin, for example) who only found their *métier* later in their careers and whose earlier work is therefore considerably less interesting or accomplished, Turner's earlier work is outstanding, and would alone have assured his place among the finest of British painters. His sea-scapes, such as *Calais Pier* of 1803 or *The Shipwreck* of 1805, with ships tossed helplessly on the surface of a raging ocean, provide an awesome depiction of the impotence of man before the uncontrollable forces of nature. And as part of that outlook, they present, paradoxically, the aggrandizement of the human imagination implied by the artistic work itself – an imagination which, inspired by such might, partakes of Nature's power, recreating it artistically, as Shelley was to demonstrate so forcefully in his *Ode to the West Wind*. But while such paintings added a new dimension to the contemporary concern with the sublime, they were not radical departures from tradition. In these sea-scapes, Turner was consciously imitating the Dutch school. In this instance, he had been specifically commissioned in 1801 by the Duke of Bridgewater to produce a canvas which could be hung as a companion piece beside a Van de Velde in the Duke's possession. In subsequent years, Turner's sea-scapes were continually compared to the Dutch works upon which they were acknowledgedly modelled. In 1837, the Duke's successor lent both canvases, the Van de Velde and the painting by Turner, to the British Institution, thereby encouraging critics to evaluate the relative merits of the two works.[23] The same holds true for his paintings in the style of Claude Lorrain, which were intended from the first to preserve and continue the tradition. His *Appullia in Search of Appullus* was in fact the entry submitted by him in a competition organized by the British Institution, whose declared purpose was to encourage imitation of such conventional pastoral scenes, the prize being offered for the best landscape '. . . appropriate as a pendant for a work by either Claude or Poussin'; and his extraordinarily fine *Crossing the Brook*, exhibited in the Royal Academy in 1815, however British in its setting – the depiction of a Devonshire scene which had impressed him on a recent tour, with Calstock Bridge spanning the River Wear in the background – makes no attempt to conceal its indebtedness to the revered Italian mode. There is the characteristic tree dominating one side of the canvas, the small foreground figures, the calm water inducing a mood of tranquillity, the Italian-type buildings in the background, and the hazy horizon in the distance, all echoing the Italian idyll. The express condition in his will bequeathing such canvases to the National Gallery, the stipulation that they were to be hung beside paintings by Claude, is sufficient evidence that he preserved until the end a conscious desire that those paintings should be seen as emulating the tradition of seventeenth-century classical landscape.

The turning-point occurring during his sojourn at Petworth, when he deserted such imitative practice in favour of an autonomous form of art, marked though it was in dividing off this latter stage in his career, had not been entirely without precedent in his own works, at least with the hindsight which the knowledge of that change now affords to the historian. Occasional canvases, such as his luminous view of the interior of Christ Church Cathedral, Oxford, dating from 1800, reveal hints of future trends; and his oil painting from 1822, never exhibited, of *George IV at the Provost's Banquet in Edinburgh* glows with the blurred yellow brilliance of the candle-lit scene in a manner anticipating the fascination with diffused light that was soon to absorb his interest. But it was in 1828 that he provided, for a public not yet aware of the new direction he was about to take, a thematic presentation of his developing concerns. His painting entitled *Regulus* (Fig. 1) puzzled many by the absence from within the scene of any figure identifiable as the eponymic character. As John Gage has convincingly shown, it is the viewer himself who is assumed to be standing in the place of Regulus, and the story which the scene depicts is highly significant for our present concerns. The Roman general, having refused to negotiate an exchange of prisoners with the Carthaginians, had been condemned by them to have his eyelids cut off as a prelude to being exposed to the glare of the sun until blinded. Turner's choice of that scene evinces his own growing interest in the dazzling power of bright sunlight, with the artist and, by extension, ourselves, subjected through the medium of his art to the awesomely painful splendour of its brilliance.

Any discussion of this painting in terms of Turner's chronological development must pause at this point, since only the thematic aspect and overall design is relevant here. Although it was exhibited in 1828 in Rome, the canvas as it now exists is the result of a thorough reworking of it undertaken some nine years later in 1837 in preparation for its first exhibition to an English public, at a time when he was already at the height of his mature phase. His later reworking of the canvas was, however, itself an indication of his progressive interest in such solar effects, the culmination of a movement beginning with his thematic choice of enforced exposure to the sun's glare, and intensified a few years later, as a contemporary account of that re-working informs us. A fellow exhibitor, Sir John Gilbert, watched with admiration the process whereby Turner enhanced the already vivid hues of the original painting:

> The picture was a mass of red and yellow of all varieties. Every object was in this fiery state ... The sun, as I have said, was in the centre; from it were drawn – ruled – lines to mark the rays; these lines were rather strongly marked, I suppose to guide his eye. The picture gradually became wonderfully effective, just the effect of brilliant sunlight absorbing everything and throwing a misty haze over every object.[24]

The painting in its final form is indeed an astonishing achievement. Overcoming the limitations inherent in pigment spread over a two-dimensional fabric, Turner succeeded in recreating, as the *Literary*

Gazette described it on its first exhibition in England, a sun that
'. . . absolutely dazzles the eyes'.[25]

The radical departure from his previous style, motivating the
original 1828 painting as well as the reworked version, derives in
part from his decision to face directly towards the sun, confronting
it in its full force rather than employing it as the background for a
traditional scene, as he had in his *Sun Rising Through Vapour* of 1807
with a group of fishermen cleaning their nets in the foreground.[26]
He had already experimented with the technique of confronting the
sun in his *Dido Building Carthage* of 1815 and its companion piece
The Decline of the Carthaginian Empire of 1817 but only as an intermediary stage of development, with the sun still functioning there
as a background setting rather than as the source of the painting's
power, in that respect following Claude's *Embarkation of the Queen
of Sheba* upon which they were based. In the Petworth phase, however, which his *Regulus* inaugurated, either the sun itself or the
transforming effect of its coruscating light upon all objects gener-
ates the emotional vibrancy of his canvases. Turner's lengthy visit
to Lord Egremont's estate in 1829 and the serene atmosphere of his
host's unobtrusive hospitality – permitting him full freedom to
wander through the grounds at will and devote his time to painting
with no obligations or pressures exerted upon him – seem to have
granted him the opportunity needed for his new interest to burgeon;
and the remarkable series of paintings either produced or begun
there, including his view of *Petworth Lake at Sunset*, left their impress upon his subsequent work. He becomes, at his finest, a painter
exploring the dissolution of solid forms when bathed in the brilliance
of light in its manifold variations, in the blazing power of the mid-
day sun, in its softer diffusion through mists and storms, or in the
vividness of non-solar conflagration, as in his *Burning of the Houses
of Parliament* of 1835.

Intermedia criticism has long connected Turner's paintings with
the poetry of Shelley, a relationship certainly with some foundation and especially attractive to those seeking proven connections
between writer and artist, since it rests upon historical documentation. Although Turner came upon Shelley's writings late in his career,
he was clearly impressed by them, including in the verses he appended in 1843 to his *Sun of Venice Going to Sea* echoes of Shelley's
Lines Written Among the Euganean Hills, while his *Queen Mab's Cave*
of 1846, despite the quotation appended from Shakespeare, was
probably inspired by Shelley's poetic treatment of that theme. They

did indeed share a sense of the luminescence shed upon the world, creating a dreamy sense of beauty and harmony, linking Turner's watercolours of Venice with Shelley's description:

> Lo, the sun floats up the sky
> Like thought-wingéd Liberty,
> Till the universal light
> Seems to level plain and height;
> From the sea a mist has spread,
> And the beams of morn lie dead
> On the towers of Venice now,
> Like its glory long ago.[27]

For that mood, Shelley's Neo-Platonic philosophy of life was peculiarly suited. But in the works most characteristic of Turner's major phase, it is to his immediate contemporary Carlyle that he has the closest affinities.

The reproductions offered here can offer some hint of the bonds joining the two; but, as one stands before the original paintings in their full blaze of colour, the quality they share with Carlyle's imaginative recourse to a multi-hued incendiarism is striking. The fiery *Burial at Sea* from 1842, with a brilliant shaft of light contrasting with the black hull of the ship, partakes of the same volatile luminosity as Carlyle's ominous image of France, described by him as a fireship packed with brimstone and bitumen, nitre and terebinth, sailing away into the Deep of Time.[28] During this period there is, in both writer and painter, an awareness of potential cataclysm, of latent forces liable to erupt into explosive force, yet at the same time a fascination with the energy and brilliance of the power displayed, however ominous it may be. The revolutionary scene in France, studied by Carlyle beforehand in scrupulous detail, emerges in his prose in a transmuted form remote from the specifics of historical minutiae, emotionally transfigured into vivid metaphor: '. . . mad-blazing with flame of all imaginable tints, from the red of Tophet to the stellar-bright, blazes off this Consummation of Sansculottism'. And in quieter, less fervent mood, when his imagery recreates in refracted form the historic events upon which he is focusing, the scene takes on a chromatic mistiness evocative of a late Turner canvas, such as the pellucid view of Venice from 1841, now in the Art Institute of Chicago, in which the majestic Renaissance and Baroque churches of S. Giorgio Maggiore and S. Maria della Salute dissolve into a delicately-hued insubstantiality:

In such succession of singular prismatic tints, flush after flush
suffusing our horizon, does the Era of Hope dawn on . . .[29]

Behind these similarities in artistic expression lay, as always, an
ideological motivation. Carlyle's indebtedness to post-Kantian
philosophy as developed by Fichte and Schelling, with its rejection
of the authenticity of empirical reasoning in favour of a belief in
subjective *a priori* knowledge, has been thoroughly documented.[30]
But Turner was not especially interested either in philosophy or in
German culture except when it had a direct bearing upon his own
work, such as Goethe's theory of optics.[31] If we are to speak of a
shared climate of opinion, it is the specifically British manifestations
rather than the continental forms that should prove most relevant,
particularly those prevailing during the period when these artistic
changes were occurring.

John Holloway, in identifying the phenomenon of the Victorian
Sage, in which category he included Carlyle as a major representative, noted some years ago how, as part of their moral earn-
estness, they tended to rely upon prophetic assertion rather than
reasoned argument, their beliefs emanating from some form of
mystical inner apprehension. Coleridge declared in his *Aids to
Reflection* of 1825:

I assume a something, the proof of which no man can give to
another, yet every man can find for himself. If any man assert,
that he can not find it, I am bound to disbelieve him! I cannot do
otherwise without unsettling the very foundations of my own
moral Nature.

Newman from a similar viewpoint devoted his entire *Grammar of
Assent* to demonstrating his distrust of rational persuasion as a means
of winning converts to his faith, rejecting any supposedly logical
proofs as being mere sophistry or 'smart syllogism'. The method he
favoured was a touching of the heart in preference to the mind,
until in the potential believer smaller truths absorbed along the
way would converge irresistibly to form an integrated moral outlook. Schopenhauer in Germany and Whewell in England similarly
abandoned Lockean reason, insisting that the mind must create new
truths.[32] It is in that context that we must place Carlyle's constant
reliance upon his own intuitive apprehension of truth and his
conviction that, for his reader too, the inner vitalism of individual

determination must overcome the disparities, the pettiness, and the deformities of worldly existence to impose its own vision upon the larger whole. As he insisted in *Past and Present*, again using a sun image, the inner soul must irradiate and beautify the outer body with its own nobleness:

> . . . all human things do require to have an Ideal in them; to have some Soul in them . . . were it only to keep the Body unputre-fied. And wonderful it is to see how the Ideal or Soul, place it in what ugliest Body you may, will irradiate said Body with its own nobleness; will gradually, incessantly, mould, modify, new-form or reform said ugliest Body, and make it at last beautiful, and to a certain degree divine![33]

The Romantic poets had conceived the process of artistic creativity differently, seeing themselves primarily as instruments of Nature, stimulated, like the Aeolian harp, by its spirit and animated by its 'correspondent' breeze to give voice to its harmonies. Impelled by it, they might share in its rapturous force, but without it they were powerless. Now, however, the philosophy has changed, and with it the image representing the process. The source of inspiration is not Nature but a self-generated inner blaze whose function is to illumine for others the truths of the universe. Such are the terms whereby Carlyle's favourite poets are described:

> Dante, deep, fierce as the central fire of the world; Shakespeare, wide, placid, far-seeing, as the Sun, the upper light of the world.

and Goethe illuminating all with his '. . . celestial radiance'.[34]

In a seminal passage in his essay *On Heroes, Hero-Worship, and the Heroic in History*, recalling the pervasive clothes metaphor of his *Sartor Resartus* but now applying it to the creative artist rather than to the social historian, Carlyle defined as the characteristic quality of both prophet and poet their ability to exploit their revelatory power of illumination and thereby to see through the deceptive 'clothes' of worldly appearance to the sacred mystery of the universe. Here too, perception is an intuitive, self-generated faculty, not requiring outside stimulation:

> But now, I say, whoever may forget this divine mystery, the *Vates*, whether Prophet or Poet, has penetrated into it; is a man sent

hither to make it more impressively known to us. That always is
his message; he is to reveal that to us, – that sacred mystery
which he more than others lives ever present with. While others
forget it, he knows it; – I might say, he has been driven to know
it; without consent asked of him, he finds himself living in it,
bound to live in it. Once more, here is no Hearsay, but a direct
Insight and Belief . . .

Mahomet, as a representative of the religious *vates*, must undertake
as his prophetic task to express not some outer truth but the self
that is within, turbulent, chaotic, rude, and untutored, but redeemed
by fervency; a soul '. . . struggling vehemently to utter itself in words.
With a kind of breathless intensity he strives to utter himself.'[35] The
idiosyncrasies of Carlyle's style are a reflection of that new conception of artistic creativity. His duty as the *vates* of modern history, indeed his irresistible urge, was not to present the details of
the French Revolution familiar to him from prolonged study, but
rather the essence of human events, the confusion, incoherence,
and turbulence in the labyrinthine multitude of petty incidents for
which only the historian can provide an effective overview and illumination. The capitalized abstract nouns appearing within his prose
are not a thoughtless importation from German, but a device for
elevating discourse into the ideal, for transforming particulars into
an overall, allegorical embodiment of truth.[36] Hence also that strange
recourse throughout his writing to imagery serving not as illustration
or elaboration but as a substitute for rational argument, the developing of his themes as it were in metaphorical parallel in order to
create a subjectively-interpreted vision in place of the logical progression, buttressed and substantiated by facts, associated with
conventional historical accounts. The novel presentation resulting
from that approach, as his readers came to realize, proved truer in
essence than any learned parade of confirmable evidence. Although
that element in his writing was not fully grasped at first, it was at
least hinted at in John Stuart Mill's review of the work on its initial appearance, a work which he realized was '. . . so strange and
incomprehensible to the greater part of the public, that whether
it should succeed or fail seemed to depend upon the turn of a
die.' What he at once noted was that its excellence consisted in
its departure from the '. . . jog-trot characterless uniformity which
distinguishes the English style of this age of Periodicals', especially in its rejection of the literalistic accounts of battles, tumults,

and insurrections familiar from the works of Hume and Gibbon. Mill went no further in defining the innovation, vaguely gesturing towards Carlyle's penetration into the minds of characters instead of merely describing their outward appearance or actions. But the stylistic difference that Mill highlighted was, as I have suggested, in fact a fundamental part of his philosophy, a literary expression of his artistic creed. The historical detail, alluded to or assumed rather than carefully recorded, is there solely to be absorbed into some larger idea, to be employed as a leaping-off point for an intensely personal and impressionistic reading of the period in its totality. Since the time of Locke, Carlyle complained, not only history but even metaphysics had become mechanical, a material philosophy: 'But the grand secrets of Necessity and Free-will, of the Mind's vital or non-vital dependence on Matter, of our mysterious relations to Time and Space, to God, to the Universe, are not, in the faintest degree, touched on in these enquiries . . .'[37] In a passage justifying his own predilection for symbol rather than literalism, he not only defined that process but exemplified it while doing so. He intimates an incident without specifying its time or place, as though the only significance of the occurrence is its larger implication, the universal lesson it conveys concerning the symbolic value of a piece of cloth: 'Have not I myself known five-hundred living soldiers sabred into crows'-meat for a piece of glazed cotton, which they called their Flag; which, had you sold it at any market-cross, would not have brought above three groschen?' And from that recalled event he deduces the general proposition that man, consciously or unconsciously, lives, works, and has his being in symbols, that history too must therefore see through the external significance of events to their intrinsic meanings. 'Of this latter sort are all true Works of Art: in them (if thou know a Work of Art from a Daub of Artifice) wilt thou discern Eternity looking through Time . . .' The factual and visible remain essential to the historian as the material for his creative work. The more clearly he sees them, the more accurate will be his ultimate perception. But they are no more than raw material, the reality exposed to the historian's eye. The eye, as he describes it in this passage, represents the faculty of the imagination, of what he terms Fantasy, alone empowered to transform such details into the authentic vision: 'The Understanding is indeed thy window, too clear thou canst not make it; but Fantasy is thy eye, with its color-giving retina, healthy or diseased.'[38]

That metaphor drawn from ocular perception, the endowing of

events with their appropriate hue, may serve as a bridge to lead us back to Turner. Since Carlyle had distinguished between the prophet as the preacher of morality and the poet as the servant of beauty, that latter definition, embracing all aesthetic pursuits, extends his remarks on literary creativity to apply to the painter too, even though Carlyle himself seems to have evinced little interest in the visual arts. Neither Leonardo nor Michelangelo nor any other great painter is included in his gallery of heroes as counterpart to his beloved Dante and Shakespeare; and, on the few occasions when he does mention painting, he appears content to rely on hearsay rather than personal knowledge.[39] But our concern here is not with supposed influences or interactions between writer and artist. It is with their independent expression of shared cultural conceptions as appropriate to their own media, adapted there to the disparate requirements of each, yet revealing affinities in aesthetic assumptions, including their conception of the creative act itself.

The task of identifying those assumptions is more difficult in connection with Turner's work, as he was verbally almost inarticulate, his lectures on perspective at the Royal Academy, for example, being notoriously difficult to follow not only because of his extraordinarily poor delivery, a tendency to mumble, but, more relevant for the written record, his proclivity for using words in strange and esoteric ways. His lectures were, moreover, historical in content so that very little has been recorded of his personal views on art, apart from a few testy replies to adverse criticism. The principles he adopted for his own work, especially during his most innovative phase from the late 1820s, must be deduced from a study of the paintings themselves, assisted by our understanding of the new view of the artist's creative function concurrently being expressed in the writings of Carlyle.

The complex traditions of sun-symbolism available to Turner have been to some extent explored by Ronald Paulson, although with more attention to the connotations of such symbolism in western culture at large than to specific applications in the paintings themselves. The associations accumulated before Turner's time, he points out, included the apprehension of the sun as the god-like source of all power, with the monitory corollary that whoever gazes upon the face of God will die. There was the sun in Plato's myth, so dazzling to the philosopher that, on his return to the cave, he could with difficulty distinguish the shadows previously so clear to him; the blind Milton's invocation to Celestial Light to shine

inward that he might see things invisible to mortal sight; its association with reason during the period of Louis XIV; and, chronologically closer to the execution of these paintings, its identification
with the Burkean sublime. Such listing of the various iconographic
interpretations, however, take on deeper significance if we recall
that these symbolical conceptions of the sun were not cumulative,
a body of associations from which the writer or artist could select
whatever suited his need, but that each had been integral to the
cultural perceptions prevalent in its period. For a metaphysical poet
such as Donne, reaching beyond the actualities of mortal existence
to the eternal, the sun in its material form had been relegated to the
status of a minor functionary. In his *Sunne Rising*, it disturbs, like
some meddlesome Peeping Tom, the lovers' joy, and is dislodged
by their spiritual experience from its Copernican centrality in the
universe; and in the religious setting of his *Goodfriday 1613, Riding
Westward* it is similarly subordinated by the transcendental para-
doxes of the other Son/Sun, being raised upon the Cross:

> There I should see a Sunne, by rising set,
> And by that setting endlesse day beget.

For the baroque artist, absorbing the scientifically enlarged cosmos
into his Christian faith, it had again been seen differently, as representing the dazzling creative light of God himself. Placed radi-
antly above the high altar with the emblem of the Jesuit order within,
or, as in Bernini's church of S.Andrea al Quirinale, constituting the
interior of the dome, the sun image dominates the scene, drawing
together the ancillary elements of the structure, as in Milton's invocation: 'Hail holy light, offspring of Heav'n's first born . . . Bright
effluence of bright essence increate . . .'; while for the subsequent
era, presuming not God to scan and turning away from cosmic
scenes in favour of observing social manners, the light of the sun
functioned like other aspects of the natural world as little more
than a pleasing background for human activity, ornamenting the
scene for the pleasure of the viewer, symbolizing the similar decorative function which the poet was to perform:

> But true Expression, like th' unchanging Sun,
> Clears, and improves whate'er it shines upon,
> It gilds all Objects, but it alters none.

Paulson's listing of various past associations with the sun, therefore, helpful though it may be as a reminder, offers little assistance
for an understanding of Turner's own individualistic response to it,
and the deeper significance of its iconographic meaning to him, as
a member of a different generation.[40]

A remark by one of Turner's more hostile critics, William Hazlitt,
delivered during the period when the artist had not yet moved into
his major phase, may prove to have been more relevant than has
often been thought. He commented that Turner tends '. . . to go
back to the first chaos of the world, or to that state of things when
the waters were separated from the dry land, and light from darkness, but as yet no living thing nor tree bearing fruit was seen upon
the face of the earth. All is without form and void.'[41] That comment has caused considerable puzzlement to historians, since it
seems quite irrelevant to the two rather traditional Claudean-type
paintings entitled *The Temple of Jupiter Panellenius* exhibited at the
Royal Academy in 1816, which Hazlitt was ostensibly reviewing. It
has been interpreted, therefore, as a strangely prophetic utterance,
appropriate to the transformations in Turner's art which were yet
to manifest themselves. But the clue may lie elsewhere. A painting
whose authenticity has long been in doubt and of which Alexander
J. Finberg had written 'I do not accept this as genuine. Probably a
fake, from Chas. Turner's Engraving' has, after its inclusion in the
recent Bicentenary Exhibition, been subjected to further study, and
is now acknowledged to be Turner's '. . . beyond any doubt.'[42] The
re-instatement of this striking painting, *The Eruption of the Souffrier
Mountains*, may offer a more acceptable reading of Hazlitt's comment, if we bear in mind that the canvas had been exhibited at the
Royal Academy only the previous year, and would have been very
much in the minds both of the reviewer and his readers. It does
indeed display the chaos of a world in uncontrollable turbulence,
with the grim darkness broken only by the lurid glare of volcanic
eruption. The new attribution of the painting gives deeper import
to Hazlitt's remarks as indicating not some extraordinary presaging
on the critic's part but his recognition of the growing importance
of such scenes of chaos in Turner's work, an interest visible in
the latter's *Destruction of Sodom* (1804), his *Cottage Destroyed by an
Avalanche* (1810), and even such supposedly historical paintings as
Hannibal and his Army Crossing the Alps, exhibited only three years
before.[43] There the raw violence of soldiers in the left foreground,
despoiling corpses of their clothing or fighting with naked daggers

over a dying woman, intensify the sense of lawless turmoil, with the sun incapable of breaking through the dark snow clouds which swirl ominously about the scene.

In Carlyle's writing too, as we have seen, that apprehension of universal chaos predominates. Yet the turmoil is countered in his work by a recurrent image of dazzling brilliance, an allusion to the historic moment at Creation when the divine word conjured up light to drive forth the darkness. For him, that act was less a specific event during the formation of the universe than a paradigm offered to mankind, an encouragement to the heroic individual to imitate the divine act by his own visionary and illuminatory power. It was to serve him as a prefiguration of the human will asserting itself to impose order upon the turbulence around it. 'Fire-baptism' was the religiously connotative term that he coined for that act, for the soul's self-enfranchisement from its pusillanimous subservience to the authoritarian bonds of tradition. But freedom from such bondage was for him insufficient. The climax of that progression must, he urged, be a totally new way of perceiving the universe, a dazzling vision paralleling the original *Fiat lux*:

> ... it is with man's Soul as it was with Nature: the beginning of Creation is – Light. Till the eye have vision, the whole members are in bonds. Divine moment, when over the tempest-tost Soul, as once over the wild-weltering Chaos, it is spoken: Let there be Light![44]

As part of his recourse to metaphors of light and fire, the imagination of man is conceived by him as dull and somnolent until, in response to the revitalizing brilliance of heaven, it awakens and, in its turn, bathes the turmoil it gazes upon in coruscating refulgence, transforming the entire scene, the human and the terrestrial, from chaos to glory:

> But is there not, human at the heart of all, strangely hidden, sunk, overwhelmed yet not extinct, a light-element and fire-element, which if you but awaken it shall irradiate and illuminate the whole, and make life a glorious fixed landscape ... ?[45]

Once granted that awakening of the soul, as he asserts elsewhere, '... how were thy eyesight unsealed, and thy heart set flaming in the Light-sea of celestial wonder!'[46]

The evolution in the concept of the poetic imagination during the eighteenth century from the mimetic to the creative, from what M.H. Abrams once termed the image of the mirror to that of the lamp, did not remain static. As these passages suggest, it underwent a further metamorphosis a few decades later, as the intensity attributed to the creative process became heightened. And the image shifts accordingly. R.A. Foakes has perceived that, for the Romantic poet, it was the gentle moon that functioned as the symbol of creativity. Throughout Coleridge's poetry, he notes, '. . . the moon in particular seems, as a light that shines in darkness, to symbolize the work of the imagination'; in the final book of Wordsworth's *Prelude*, it reigns in single glory over the grand vision; and in Keats' *Endymion*, a human being becomes immortalized by love of the moon.[47] But the moon could no longer serve that function in the next generation, the power of creativity being now conceived as a flaming force, for which the symbol was to be the sun shining in its full splendour.

Turner's *Ancient Italy – Ovid Banished from Rome* of 1838 (Fig. 2), constitutes, I believe, despite the absence of any known contact between the two, a visual embodiment of Carlyle's conception of the creative imagination, his interpretation of it as 'a light-element and fire-element, which if you but awaken it shall irradiate and illuminate the whole'. The sun transfigures the entire scene, absorbing into an overriding harmony the social disorder represented by the foreground figures escorting the exiled poet from the city through the objects randomly scattered in their path. But to attribute that function exclusively to the sun is to beg the question, for it is, of course, ultimately the artist's imagination that has imposed that order upon the scene. Schelling, as the heir of Kant, had described the surge of unconscious energy from which artistic creativity derives as '. . . the eternal sun in the realm of the mind', and it is in that co-existently symbolic sense that the depiction of the sun in these paintings is to be read.[48] Its placing in these canvases in a commanding position, as the element from which the energy of the scene derives, a process already perceptible in the earlier Carthage canvases but reaching its fulfilment in *Regulus*, continues with increasing power through the later 'fiery' paintings, indicating how integral that symbolism was to his new, developing conception of the purpose of the artistic act – to impose by the power of his flaming imagination an aesthetic harmony upon the incoherence, violence, and inexplicable fortuitousness of terrestrial events. It parallels Carlyle's view of history whereby chaos is controlled by the overview of the historian, scorning the pusillanimity or foolhardiness of those succumbing to the dictates of fortune, and searching at all times for the heroic will, able to impose its vision upon the anarchic confusion and, with fiery, god-like power, to direct the course of events:

> Despicable biped! what is the sum-total of the worst that lies before thee? Death? Well, Death; and say the pangs of Tophet too, and all that the Devil and Man may, will or can do against thee! ... And as I so thought, there rushed like a stream of fire over my whole soul; and I shook base Fear away from me forever. I was strong, of unknown strength; a spirit, almost a god.[49]

Behind that shared response lay a crisis of belief recently explored by John P. McGowan, the transition from the Lockean epistemological tradition, relying for its perception of truth upon the sense-data transmitted to the human mind, and the Romantics' apocalyptic yearning, their awareness of a transcendent truth, divine in origin, which they hoped would be revealed to them through the mediation of the natural scene.[50] With faith in the divinity of such truth now weakened in subsequent decades, it would seem that both Carlyle and Turner located the source of revelation exclusively in the power generated by the artist himself, 'the Priest or Interpreter of the Holy' as Carlyle called him, whose function was no longer to transmit received truths but, as a hero in his own right, to comprehend and to re-create the sacred verities through his art.

The Romantic concept of the sublime, in line with Burke's treatise, as an awed apprehension of the intimidating powers of the universe – the view reflected in Wordsworth's revelatory experience on stealing the boat in his *Prelude* as the huge mountains seem to pursue him with their moral lesson, or in Friedrich's *Arctic Shipwreck* of 1824, where human activity is crushed or dwarfed by the forces of nature – is replaced in this period. The intuitional discovery of cosmic truths is no longer an event induced by the effect of the environs on an essentially passive viewer but arises from a bold assertion of self, the writer's or artist's domination of the scene. Fichte's modification of Kant's philosophy had involved precisely that change. For him, intellectual apprehension of the sublime truths of the universe result from willed acts, ensuing from a religiously-motivated dissatisfaction with one's own knowledge and a determination to discover metaphysical verities. So indeed is Carlyle's

climactic moment of revelation, his 'Baphometric Fire-Baptism' a
willed assertion of self:

> ... then was it that my whole ME stood up, in native God-
> created majesty, and with emphasis recorded its Protest ... The
> Everlasting No had said: 'Behold, thou art fatherless, outcast, and
> the Universe is mine (the Devil's)'; to which my whole ME now
> made answer ...[51]

In the context of that cultural shift, Turner's indebtedness to and
admiration for Claude Lorrain may be seen as representing his earlier affinity to the Lockean tradition, while such canvases as his *Shipwreck* express his proclivity to the Burkean sublime. But the Petworth
phase, culminating in the 1830s, reflected his transition to the newer
conception of the artist as suffusing and metamorphosing his material with the transcendent power of his glowing vision, a process for
which the sun served as the perfect symbol.

In response to deconstructionist readings, Anne Mellor has perceptively drawn attention to the irony or paradox within Romanticism, the self-destructive quality of the creative process in that period
whereby the poet, acknowledging the fluidity and impermanence
of nature, recognized that his own finite attempts to preserve the
scene for perpetuity were themselves equally doomed. Conscious
of his own ephemerality, he oscillated between self-creation and
self-annihilation, alternating, as did Byron, between commitment
and aloofness.[52] But by the time of Carlyle and Turner, it may be
argued, the scepticism implicit in that view had been replaced by
a new confidence, the conviction that the artist is indeed capable
of emerging from the chaos around him and, by the power of
his personal vision, can play God. The vortex effect in so many of
Turner's paintings is not a despairing vision of universal disorder.
If so, how does one account for the invigorating stimulus and
splendour imparted by his canvases? The maelstrom effect is only
one component in a more complex and ultimately more positive
apprehension of reality. The vortex does represent the ephemeral
and uncontrolled, whether it be the confusion and savagery of
conquest in his Hannibal, the advent of typhoon and storm in his
sea-scapes, or the distorted passions of human greed and vicious-
ness expressed in the powerful canvas dating from 1840 of *Slavers
Throwing Overboard the Dead and Dying in the Turmoil of an Approach-
ing Typhoon*, with the frail ship tossed helplessly in the blackening

waves, human limbs torn apart by predatory creatures, and the sky a mass of whirling movement in warning of the oncoming storm. But that vortex in his major phase is set against the stabilizing centrality of the sun itself, the compelling symbol of the artistic imagination, present either as a glowing sphere visibly co-ordinating and harmonizing the whole in its mellowing incandescence or, in such paintings as *Slavers* . . . , as the hidden source of illumination in the bright right-hand side of the canvas, awaiting its opportunity to break through the darkness and to impose order upon the haphazard, the vicious, and the impermanent. Indeed, as social protest, as a call to mankind to eradicate from its midst such appalling inhumanity, the painting assumes man's ability to rectify the chaos.

Critics of Turner's paintings have long stressed the darker side of his character, Jack Lindsay, for example, identifying the vortexes, in his psychoanalytical reading of the paintings, as representing the dreadful convulsions and spasms of his insane mother which the artist so long had to witness and endure. John Gage has similarly interpreted his work as identifying the sun with a terrible avenging God, '. . . a true source of Turner's growing pessimism which expressed itself not alone in darkness but also in the more awful sublimity of light.'[53] That Turner had cause to be of a melancholy turn of mind as a result of his filial suffering is certainly true, but there is no solid evidence to support the claim that he was in fact melancholy, and psychoanalytical deductions can be notoriously misleading. It is, for example, a platitude of critical history that the darker elements in Byron's personality are to be attributed in large part to his physical disability, the club foot with which he was born; but it is rarely noted that Sir Walter Scott suffered from a similar malformation, and yet was of a genial and optimistic disposition. Without actual evidence of Turner's tendency to gloom, it is mere conjecture to assume it and to read such dark imaginings into his paintings. There is, of course, the testimony of the poem he wrote and from which he frequently drew the lines appended to his paintings, *The Fallacies of Hope*. The title alone might seem to indicate a profound pessimism and has served as a basis for such assumptions among historians. But the poem was, in fact, a very conventional and rather weak imitation of James Thomson's verse with its echoes of the graveyard poetry still fashionable at that time, the quotations from it being intended to evoke for his canvases the solemnly meditative mood associated with such scenes. To his view of *Dolbarden Castle*, for example, he attached the lines:

How awful is the silence of the waste,
Where nature lifts her mountains to the sky.
Majestic solitude, behold the tower
Where hopeless OWEN, long imprison'd, pined
And wrung his hands for liberty in vain.

To deduce from this conventional pose a fundamental melancholy of disposition is scarcely justified, especially in relation to the major phase of his painting, his brilliant series of sun-drenched canvases glowing with vitality and vigour, where the appended quotations from his poem now refer generally to mythological incidents rather than moods of melancholy.

The threat of cataclysm portrayed by both artist and writer was, as their shared response suggests, not a personal threat to their private lives. The foreboding implicit in their sense of impending doom would seem, at least on the evidence of Carlyle's writings, to have arisen from one of the central anxieties of the Victorian era, from fears social, religious, and political in origin. No reader familiar with that period needs to be reminded how ominously the dread of a Jacobin uprising in England loomed in people's minds. Although historically the threat was never to materialize, the fear of a violent overthrow of the established class structure such as had been witnessed across the Channel, a revolution created by rioting mobs surrendering to the basest human passions, was ever-present. Pitt's imposition of the death penalty for rioting in 1793 had contained for the moment the restlessness among the working class, and the subsequent carnage at Peterloo had shocked both sides into temporary immobility; but by the late 1820s, introducing the period we are examining, the appalling poverty created by a series of failed harvests, by common-land enclosures, by the unemployment resulting from mechanization, and by the drift of the population into the crowded cities, had brought the threat of revolution once more to the fore, evidenced in the grim prophecies in Southey's *Colloquies on the Progress and Prospects of Society* published in 1829. 'The country', as Arthur Hallam recorded in 1830, 'is in a more awful state than you can well conceive. While I write, Maddingley, or some adjoining village, is in a state of conflagration, and the sky above is coloured flame-red ... The laws are almost suspended; the money of foreign factions is at work with a population exasperated into reckless fury.'[54] If the social fabric seemed about to be rent, the haven of religious faith appeared equally insecure in the light of Strauss's *Leben Jesu* of 1835 soon to be translated by George Eliot, coupled with the accumulation of scientific evidence contradicting the accepted biblical account of creation. There was Lyell's *Principles of Geology* of 1830–3, which was to elicit from Ruskin the bitter complaint: 'If only the geologists would let me alone, I could do very well, but those dreadful Hammers! I hear the chink of them at the end of every cadence of the Bible verses . . . I would give all the poetry of Isaiah and Ezekiel willingly for one or two clear dates.' Intimations of chaos were in the air. John Martin's *The Expulsion of Adam and Eve* of 1827, although commissioned to illustrate Milton's epic, instinctively transforms the quiet hopefulness of the poem's concluding lines into one of grimness and horror. In the original, the sorrowing couple, comforted by the archangel Michael, pass hand-in-hand through the gateway of Eden to find that

> The World was all before them, where to choose
> Thir place of rest, and Providence thir guide . . .

Here, the gloomier vision of Martin's own time prevails, a threatening, cataclysmic landscape inhospitably composed of jagged rocks, dark chasms, and dangerous precipices beneath a stormy sky. And across the ocean in the same year, Thomas Cole confirmed that pessimistic mood in his own horrific version of the same scene, with the added element of trees almost plucked from their roots by powerful winds and, in the left foreground, a deer's carcass being torn apart by a ravenous wolf. The ominous element in Cole's paintings is particularly notable in the light of R.W.B. Lewis' identification of the more positive and optimistic 'Adamic' quality in American culture, whereby the pioneer on that continent saw himself as a figure of heroic innocence poised at the start of a new history.[55] But here the fears and uncertainties of that generation dominate the scene.

The prominence of the theme of cataclysm during the period we are examining has been recently examined by George Landow, who notes how images of shipwreck, plague, volcanic eruption, and other such disasters recur throughout the literature and art of the time.[56] It was that general mood which clearly motivated the simultaneous convergence of Carlyle and Turner on to that theme. But the negative aspect of those manifestations should not be seen in isolation. They did not only represent crisis but suggested concomitantly the

means of overcoming it. As J. Hillis Miller has reminded us, the
sense of *Deus absconditus* in this period cast the poet or artist back
on his own resources, forcing him to search within himself for a
method of overcoming the black void.[57] With the sense of threatening doom, there may be seen to arise simultaneously a conviction
that the artist's function was in some way to control or impose
order on the envisaged turmoil. Carlyle found his solution in the
creative faculties of the individual poet, artist, or heroic leader,
drawing his strength from the divine, yet to a large extent expressing his own innate powers. What is man, Carlyle asks, but '. . . a
Symbol of God; is not all that he does symbolical; a revelation to
Sense of the mystic god-given force that is in him.'[58]

To that mood may be related one of the most enigmatic paintings
of Turner's final years, *The Angel Standing in the Sun* (Fig. 3) from
1846. Ostensibly it is a depiction of the vision recorded in *Revelations*
19:17, 'And I saw an angel standing in the sun; and he cried with
a loud voice, saying to all the fowls that fly in the midst of heaven,
Come and gather yourselves together unto the supper of the great
God . . .' But why Turner, who was not of a religious bent, should
have chosen that theme remained puzzling until comparatively
recently, when Jack Lindsay recognized it as related to Ruskin's
laudatory description of the artist some three years before in the
first volume of *Modern Painters*. In a passage criticized as blasphe-
mous in its extravagant praise and accordingly removed from the
next edition, his admirer had pictured him

> . . . sent as a prophet of God to reveal to men the mysteries of His
> universe, standing, like the great angel of the Apocalypse, clothed
> with a cloud, and with a rainbow upon his head, and with the
> sun and stars given unto his hand.[59]

Turner, however, while capturing the spirit of Ruskin's description,
did not reproduce it exactly, and the changes are fascinating, especially in the context of the theme being explored here. The angel,
instead of heraldically holding an emblem of the sun in his hand as
Ruskin had described him, is here placed within the dazzling radiance itself. At his feet is a serpent whose presence had often been
interpreted by art historians as indicating once again the innate
pessimism of the artist. But seen in the context of this contemporary conception of the artist's task as the heroic imposition of
order upon chaos, his location within the dazzling solar radiance

transforms him in effect into an emissary of the triumphant sun, driving forth by its purifying power the forces of evil from the world, that evil represented by the chained serpent writhing in the foreground, beside the figure of the murdered Abel and the fleeing, skeletal symbol of death.

This shared assumption that artist, writer, and heroic leader were to appropriate the faculties of the divine and create light and harmony out of chaos may be relevant to an aspect of Turner's practice widely remarked upon at the time, and an unfailing source of awe to his contemporaries. During his major phase, it was his habit to submit his canvases for exhibition in an unfinished state, the paintings often consisting of no more than a few smudges or blotches, which he proceeded, on the allotted Varnishing Days before the official opening, to transform into finished works of art before the eyes of his colleagues. Rather than mere eccentricity as it has usually been regarded, such practice was, it would seem, a public demonstration of that very conception of the artist's function which he held dear, his desire, with more than a touch of showmanship, to 'play God' before an audience of his colleagues, ostensibly ignoring the crowd of curious professional onlookers yet clearly delighting in displaying his own version of the *Fiat lux!* as, before their eyes, he transfigured the chaotic rudimentary smears into a brilliantly integrated painting. The familiar account by E.V. Rippingille, who witnessed such a demonstration of Turner preparing his *Burning of the Two Houses of Parliament* for the 1835 Exhibition at the British Institution, takes on a deeper meaning in the light of this interpretation, the opening comments being especially relevant to this reading. Turner, Rippingille recalls, arrived well before the others:

> Indeed it was quite necessary to make the best of his time, as the picture when sent in was a mere dab of several colours, and 'without form and void', like chaos before the creation. The managers knew that a picture would be sent there, and would not have hesitated, knowing to whom it belonged, to have received and hung up a bare canvas, than which this was but little better. Such a magician, performing his incantations in public, was an object of interest and attraction.

He describes the intensity of the artist's concentration and his refusal to exchange even a word with his colleagues until, at the end of the performance, with lordly disdain for the onlookers:

... Turner gathered his tools together, put them into and shut up the box, and then, with his face still turned to the wall, and at the same distance from it, went sidling off, without speaking a word to anybody, and when he came to the staircase, in the centre of the room, hurried down as fast as he could. All looked with a half-wondering smile, and Maclise, who stood near, remarked, 'There, that's masterly, he does not stop to look at his work; he knows it is done, and he is off.'[60]

Other accounts, such as that of Sir John Gilbert cited earlier in this chapter, stress the transforming 'fire' he seemed able to create by those late touches. There was the incident from 1832 when one of his sea-scapes was hung nearby Constable's *Opening of Waterloo Bridge*. C.R. Leslie recounts how Turner stood there comparing the two works, and then, putting a round daub of red lead somewhat bigger than a shilling on his grey sea, went away without saying a word, thereby making Constable's painting look weak in comparison:

... I came into the room just as Turner left it. 'He has been here', said Constable, 'and fired a gun.' On the opposite wall was a picture, by Jones, of Shadrach, Meshach, and Abednego in the furnace. 'A coal', said Cooper, 'has bounced across the room from Jones's picture, and set fire to Turner's sea.'[61]

Lawrence Gowing noted some years ago how Turner's witnessing of the burning of the Houses of Parliament in 1834 released '... a fantastic force' in his work whereby the barrier between reality and imagination vanished, an incandescence of fiery, hot colour dominating his subsequent paintings.[62] The change may have occurred a little earlier in his career, either during his two visits to Italy in 1819 and 1828, or, as in the view I have adopted here, during his stay at Petworth, with his witnessing of the Parliament fire a few years later intensifying the process; but the principle argued by Gowing is undoubtedly correct, that from this period onward the marks of pigmentation on his canvases cease to conform mimetically to any identifiable object in the actual scene. They convey instead the essence of the view or object, serving often as little more than an allusion for which the viewer was required to supply the associative link. The fish attacking a drowning man in the right-hand corner of *Slavers* ... are of no recognizable species, and are no more than intimations of sea creatures. Ruskin, committed to the principle in art of accurate and detailed copying of nature, was, of course, to educate the public in later years to appreciate Turner's supposed truth to detail, explaining how the chalky appearance of his waves, condemned by contemporaries as incongruously resembling veined marble slabs, arose from his refusal to accept the unrealistic blue-green transparency conventionally accepted by earlier painters. But if Ruskin's defence on the grounds of verisimilitude held true for *Calais Pier* and the canvases belonging to his naturalistic phase, it was markedly inappropriate when applied to the later period, however hard Ruskin tried to apply that mimetic principle even there.[63] It should be seen rather as Turner's attempt to reach beyond the tactile to the quintessential.

That, as we have seen, was the distinguishing quality of Carlyle's writing too, reflecting his insistence that the true poet penetrates the clothes or disguise of the mundane, possessing an '... eye that flashes direct into the heart of things, and sees the truth of them.'[64] Accordingly, he offered like Turner a refraction of each scene into metaphors communicating the writer's emotional engagement, in a manner whereby his own pulsating vision energized the depiction. At times, the employment of this technique by writer and artist draws remarkably close, as in the following passage by Carlyle, presaging the swirling rush of Turner's famed *Rain, Steam, and Speed* (Fig. 4), not necessarily in theme (the word *train* being used here in its military sense) but in its artistic treatment of the image:

> Thus, like some wild-flaming, wild-thundering train of Heaven's Artillery, does this mysterious MANKIND thunder and flame, in long-drawn, quick-succeeding grandeur, through the unknown Deep. Thus, like a God-created, fire-breathing Spirit-host, we emerge from the Inane; haste stormfully across the astonished Earth; then plunge again into the Inane.[65]

The bond they share is their authors' desire, transcending the detailed and particular, to capture instead the speed and excitement of their swirling visions, their passionate personal response to the scene. Lady Simon, in a frequently-quoted account, recorded how, during a storm, her fellow traveller Turner thrust his head out of the window as they were speeding along in order to experience the full force of the elements and the rushing movement. That incident, as she afterwards recognized, served as the basis for this painting. What may be easily overlooked in that account is that

Turner was on that occasion inside the vehicle and not, as in the painting, observing it from a fixed point some distance away. His brilliance here has been to merge the two experiences and thereby to achieve a distillation or universalizing of the whole. The train is seen hurtling forward from the vantage point of a stationary onlooker, while at the same time imposed upon that scene is the sensory response of the passenger, the blurring of landscape and thrill of swift movement encountered when travelling at such unprecedented speed.[66]

Such confident creative energy is at the opposite pole to the 'lost vision' of the Romantics. The vein of weariness and nostalgia in that earlier phase, in Wordsworth's despair of ever recovering the freshness of childhood response, in Keats' sense of the fret of living, or in Byron's self-portrait as 'grown agèd in this world of woe', is replaced in the 1830s by the phoenix image of rebirth and revitalization, in which the artist-writer is a vigorous participant, not waiting passively for the World-Phoenix to

> ... burn-out, and lie as a dead cinereous heap; and therefrom the young one start-up by miracle, and fly heavenward. Far otherwise! In that Fire-whirlwind, Creation and Destruction proceed together; ever as the ashes of the Old are blown about, do organic filaments of the New mysteriously spin themselves: and amid the rushing and waving of the Whirlwind-Element come tones of a melodious Deathsong, which end not but in tones of a more melodious Birth-song. Nay, look into the Fire-whirlwind with thy own eyes, and thou wilt see.[67]

Carlyle's flaming whirlwind is Turner's vortex, with the vital addition that out of each the creative force of the artist can produce a new and fully integrated vision. How close they were in their artistic technique may be indicated by a remark of Carlyle's on his own stylistic purpose. While engaged in preparing the last volume of *The French Revolution*, he wrote to inform his wife that he had completed his detailed study of the period and was now ready for the act of writing itself. His description of that creative process might have been taken from the catalogue of a Turner exhibition, his determination

> ... to splash down what I know in large masses of colours, that it may look like a smoke-and-flame conflagration in the distance ...[68]

2

The Fallen Woman

The degree of 'circulation' between contemporary social events and literary works, even when the former seem entirely divorced from the central concerns of the work, has emerged as a major pursuit in New Historicism (or, as its founder prefers to call it, 'the poetics of culture'). Louis Montrose's legal and ethnographic exploration of the inheritance rights of younger brothers during the Elizabethan period has proved illuminating for *As You Like It*; and Marjorie Levinson has convincingly demonstrated how indispensable to an understanding of *Tintern Abbey* is a knowledge of the industrial changes taking place in the Wye Valley – changes deeply disturbing to the poet and functioning as a subdued theme in a work ostensibly musing on the quality of his own creativity.[1] Tzvetan Todorov's theory of *vraisemblance*, the reader's instinctive interpretation of all texts in the light of other texts, a principle applied by him beyond the parameters of the written word to encompass broader aspects of cultural interpenetration, opens the further possibility of expanding the exploration of such social changes to include the visual arts.[2] I should like to investigate an instance of such cross-media interrelationship in the light of recent gender studies.

Thematic convergence, the noticeable recurrence at a moment in history of a topic or image repeatedly selected by writers and artists often unaware of their colleagues' interest and, at times, only faintly conscious themselves of the deeper attractions it holds for them, can prove a valuable indication in synchronic enquiry, suggesting the relevance of that theme to some fundamental concern of the time. Within the painting, drama and literature of this period there is a striking instance of such convergence, a concentration upon the image of the Fallen Woman.[3] The interest was directed not to the hardened professionals who had amused the dramatists of the Restoration, the unashamed courtesans and easy-living actresses of the theatre, nor upon the rustic laxity of morals typified by Fielding's Molly Seagrim.[4] For the Victorian, it was the fallen woman wakened into remorse for her past actions, and yearning for forgiveness and compassion. Although further instances continued to

occur through the later years of the century, often with shifting
emphases, the main concentration upon that theme within the novel
emerges in the period around 1850. Most representative are the
seduction of Little Em'ly by Steerforth in *David Copperfield* (1849–50),
Henry Bellingham's dalliance with and desertion of the orphan girl
in Mrs Gaskell's *Ruth* (1853), Barnes Newcome's affair with a factory girl whom he eventually '. . . flung out of doors without a penny,
upon some pretence of her infidelity towards him' in Thackeray's
The Newcomes (1854), the thoughtless corruption of Hetty by Arthur
Donnithorne in George Eliot's *Adam Bede* (1858–9) and, across the
Channel, Alexandre Dumas's *La Dame aux Camélias* of 1848 leading
to Verdi's *La Traviata* of 1853, both of which aroused great interest
in England, the play version of Dumas's novel becoming one of the
most popular dramas on the English stage.[5] How intense that interest was in the mid-century may be indicated by a remark in 1860
in the *Saturday Review*: 'We seem to have arrived at this point – that
the most interesting class of womanhood is woman at her lowest
degradation . . . and painters, preachers, and sentimentalists have
kept the excitement at fever-pitch.'

As that comment indicates, the interest of the novelist in that
subject was, during those same years, matched by the painter.
Richard Redgrave's *The Outcast* of 1851 depicted what was now to
become a recurrent Victorian theme, a father's expulsion of his
errant daughter from the home, together with her illegitimate baby;
Rossetti's *Found*, begun in 1851, chose as its sentimental subject
the country drover's discovery on his way to market of his former
sweet-heart corrupted by the city, the calf enmeshed in a net on
the cart beside him symbolizing her plight;[6] Holman Hunt's well-
known canvas *The Awakening Conscience* (Fig. 5) of 1852 explored
the dawning remorse of a kept mistress; the popular sequence of
three paintings by August Leopold Egg, *Past and Present* (Fig. 6) of
1858, narrated pictorially the exposure of an adulterous wife and
the consequent tragedy brought upon herself and her family; while
Ford Madox Brown provided the most dramatic version in his
startling vignette of an unmarried woman thrusting her child at
the delinquent father in *Take Your Son, Sir* of 1857. The viewer,
placed there in the uncomfortable position of the irresponsible
parent, glimpsed only as a reflection in a mirror behind her, is
thereby compelled, as it were, to undergo the harrowing experience and share the guilt.[7] Associated with these works, to which we
shall return, were such themes as George F. Watts's *Found Drowned*

(1848–51) and Thomas Hood's poem *The Bridge of Sighs* (1844) with their assumption (the latter based upon a specific case) that such female suicides usually resulted from the shame of extramarital pregnancy or the life of prostitution dictated by poverty and starvation:

> Touch her not scornfully;
> Think of her mournfully,
> Gently and humanly;
> Not of the stains of her,
> All that remains of her
> Now is pure womanly . . .

And, together with them, was Martha Edell in Dickens' *David Copperfield*, about to fling herself into the Thames, and identifying herself there with the dark, tainted river as the symbol of her own corruption: 'I know that I belong to it. I know that it's the natural company of such as I am. It comes from country places, where there was once no harm in it – and it creeps through the dismal streets, defiled and miserable – and it goes away, like my life, to a great sea, that is always troubled – and I feel that I must go with it!'

In real life too, there was manifold evidence at this time of the prominence of that theme in men's minds, including Gladstone's nocturnal wanderings, so embarrassing to his parliamentary colleagues, through the streets of London in search of prostitutes to reform, and Dickens's establishment of a home, Urania Cottage, for repentant sinners of that class.[8] The initial model for the mistress in Holman Hunt's painting was, appropriately enough, a woman of easy virtue, Annie Miller, whom the artist himself undertook to rehabilitate. But the appropriateness to the painting's theme ended there, his attempt at improving her morals meeting with conspicuous lack of success.[9] As Gladstone was to discover to his chagrin, the recurrent depiction of the fallen woman in art and literature as the 'repentant sinner', longing to be re-accepted into society, bore only a limited resemblance to reality. A considerable proportion of the members of that trade were, as at all times, hardened professionals, many becoming successful and impenitent courtesans like the famous Catherine Walters, known as 'Skittles', who ended her days living in wealth and comfort in Mayfair, while numerous others exploited their professional contacts to marry into the wealthy upper classes, their previous prostitution being regarded by them, we are informed by a survey of the time, as a necessary and unregretted preliminary for such social and financial promotion.[10] As *The Times* wrote in a leading article in 1858:

> The great bulk of the London prostitutes are not Magdalens either in esse or posse, nor specimens of humanity in agony, nor Clarissa Harlowes. They are not – the bulk of them – cowering under gateways, nor preparing to throw themselves from Waterloo Bridge, but are comfortably practising their trade, either as the entire or partial means of their subsistence. To attribute to them the sentimental delicacies of a heroine of romance would be equally preposterous. They have no remorse or misgivings about the nature of their pursuit; on the contrary, they consider the calling an advantageous one, and they look upon their success in it with satisfaction.

James Brown has rightly pointed out that Dickens' novels are not social documentation, as Humphry House and others had implied, but specifically literary depictions, often sentimentalizing the contemporary scene;[11] and that marked discrepancy between the picture of the fallen woman as presented in the art and literature of the day and the genuine situation has, I would suggest, wider implications.

The traditional explanation of this mid-century artistic convergence has been patently sociological. It has been assumed that the new focus upon that theme resulted from an alarming increase in prostitution and in related instances of sexual licence in the Victorian period, an increase which had transformed the problem into the Great Social Vice of the age. In a recent study, Amanda Anderson has, for example, suggested that the Victorians saw the sudden proliferation of fallen women as representing a contemporary weakness within society, a failure to exert that kind of self-determination and control which J.S. Mill had been advocating.[12] But the basic assumption that a major escalation in such activities did occur at that time deserves closer scrutiny. It is true that the pressures of society upon young men to postpone marriage until they could afford to support an establishment at a level appropriate to their rank left them with an unenviable choice. They had before them the alternative of prolonged celibacy or of indulgence in the kind of discreetly conducted affairs which Victorian society, if it did not condone, at least recognized as an inevitable part of the system (involving, of course, a reprehensible double standard for the sexes).

It is true also that the number of prostitutes known to the police throughout England and Scotland in 1850 had risen to the figure of 50,000, with 8,000 recorded for London alone. But despite the impressive statistics – and such investigators as E.M. Sigsworth and T.J. Wyke have expressed doubts concerning their reliability – there is no evidence that these figures reflected any more than a proportional rise in prostitution matching the growth of the city.[13] In the Elizabethan era, we should recall, London had been equally notorious as a city teeming with whores, as is evidenced, among many other instances, in Robert Greene's *A Looking Glass for London* condemning the lewdness and debauchery of the city as a modern Nineveh, or in his confessional work *A Groatsworth of Wit Bought with a Million of Repentance,* as well as in the numerous 'conycatching' pamphlets produced by his fellow writers revealing the seamy world of the city's brothels. In the eighteenth century, Hogarth had addressed in *The Harlot's Progress* what he saw, no less than his Victorian successors, as a major concern of the day, a period when severe agricultural unemployment was forcing families to send their young daughters into the cities in search of work and, only too often, onto the streets in a manner to be repeated during the following century. If Hippolyte Taine was to report in 1850 that on the Haymarket and the Strand '. . . every hundred steps one jostles twenty harlots', that scene was certainly not unprecedented, Defoe having described London over a hundred years earlier in 1725 as similarly '. . . swarming with strumpets'.[14]

Quite apart from the specific profession of prostitution, the sexual licence existing behind the façade of Victorian propriety would also seem not to have been intrinsically different from that existing in earlier periods, and that continuity would again weaken the theory that contemporary profligacy had achieved some new prominence as the Great Vice. The tradition of employers taking advantage of conveniently available housemaids and the general frequency of extra-marital affairs in the middle to upper classes is amply attested for the seventeenth and eighteenth centuries by Pepys' diary and by Boswell's *London Journal,* both of which, by their chance survival as private journals not intended for publication, may be accepted as truthful accounts. The series of frequent sexual encounters they record no doubt typified the activities of many men of their time and, conversely, characterized the readiness of their paramours to comply. To argue, therefore, that the sudden emergence of the theme of the fallen woman in Victorian art reflected a significant

contemporary increase in prostitution or in sexual licence is historically dubious.[15]

In searching for the deeper motivation, it is well to remember
the weighty emphasis upon symbolism in the art and architecture
of the mid-nineteenth century, marking a conscious return to the
practice of medieval thought. A major impetus in the revival of
Gothicism, especially in the more serious phase characterising the
Victorian era, had been the desire to reintroduce a sacramental spirituality into a world becoming increasingly materialistic. Religiously
that tendency expressed itself, even among the most fervent opponents of Rome, in a re-emphasizing of the typological aspects of
Christian ritual and of ancient church architecture. The influential
Ecclesiologist, published from 1841 by the Camden Society, directed
church builders to recall at all times that the aisles on either side
of the nave were intended originally as visual affirmations of the
Undivided Trinity and should be constructed with that purpose in
mind; and that the overall shape of the church had, from the medieval period, been planned, as the term *nave* indicated, to express
its function as the ship or ark of salvation.[16] Ruskin was to incorp-
orate the revived typological approach into the aesthetic principles he advocated for the secular art of his time, recommending
the readoption by artist, sculptor, poet, and craftsman of '. . . that
great symbolic language of past ages, which has now so long been
unspoken'; and Holman Hunt recorded the thrill he experienced,
marking a turning-point in his own art, when he first read Ruskin's
explication of Tintoretto's *Annunciation*, with its enlightening comment that the tumble-down building in that canvas adumbrated the
crumbling Jewish Church and that Joseph's presence as carpenter
pointed towards the future reconstruction of the new Church.[17] Pre-
Raphaelite painting was redolent with such symbolism, the viewer
being instructed in the correct reading of detail where it was felt
that its significance might be missed. Rossetti thought it necessary
to append to his painting of *The Girlhood of Mary Virgin* (1848–9) a
sonnet providing a key to its complex iconographic allusions:

> These are the symbols. On that cloth of red
>   I' the centre is the Tripoint: perfect each,
>   Except the second of its points, to teach
> That Christ is not yet born. . . .
> The seven-thorn'd briar and the palm seven-leaved
>   Are her great sorrow and her great reward . . .[18]

Hunt's *Hireling Shepherd* of 1851 (Fig. 7) may, to the modern viewer, appear to be a light-hearted depiction of a pastoral flirtation; but for the Victorian viewer, the painting carried a more weighty moral message. Appended was a quotation from Edgar's song in *King Lear*:

> Sleepest or wakest thou, jolly shepherd?
> Thy sheep be in the corn:
> And, for one blast of thy minikin mouth,
> Thy sheep shall take no harm.

With that hint, the viewer would be expected to discern in the background one sheep that has already invaded the field, its head just visible above the corn, a second about to enter the prohibited area, while others, to the left of the tree, prepare to follow. But the artist's intent was more specific than an animadversion on moral responsibility. The scene was to be understood, he explained, as an attack upon the failings of contemporary churchmen, '. . . a rebuke to the sectarian vanities and vital negligencies of the day', the shepherd serving in the scene as a type of '. . . muddle-headed pastors who instead of performing their services to the flock – which is in constant peril – discuss vain questions of no value to any human soul'. Further emblems within the painting reinforced the message. The shepherd, displaying to the girl a pretty moth which he has caught in his hand, employs it as a means of sidling up and cuddling close; but the moth, as W.M. Rossetti noted in a contemporary review of the painting, is in fact a Death's-head Moth, an omen which causes the girl to draw back momentarily from his embrace – that latter reading being confirmed later by the artist himself.[19] The title of the painting was, moreover, a reminder in Gospel terms that the labourer, clergyman as well as shepherd, should be worthy of his hire.

This Victorian tendency to allegorical or heavily moral readings of art was extended to the novel, the story of Dorothea, as the prelude to *Middlemarch* takes care to inform us, relying upon hagiographical associations, the heroine intended to be 'read' as a Saint Teresa of Avila transposed into the Victorian age, with the fineness of her hand and wrist iconologically evocative of the Blessed Virgin as she had appeared to Italian Renaissance painters.[20]

The focus in post-modernist critical strategy upon art as representation rather than mimesis, together with its growing sensitivity

to mythic substructures in art and literature offer some encouragement for eschewing the established literalist or sociological reading of the prominence of the Fallen Woman in search of a deeper
motivation, a reading perhaps more appropriate to a Victorian period
nurtured upon weighty symbolism.[21] The renegotiation of literary
interpretation in terms of the politics of power as exemplified in the
works of Stephen Orgel and Roy Strong or in terms of class struggle
as in the work of John Barrell and others,[22] provides, as has been
noted, added incentive for exploring the phenomenon in an extra-
literary context. In contrast, however, to Marxist criticism which
has predominated in such enquiry, focusing especially upon bourgeois exploitation of the weaker elements in society, I should like
to consider the problem from an opposite viewpoint, as manifesting in the bourgeoisie itself, among middle-class writers and artists
of the day, a dawning and rueful recognition of their own guilt
in having exploited that power to excess.

The starting-point for the enquiry is, fortunately, so well-
established as to require no substantiation here. For I propose to
argue that the Fallen Woman, in a remarkably subtle way, constituted the obverse of one of the most familiar Victorian images, the
Angel of the House. The salient elements in that latter image had
involved the elevation of the virtuous woman into an idealized
model of purity, chastity and selfless devotion. She became, in the
phrase coined by Coventry Patmore, not merely the refined object
of male love but, in a more profoundly symbolic sense, the repository of certain moral and religious values not always adhered to in
the masculine world. She presided in her husband's absence over
a home which was to serve as a haven of spiritual refreshment
after the pressures of mercantile activity in the city. That change in
familial patterning, with the function of domesticity assigned to the
female, had been prompted in part by the Evangelical revival, urging
at the turn of the century, notably under the leadership of the Clap-
ham Sect forming around Henry Thornton, that the home should
serve as the source and protector of moral integrity. These were
principles popularized, in strong opposition to Mary Wollstonecraft's
Vindication of the Rights of Women, in Hannah More's celebrated novel
of 1807, *Coelebs in Search of a Wife: comprehending observations of
domestic habits and manners, religion, and morals*.[23]

But the institutionalizing of the home as the focal point of Victorian life in the 1830s was no less indebted to an economic and
social change of the time, a new conception of respectability for the

upper-middle-class wife, now connected with her place of residence. There emerged a clear line of demarcation, a division of status, between those families still living over the business premises from which they derived their income, where the wife served in the shop below or supervised whatever commercial enterprise was pursued there, and those more wealthy families which could afford to move their homes from the place of their trade to residential districts, with the husband now departing each morning for his mercantile engagements, leaving his wife unsoiled by business pursuits and free to care for the home, to attend to the children, and to prepare for his evening return.

John Cadbury exemplified this mid-century process. Setting up as a tea and coffee merchant in Birmingham in 1824, he followed the norm by moving into premises over his shop in Bull Street, where both his first wife and, after her premature death, his second wife assisted him in the business each day. But by 1832, he had prospered sufficiently to purchase a house in the more prestigious suburb of Edgbaston, his wife now remaining there to fulfil the new duties appropriate to a Victorian matriarch. Coupled with this display of prosperity and the demonstrable fact that the wife no longer needed to contribute to the family income was the growing conception that 'manhood' included a husband's ability to maintain his wife and family in a worthy manner, protecting them from any contamination through commercial activities. As Henry Broadhurst summarized that sentiment in a speech at the Trades Union Congress, men

> . . . had the future of their country and their children to consider, and it was their duty as men and husbands to use their utmost efforts to bring about a condition of things, where their wives would be in their proper sphere at home, instead of being dragged into competition for livelihood against the great and strong men of the world.[24]

In a manner which feminist criticism has so effectively revealed in recent years, the patriarchal society of the nineteenth century resulting from those and other changes saddled the woman with a passive task, the burden of embodying the male's spiritual ideals. She became, as Helena Michie has described the process, a text upon which the male inscribed his own cultural needs.[25] In a lecture delivered in 1864, Ruskin eloquently epitomized that Victorian assumption, describing how, while man must go out into the world and be hardened by failure, offence, and error, '. . . he guards the woman from all this; within his house, as ruled by her, unless she herself has sought it, need enter no danger, no temptation, no cause of error or offence. This is the true nature of home – it is the place of Peace . . . it is a sacred place, a vestal temple, a temple of the hearth watched over by Household Gods, before whose faces none may come but those whom they can receive with love . . .'[26] And William Wilberforce wrote to his wife from London asking her to pray for him, as it '. . . will be a comfort for me to know that you all who are, as it were, on the top of the mountain, withdrawn from and above the storm, are thus interceding for me who am scuffling in the vale below.'[27] Hence the prominence of domestic interiors in the painting of the time as hallowed precincts of comfort, shielded from the hurly-burly of the outside world. Drawing upon Dante, Petrarch, and the troubadour poets, the Victorian evolved a spiritualized religion of love in which woman was to be worshipped in a manner paralleling that of the Virgin Mary in the Middle Ages, as the embodiment of goodness and mercy, shedding a beneficent influence upon the rougher, more worldly male.[28] For many women that feminine ideal, created by male needs, provided a role which they willingly fulfilled in real life, Tennyson's wife Emily being seen by her admirers as an exemplary instance:

> Her great and constant desire is to make her husband more religious, or at least to conduce, as far as she may, to his growth in the spiritual life. In this she will doubtless succeed, for piety like hers is infectious, especially where there is an atmosphere of affection to serve as a conducting medium.[29]

As Samuel Smiles maintained in his widely-admired manual of 1859, the family home was '. . . the very nucleus of national character; and from that source, be it pure or tainted, issue the habits, principles, and maxims, which govern public as well as private life.'[30]

That image of female purity has long been recognized, then, as an attempt on the part of the Victorian to translate into symbolic terms the spiritual values to which he subscribed, embodying them in the image of the ideal wife. But the theme of the fallen woman, emerging so prominently in the art and literature of the mid-century, has, for some reason, been interpreted exclusively at the literal level, as a reflection of certain vices in the contemporary social scene. It

would seem, however, that her pejorative projection was more in-
tegrally related to its nobler counterpart. For if the Angel image
may be seen as a male exploitation of the female in terms of a
document on which to inscribe his own cultural text, there exists
in this instance what Bakhtin would call a dialectical sub-text,[31] a
cultural antithesis thrusting against it, to provide for that generation a two-fold metaphor of woman – as the exemplar of man's
moral ideals and at the same time as a personification of his failure
to attain them. Indeed, implicit within the image of 'the Angel in
the House' itself, even in its purest form, may be perceived a hint
of its negative reflection; for the very attempt of the Victorian male
to sanctify within that womanly figure the ideals and ethics of the
Christian faith in order to insulate her from the aggressive com-
mercialism of his business affairs reveals a recognition that whatever lay outside the home was in some way profane. It implied an
uncomfortable presentiment that those mercantile activities were
ultimately incompatible with the high moral principles enshrined
in the domestic refuge; and it was to image forth that latter feeling
of male guilt that the Fallen Woman emerged in the art and literature of the time. That moral dichotomy between the sacred and profane, the sense that the world of economic activity was unholy was,
we may recall, not part of earlier Protestant tradition which had
always urged the faithful Christian to carry his moral principles into
all aspects of his life, the Quakers, for example, establishing large
banking concerns in America and elsewhere through their reputation for scrupulous honesty and fairness in financial dealings.

Within the theme of the Angel in the House in its positive form,
that discomfort concerning commercial affairs remains no more
than a faint suspicion, pleasantly camouflaged by the convenient
assumption that women were too delicate to deal with mundane
affairs and that chivalrous man must protect them accordingly. But
in the context of the separation of the two worlds, the emerging
image of the fallen woman takes on a profound symbolic force,
representing a grave doubt whether the process of secluding the
Christian home from the realities of vigorous competitiveness
was feasible after all. As society became increasingly aware of the
appalling conditions in the sweat-shops, factories, and mines, conditions created by the remorseless cost-cutting which lay at the
foundation of the commercial and industrial expansion of Victorian
England, there emerged a guilty perception of the incompatibility
of such vigorous, competitive, and often ruthless self-advancement

with the basic principles of Christian compassion, altruism, and love for one's fellow creature.[32] The Victorian home, resting upon the wealth accumulated by those callous methods, could no longer be isolated from its profiteering source, becoming, on that metaphorical level, itself tainted and corrupt. The Angel of the House, representing the virtues of gentleness and charity, becomes, therefore, transformed allegorically into the Fallen or Prostituted Woman, a symbol of moral purity seduced by the heartless self-interest of the male.

The outcrop of works on that latter theme occurred, we should note, in the 1850s, at a time when the gap between the idealized world of the spirit and the unscrupulous exploitation of the poor by the business world had begun to be exposed.[33] While the Great Exhibition, providing firm evidence of England's leadership in industrial development and design, had served to consolidate the Victorian's pride in his country's material achievements, there emerged concurrently a counter-movement, a growing awareness of the grim cost in moral terms involved in creating the human infra-structure upon which that progress had been based. The previous decade, the 'hungry forties', had witnessed the most appalling poverty among the lower classes as the gap widened drastically between Dives and Lazarus, between the rising middle-class enriched by industrialist expansion and the low-paid factory operatives from whom their prosperity derived. Handloom weavers were being dismissed in the Midlands, destitute Irish immigrants were crowding into the cities, making the search for the few jobs available even more desperate, and the results were visible to all when, as the *Manchester Times* reported in July, 1842, '... hungry and half-clothed men and women are stalking through the streets begging for bread'. The petitions of the Chartist movement, restrained and reasonable though they were compared to the revolutionary events that had been occurring on the Continent, had been harshly rejected by Parliament, leaving the starving poor in even greater despair.

But if their case had been rejected politically, it was now being vigorously taken up by the writers of the day; and the dates are instructive. Elizabeth Gaskell's widely-read novel *Mary Barton* of 1848 brought home to the middle-class reader, to whom it was directed, an uncompromisingly vivid picture of the heart-rending hopelessness of a labourer deprived of his labour and compelled by prevailing economic forces, so incomprehensible to him, to watch his wife and children die of malnutrition or typhus in the over-crowded, stench-filled cellars to which they were condemned. Such suffering had existed previously, but had then been attributed with some justice to natural calamities over which man had no control, such as the successive failure of harvests. Moreover, the social distance between the classes had made it comparatively easy to salve conscience by resorting to such glib beliefs, often reinforced from the pulpit, that the cause lay in the workers' squandering of their earnings on drink and their reprehensible inability to save for lean times. Joseph Adshead's sociological study *Distress in Manchester: evidence of the state of the labouring classes* of 1842, testifying to the existence, in only four districts of the city, of over 2,000 fetid cellar homes in which thousands of children were being reared, quoted the Reverend R. Parkinson's comment that: 'The separation between the different classes, and the consequent ignorance of each other's habits and conditions' was the greatest impediment to any judicious and effective relief of the poor.

In the 1850s, that ignorance was swept away. Dickens' *Hard Times*, first published serially in 1854, exposed with unprecedented severity, coupled with a withering scorn more effective than Elizabeth Gaskell's sympathetic veracity, the ruthless maltreatment of workers by the Gradgrinds and Bounderbys of the age, whose sole consideration was the profit that could be extracted from them, '. . . ready to weigh and measure any parcel of human nature, and tell you exactly what it comes to.' It revealed the shocking inhumanity intrinsic to the new business ethic, the principle adopted by the great manufacturers of the age that 'two and two are four and nothing over', with the final line of the firm's financial balance sheet supplying the ultimate justification for their activities, whatever the sacrifice in human suffering.

It is precisely at that time that the image of the Fallen Woman emerges as a central theme in both art and literature, representing, as a counter-image to the Angel in the House, the growing perception that the morality of the Victorian era which she had symbolized was itself sullied. It reflected an uncomfortable suspicion that the discarding of the Christian values of selflessness, love and charity within the brutal cost-cutting factories and sweat-shops was, since it constituted the very source of the wealth upon which the home rested, too integral to it to allow of any neat separation.[34] Indeed, in *Hard Times* itself, a primary exposer of such moral hypocrisy, that image undergoes a fascinating metamorphosis. The Angel, conventionally representing the middle-class notions of piety, is dislodged from her indigenous position within the middle-class home. She is imported instead from the lower echelon, from the working-class world of the warm-hearted circus-people, untouched, as Dickens specifically points out, by the crude business ethics of the day, and now seen as the true repository of those moral principles of altruism and mercy. There was, we are informed, '. . . a remarkable gentleness and childishness about these people, a special inaptitude for any kind of sharp practice, and an untiring readiness to help and pity one another, deserving often of as much respect, and always of as much generous construction, as the every-day virtues of any class of people in the world.' Sissy Jupe's innate moral sensitivity, derived from the circus people to whom she belongs, resists, to the despair of her middle-class teachers, all attempts to train her into the statistical callousness of the Victorian dispensation. Only twenty-five out of every million inhabitants die of starvation per year, she is proudly informed by her tutors during a catechism on the achievements of the modern age:

> . . . What is your remark on that proportion? And my remark was – for I couldn't think of a better one – that I thought it must be just as hard upon those who were starved, whether the others were a million, or a million million.

Even more striking than this importation from the working class, however, is the corruption within this novel of the traditional middle-class heroine herself. Louisa, as the beautiful daughter of a wealthy entrepreneur, is the obvious choice as the potential Angel of the home. Yet she takes on instead the attributes of the Fallen Woman. She functions here as an image of morally-tainted Victorianism, coldly selling herself to the repulsively mercenary Josiah Bounderby in order to support a brother whose worthlessness and calculating self-interest she is totally unable to perceive. And, as a symbol of this infected ethical system, she falls from grace, drifting into an adulterous entanglement, from which, at the very brink of its consummation, she flees (like Holman Hunt's figure) in a last-minute awakening of remorse. Her fall from purity is inextricably linked by Dickens to the worship of Mammon prevailing in her time. As she herself declares, it was the Victorian system itself which had corrupted her, the materialistic teachings of her father Gradgrind

1.   J. M. W. Turner, *Regulus*

2.   J. M. W. Turner, *Ancient Italy – Ovid Banished from Rome*

3.   J. M. W. Turner, *The Angel Standing in the Sun*

4.   J. M. W. Turner, *Rain, Steam and Speed– the Great Western Railway*

As he that taketh away a garment in cold weather,
so is he that singeth songs to an heavy heart.

5. William
   Holman Hunt,
   *The Awakening
   Conscience*

6. (*below*)
   Augustus Egg,
   *Past and
   Present* (3rd
   scene)

7. (*above*) William Holman Hunt, *The Hireling Shepherd*

8. Dante Gabriel Rossetti, *Mary Magdalene at the Door of Simon the Pharisee*

9. J. E. Millais,
   *Mariana in the
   Moated Grange*

10. Gustave Doré, *Over
    London by Rail*

11. James Gillray,
    *Hero's Recruiting at
    Kelsey's*

12. (*below*) Honoré
    Daumier, *Le Ventre
    Législatif*

Loudon 1833

T. King

Cabinet Makers
Sketch Book 1835

13. Upholstered
couches, 1830s

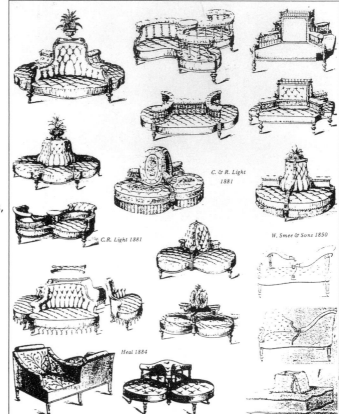

14. Upholstered couches,
1850–84

C. & R. Light
1881

C.R. Light 1881

W. Smee & Sons 1850

Heal 1884

15. 'Day-dreamer'
    armchair by H. Fitz-
    Cook from the 1851
    Exhibition

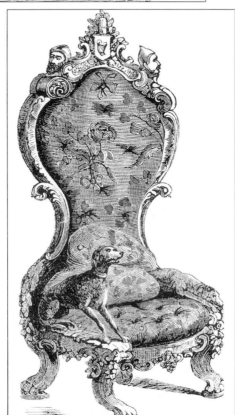

16. Armchair of Irish
    bog-wood by A. J.
    Jones of Dublin,
    from the 1851
    Exhibition

stultifying the natural love and compassion of her inner self which, under other circumstances, would have qualified her as the Angel:

> With a hunger and thirst upon me, father, which have never been for a moment appeased; with an ardent impulse towards some region where rules, and figures, and definitions were not quite absolute; I have grown up, battling every inch of my way . . . In this strife, I have almost repulsed and crushed my better angel into a demon.[35]

The web of analogues and contrasts which serve as the substructure to Dickens' novels, such as parallel father–child relationships, was impressively identified some years ago by Steven Marcus;[36] but to those which he and others have identified should be added the polarized images of the saintly and the corrupt female, with their important symbolic associations. In *David Copperfield*, the noble and generous Agnes, 'ever pointing upward . . . ever leading me to something better, ever directing me to higher things', serves most obviously as a counterpart to the self-centred child-bride Dora whom David first marries. Yet she is at the same time, in her unwavering fidelity to the principles of uprightness and morality, an anti-type to the weaker Em'ly, fallen from the status of Angel accorded her by the young David:

> I am sure my fancy raised up something round that blue-eyed mite of a child, which etherealized, and made a very angel of her. If, any sunny forenoon, she had spread a little pair of wings and flown away before my eyes, I don't think I should have regarded it as much more than I had had reason to expect.

But this potential angel, too, falls from grace, seduced by a Steerforth embodying those Victorian qualities of self-assertion and self-interest which Dickens so deplored, yet which at the same time he, like his fictional hero David, found so strangely fascinating.

In these recurrent images of the fallen woman, the character of the male seducer is equally fraught with symbol, representing the tarnished ideal of Victorianism which seduces and destroys. The oppression of the poor and the defenceless for personal gain is echoed here in a Steerforth exploiting the weaker boys at school for his own profit, heartlessly organizing the expulsion of the gentle Mr Mell from his teaching post and from his sole source of income for the sin of having a mother in the almshouse, and, in adulthood, contemptuous of the poor who, he remarks insensitively, '. . . may be thankful that, like their coarse rough skins, they are not easily wounded' by the conditions of their environment. This disdain for the indigent (which David ingenuously assumes must have been uttered in jest) is an evocation in this novel of Bounderby's callous dismissal of each and every plea for alleviation of their lot from his starving workers, on the grounds that they all '. . . expect to be set up in a coach and six, and to be fed on turtle soup and venison, with a gold spoon'. Such inclemency is the antipole to the biblical injunction to care for the widow and orphan, a charitableness represented in this novel by Steerforth's lower-class counterpart, the generous Mr Peggotty whose tiny boat-house has been hospitably and permanently opened by him to both widow and orphan, and whose beloved Em'ly, the fallen woman of the novel, Steerforth leads astray, tempting her with just such dreams of monetary gain and social elevation – the promise that she would be a lady and travel with him in luxury – as had corrupted the Victorian ideal.[37] In Mrs Gaskell's *Ruth* of 1853, whose sympathetic portrayal of the fallen woman created a sensation at the time of its appearance, the harsh working conditions described in the opening chapters are seen as the direct cause of her fall – a sixteen-year-old orphaned seamstress, drearily labouring through each night until the early hours for a miserable pittance and with no hope of reprieve, totally dependent upon the whims of her employer and, when summarily and unjustly dismissed, left with no prospect of shelter other than the support of a male friend, her future seducer.

An allegorical female polarity very similar to that in *David Copperfield* is to be found in George Eliot's *Adam Bede* of 1859, with the demure Quaker preacher, Dinah Morris, embodying the altruism, piety, and charity to which the Victorian age was overtly committed, while Hetty, with dire results, surrenders herself to Arthur Donnithorne in dreams of fine carriages, silks, and social advancement – again the very rewards that the perspiring merchant on the Exchange and the cost-cutting manufacturer in the Midlands desired for his own wife and daughters:

> . . . perhaps some day she should be a grand lady, and ride in her coach, and dress for dinner in a brocaded silk, with feathers in her hair, and her dress sweeping the ground like Miss Lydia and Lady Dacey . . .

The antithesis of Angel and Fallen in the novel is highlighted when Hetty is found at the time of her arrest for murder to have only '... a small red-leather pocket-book in her pocket with two names written in it, – one at the beginning, "Hetty Sorrel, Hayslope," and the other near the end, "Dinah Morris, Snowfield." She will not say which is her own name.' One need not remark on the implications of the place-names.

Arthur Donnithorne, a more subtle projection than Steerforth of the Victorians' uncomfortable awareness of a moral failing within the system, is no villain. He aims, indeed, to be the perfect Victorian gentleman, the ideal landowner, kind to his tenants, forward-looking in his schemes for improving the timber, generous and affectionate to those about him. But, as the authorial voice informs us, he assumes, as part of the generation into which he was born, that money, the panacea of the age, will answer for morality, endowing him with the wherewithal to purchase his way into heaven:

> ... we don't inquire too closely into character in the case of a handsome generous young fellow, who will have property enough to support numerous peccadilloes, – who, if he should unfortunately break a man's legs in his rash driving, will be able to pension him handsomely; or if he should happen to spoil a woman's existence for her, will make it up to her with expensive *bon-bons*, packed up and directed by his own hand.[38]

At first sight, the polarized pattern of noble and corrupt woman in the mid-century novel may appear to be contradicted by Thackeray's *Vanity Fair* of 1848, with the author's declaration at the very opening that his novel will possess neither hero nor heroine, as well as by the sympathy he often elicits in the course of the story for the resourceful, immoral, and lively Becky Sharp. But behind the façade of cynical worldliness – the author's pretence that we are witnessing the puppetry of Vanity Fair in performance – may be perceived the same basic motivation, the author's determination to expose the corrupting materialism and egoism of the Victorian world. For that purpose he employs essentially the same feminine contrast, however thinly disguised. No sensitive reader needs to be informed of the sentiments emerging from behind the sardonic pose of its author, that Dobbin, despite his clumsiness and his ridiculously large feet, and Amelia, for all her exasperating *naïveté*, her tardiness in appreciating Dobbin's qualities, and her abundance of tears – 'for the silly thing would cry over a dead canary-bird; or over a mouse, that the cat haply had seized upon' – ultimately embody those very Victorian ideals of compassion, selflessness, and sexual purity with which the authorial figure identifies, while Becky, as we have learned towards the end of the novel after the exposure of her adultery with Lord Steyne, has sacrificed both her body and her soul on the altar of the Victorian idol, Mammon.[39]

For a period so steeped in biblical terminology, whose leading philosophers, aestheticians, and secular sages resorted to the familiar language and rhetoric of the Scriptures in preaching their various causes, it is scarcely surprising that the image of the fallen woman should have borne connotations of the moral decadence of society, of the Victorian's whoring after strange gods, and after one such god in particular. Carlyle, whose pronouncements carried great authority for his readers, castigated his generation for deserting the biblical morality to which it paid lip-service, the principle of altruistic love of one's neighbour, in favour of what he called the 'Gospel of Mammonism' modelled on the scriptural villains. And he stressed in that forceful attack the theme central to this present chapter, the Victorian attempt to isolate their Gospel faith from their crass pursuit of wealth as if there were no connection between the two:

> ... we for the present with our Mammon-Gospel have come to strange conclusions. We call it a Society; and go about professing openly the totalest separation, isolation. Our life is not a mutual helpfulness; but rather, cloaked under due laws-of-war, named 'fair competition' and so forth, it is a mutual hostility ... 'My starving workers?' answers the rich Millowner: 'Did not I hire them fairly in the market? Did I not pay them, to the last sixpence, the sum covenanted for? What have I to do with them more?' – Verily Mammon-worship is a melancholy creed. When Cain, for his own behoof, had killed Abel, and was questioned, 'Where is thy brother?' he too made answer, 'Am I my brother's keeper? Did not I pay my brother his wages, the thing he had merited from me?'[40]

Throughout the Old Testament such desertion of scriptural teachings had been conceived in precisely the terms of the new Victorian image, as harlotry, a desecrating of the moral covenant to which the Hebrews were spiritually committed in favour of prostitution to pagan gods and pagan practices. The idolator, we are informed in

Leviticus 20:5–7, will be cut off, '. . . and all that go a-whoring after him, to commit whoredom with Molech, from among their people. And the soul that turneth after such as have familiar spirits, and after wizards, to go a-whoring after them, I will even set my face against that soul, and will cut him off from among his people.' The prophet Hosea, urging Israel to return to its rightful Lord, vividly depicted himself, representing the generosity of the divine, as a husband betrayed by his adulterous wife yet willing to accept her back without recrimination if she would prove remorseful.

Erwin Panofsky demonstrated to us some years ago how the study of iconology requires an examination not only of representational images in isolation but also of the dominant 'forms' or spatial structures within which they reside; and that observation has prompted subsequent historians to acknowledge the importance in each period of certain geometrical or other visual configurations predominating in each era and expressing the basic beliefs of the time. He himself pointed to the centrality in medieval thought of articulation or ramification, a concept underlying the structure of the cathedrals of the Middle Ages, designed not to be seen from some central position as integrated units but rather as a series of extensions or subdivisions branching off from the nave, thereby reflecting, he suggests, the intellectual process of classification and sub-heading in such contemporary compendia of knowledge as the *Summa Theologiae* of Aquinas.[41] Neoplatonism chose the perfect sphere to represent its conception of universal, cosmic harmony, the eighteenth-century Enlightenment favoured the image of equipoise – the subtly variegated symmetry of heroic couplet and arabesque expressing the rational weighing of truth. And in that context, the prominence of the Fallen Woman in mid-century literature and painting may be seen as a figurative projection of a profound disquiet of the time.

There was a further dimension to this new symbol, an adaptation of a long-established Christian tradition to contemporary concerns. In the sixteenth and seventeenth centuries, as part of the Council of Trent's determination to regain the loyalty of the backsliding and to restore the faith of souls tempted away by the Reformation, the theme of the Magdalene, the fallen woman of Christian hagiography, had achieved considerable prominence in painting, such canvases focusing, as one might expect, upon the act of penitence itself, the ecstasy of returning in piety to spiritual union with the divine.[42] In countless paintings of the time, she was portrayed, as in

Titian's version of 1560, in rapturous adoration during the moments subsequent to her conversion, with only her dishevelled garments and the flask of tears beside her to recall her sinful past. Now the theme was revived but with a different emphasis. The message is no longer an invitation to religious rapture but focuses instead on her life before her regeneration, the period of her meretriciousness, identified now with the sins of contemporary society. The scene chosen by Rossetti for his *Mary Magdalene at the Door of Simon the Pharisee* (Fig. 8) of 1858 depicts her in the moments prior to her conversion, as she faces with growing perception the choice she must make between the gaudy baubles associated with her dishonourable calling and the life of purity symbolized by the fawn gently browsing in the foreground, while a gorgeously apparelled male admirer, representing the wealth she is deserting, places a proprietary hand upon her knee in an attempt to dissuade her from leaving.[43] The scene symbolizes, therefore, with implications for the contemporary world, the choice to be made between an immoral pursuit of wealth and a life of Christian selflessness.

Hogarth's series, *The Harlot's Progress*, had, we may recall, been devoid of any religious or, indeed, of any larger symbolic meaning. It was an exclusively social protest relevant to his time, a castigation at the most literal level of the seducers and procurers of his day, such as the notorious Colonel Charteris and Mother Needham depicted in the opening engraving, entrapping innocent country girls into supposed domestic service as a gateway to prostitution. No hope of repentance was offered the victim and, after the initial scene slily comparing the fate of the foolish girl to the dead goose in her basket, she ceases to elicit sympathy, being transformed forthwith into a brazen hussy now deserving, Hogarth suggests, the sordid death consummating the moral lesson.[44] But the same does not hold true for the Victorian artist, where the final picture in the tripartite series by Augustus Egg (Fig. 9) is redolent with symbolism. She huddles with her child under a dockside arch, beside a wharf, with factories and warehouses visible on the further bank representing the source of London's commercial income, and above her a play-poster pointedly advertises *Victims*, to suggest the larger forces responsible for her plight. Before her is the dark river, the temptation to the oblivion of suicide and escape from shame associated with the fallen woman. The primary emblem, however, has been overlooked by critics, who, less responsive to symbolism than their Victorian counterparts, have traditionally interpreted the scene as allowing '. . . no hope for the sinner.'[45] But to a generation nurtured on iconological allusions in painting, the coruscating lantern at which she gazes so yearningly would have represented the star in the east, the star which appeared to the Magi in order to lead them to their spiritual rebirth. It was a symbol of salvation familiar to the Victorians, as in Dickens' *Hard Times*, when the dying Stephen directs Rachael's gaze to the heavenly star which had comforted him in the pit during his last hours, '. . . shinin' on me there in my trouble. I thowt it were the star as guided to Our Saviour's home.'[46] And for confirmation of that symbolism in painting, one may note how in G.F. Watts' *Found Drowned* of 1848–50, depicting the corpse of a woman washed up under the arch of a city bridge, a single star shines in the sky, as though offsetting the dark factory chimney and industrial tower below it. Such sentimentalism may be unpalatable to modern taste but, as Fred Kaplan has recently argued, that vein of overt emotionalism needs to be seen within the context of its time, representing in popular culture a resistance to the encroaching scientific determinism of the day, a rear-guard assertion of faith, despite all contrary evidence, in a benevolent universe concerned with the welfare of the individual and ultimately rewarding goodness and piety.[47] Within Augustus Egg's triptych, the Star of Redemption, however meagrely it may assist her within this temporal world, serves iconologically as the complement to her Fall (alluded to in the initial picture in this series by the worm-eaten apple on the floor and by a painting of *The Expulsion from Eden* hanging on the wall). It offers the hope that repentance may yet find recompense, if only beyond the grave.

The interest of these paintings in the sinner's gradual recognition of her guilt (a process absent from earlier Magdalene canvases, focusing solely on the spiritual rewards subsequent to conversion) would seem to represent the hesitant perception within the Victorian mind of their own hitherto unperceived culpability; and the penitence itself, the salvation represented by the star, emblemizes their hope that Victorian society might yet prove capable of cleansing itself. The most famous instance, Holman Hunt's *The Awakening Conscience* (Fig. 5), depicts, as its title underscores, the very moment of dawning remorse, the same moment of slow recognition as is captured by the facial expression of Rossetti's Magdalene. To view Hunt's painting in the way it has been traditionally interpreted, as an exclusively social commentary, an animadversion on the sexual modes of Victorian morality, is to miss these deeper reverberations.[48]

As Michael Baxandall has shown us for the quattrocento, there exists in each generation a 'cognitive style' for viewing art, a series of expectations predisposing the public and sensitizing them to respond to elements in contemporary painting which might not be readily discernible to succeeding generations.[49] The assumption in the mid-nineteenth century, on the part both of artists and their patrons, that allegory was intrinsic to art both for the larger scene and for each of its details was fully applicable in this specific instance, as we know from the account of its origins. An idea had arisen spontaneously among the members of the Brotherhood that they should produce works devoted to the subject of Vice as companion pieces to the portrayals of Virtue they had already produced, and the incident created some retrospective acrimony as each claimed later to have initiated the idea. What remains undisputed is that Rossetti's *Found* was consciously planned by him as a counterpart to his *Ecce Ancilla Domini*, thereby providing, as did most such thematic pairings, polarized representations of woman as Angel and as Fallen. Hunt, too, consciously conceived of his second painting as a 'material complement' to his emblematic *The Light of the World* of 1853–6, both canvases being laden with symbolic allusions.

Employing in that earlier work a form of allegory reliant upon the medieval Everyman tradition rather than upon the classical mythologizing of the Romantic poets, he had represented there the saving power of Christ in terms of a personified Divinity, holding a lantern and knocking for admission at the door of the Soul. The closed door, he explained in his book on Pre-Raphaelitism, represented the obstinately shut mind, the weeds stood for daily neglect, the orchard itself typified the garden of delectable fruit for the feast of the soul, and the bat, flitting about in darkness, adumbrated Ignorance. The painting was fraught with such allusions, as Ruskin perceived in his review of it, exemplifying in that review the task of allegorical interpretation expected from the spectator:

> The lantern carried in Christ's left hand, is this light of conscience. Its fire is red and fierce; it falls only on the closed door, on the weeds which encumber it, and on an apple shaken from one of the trees of the orchard, thus marking that the entire wakening of the conscience is not merely to committed, but to hereditary guilt . . . The light which proceeds from the head of the figure, on the contrary, is that of hope and salvation; it springs from the

crown of thorns and, though itself sad, subdued, and full of soft-
ness, is yet so powerful that it entirely melts in the glow of it the
forms of the leaves and boughs.

The music of the still small voice, Hunt added in his own description, was the summons to the sluggard to awaken and become the
zealous labourer under the Divine Master; and it was that message
which his *Awakening Conscience* was intended as counterpart to
transmit in a more 'material' or contemporary setting, the weighty
symbolism remaining despite the more realistic presentation in
this later work.[50] We should perhaps recall how embedded within
the Victorian consciousness was the idea of the soul's sudden conversion to higher ideals, whether religious or secular, many of its
leading thinkers having themselves experienced such elevation.
John Stuart Mill recorded in his *Autobiography* his emergence from
despair to hope in his younger days; Newman underwent a similar
experience in Sicily, which led him to devote his life to encouraging
the same emotional awakening in others, among them the young
poet Gerard Manley Hopkins; and the process of spiritual conversion, so characteristic of the Victorian era, was to inspire William
James to produce his brilliant psychological study of the phenomenon. The scene chosen by Holman Hunt, therefore, had wider
implications for his generation than mere sociological vignette.[51]

Within that painting, the false domesticity of the home established for the kept mistress has a special significance for this present
reading of the theme as a counter-image to the Angel in the House.
The vulgarity of the furnishings of the room, more apparent to a
contemporary, was at once noted by Ruskin. He remarked on the
significance of the cheap rosewood varnish of the piano and the
fatal newness of the embossed books unmarked by use. The art
critic of the *Athenaeum* similarly drew attention to the ostentatious
carpet, the gaudy mirror disproportionate to the size of the apart-
ment, and the flashy taste of the room as a whole. But that aspect
functions not merely as a mark of tawdriness in itself. The obtrus-
iveness of the cheap furnishings, together with the careless disorder
of dropped glove, discarded music, and tangled wool trailing on
the floor, ensured that the room would have been recognized by
any alert contemporary as a travesty of the well-run domestic interior on which the Victorian matron so prided herself, an interior
whose polished mahogany furniture and weighty centre-pieces of
genuine silver were designed to express the unimpeachable moral

and religious solidity of the Victorian household, under the responsible control of a wife devoted to her duties.

In such thematic convergences the deeper symbolic function
may, we have noted, not be consciously recognized by the writer or
artist as he responds to associations and impulses functioning at
a submerged level. On the other hand, we may justifiably enquire
whether there exists any actual evidence that Hunt himself was in
any degree aware of a broader allusion to the troubled conscience
of his generation – to the growing realization that the principles
of Christian charity proclaimed in the home were being contra-
vened at the very source of its wealth, by the oppression of the
poor in factories, mines, and workhouses. In art books, this painting is usually reproduced without its imposing frame, and hence
without the verses which Hunt had ordered inscribed upon it. Where
attention has been drawn to the quotation, it has evoked comment
only for its seeming irrelevance to the subject-matter of the painting
itself, or (with the familiar twentieth-century emphasis upon Victorian hypocrisy) has been explained away as a half-hearted attempt
on the part of the artist to camouflage his voyeurism – as Christopher
Wood puts it, '. . . to lend religious seriousness to such a risqué
subject.'[52] But the motto, which the artist directed William Combe
to inscribe on the frame 'as large as possible', cannot be so easily
dismissed. It reads: '*As he that taketh away a garment in cold weather,
so is he that singeth songs to an heavy heart*' (*Proverbs* 25:20). The latter
part of the verse is appropriate to the scene, but what relevance has
the initial section, the reference to the garment? – particularly if one
notes that Hunt has carefully suppressed the intervening words
'. . . *and as vinegar upon nitre*', presumably because he wanted the
opening phrase to carry its full weight. The verse from *Proverbs* –
as the Victorian immersed in Bible readings would have recognized – was a reference to a biblical prohibition concerning business
affairs. The Psalmist here echoes the command in *Exodus* 22:26
that commercial dealings must at all times be subordinated to the
demands of humanity and compassion, responsive to the cry of the
weak and the suffering. It specifies there the duty of returning each
evening any pawned or pledged garment, since it is required by the
debtor for warmth at night, even when that garment constitutes the
sole security for the financial transaction:

> If thou take thy neighbour's garment to pledge, thou shalt return
> it to him by the time that the sun goeth down; for that is his only

covering, it is his raiment for his skin: wherein shall he sleep? And it shall come to pass if he crieth unto me, that I will hear . . .

The scene of profligacy and guilt in the painting was linked, therefore, in Hunt's mind with the larger issue of business ethics and, in particular, with the immorality of exploiting the indigent. And the symbols within the picture fortify the message. On the wallpaper in this room, as Hunt himself explained, the corn and vine have been left unguarded by the sleeping watchers '. . . and the fruit is left to be preyed on by thievish birds'. It is a metaphor scarcely appropriate to an interpretation of the painting as a commentary on sexual mores, but highly relevant in terms of the Fallen Woman as examined here, a recognition of society's failure to fulfil its moral duties and, like the cat beneath the table playing with a helpless bird, cruelly ill-treating those weaker members within its power. Lest it be thought that those symbols of the abuse of the weak relate to the woman in this painting, forced, as it were, by starvation into prostitution or driven by society into the profession of a kept mistress (as Mrs Gaskell had argued of the indigent seamstress in *Ruth*), one may note that the female figure here bears no sign of being herself exploited, of being compelled against her will to follow that profession. She is, by all signs, a willing paramour whose consciousness of sin has only just arisen in her mind, tardily awakened by the notes played casually upon the piano. It is not she, therefore, who is to be equated with the helpless bird. As the inscription suggests, in her capacity as tainted woman she functions as a broader image of compromised morality, of a Christian society voluntarily selling itself for profit. If in this instance the fallen woman is a willing paramour, it should not be forgotten in this connection that from the time of the widely-read publications by both Greg and Mayhew, the prostitute had been recognized as in many instances forced into that trade by her dire financial needs, and she thus functioned literally as well as metaphorically as a visible symbol of society's exploitation of its weaker members. It is, indeed, in that latter context of society's meretriciousness that we may appreciate more fully the poignancy of the climactic scene in *La Dame aux Camélias* and *La Traviata*, the shock to the assembled company as the embittered lover contemptuously flings his gambling profits in the face of the courtesan, publicly exposing the pecuniary aspect of her trade while tragically unaware that she has already, as in Hunt's painting, awakened into remorse.

With the Fallen Woman recognized as the antipole to the Angel, another theme emerging into prominence at just this time may be identified as an associate symbol, an exploration of that same central concern from a different angle. The forsaken woman, deserted by her lover, represents, this time with the male figure bearing the full guilt, the same idea of moral domesticity frustrated by the Victorian pursuit of wealth, the potential Angel in the House unable to fulfil her desired role. Here too, poetry, novel, and painting of the mid-century converge upon the theme. There is Tennyson's *Mariana* rejected by her affianced Angelo to grieve in solitude in the moated grange, together with Millais' admirable depiction of that same scene. There is Miss Havisham of *Great Expectations* (1860), forsaken by her bridegroom on the day of the wedding to live on in embittered spinsterhood, and Lily Dale in Trollope's *The Small House at Allington* (1864) cruelly jilted by Adolphus Crosbie, so deeply hurt that she can never consider marriage again. As part of the eclecticism directing creative artists in all periods to choose only those elements relevant to their immediate needs, one may note how Tennyson has focused upon what is in fact a very minor element in Shakespeare's play and how neither he nor Millais even hints at the reunion and marriage in fact achieved by Mariana at the end of the play, presenting instead only the scene of her abandonment and despair, the aspect shared by the other images of deserted women from that period.

In Millais' painting of *Mariana in the Moated Grange* (Fig. 9), the contemporary conception of woman as the shrine of moral and religious values achieves full expression. The haloed saints, copied from the stained-glass windows in Merton College Chapel, and the table substituting as altar, with holy lamp, triptych, and incense, transform her room into a conventual cell. But the dreadful weariness expressed in her stance and the rich blue velveteen of her dress remind us that she is no celibate preferring a religious life of asceticism and withdrawal from the world, but a woman yearning to take her rightful place as a wife and mother within the Victorian home. The dominant imagery of the poem upon which Millais based this picture, echoed here by the mouse running undisturbed in the foreground of the painting, is of a house neglected and dilapidated:

> With blackest moss the flower-pots
> Were thickly crusted, one and all:

> The rusted nails fell from the knots
> That held the pear to the gable-wall . . .[53]

The ordered domesticity upon which the Victorian male prided himself as his sanctuary of morality and faith presided over by a loving wife has, in this thematic treatment, been vitiated. Miss Havisham's home is the embodiment of household disintegration and neglect, with its decaying wedding-cake (the frustrated promise of the familial home about to be established) overhung by cobwebs and crawling with black beetles. From behind the panelling can be heard the ceaseless scurrying of mice, the bars over the windows are rusting away, and the garden is grievously overgrown with weeds. Moreover, uniting these various instances into a consistent pattern is the crude financial motivation for the breaking of each engagement. Shakespeare's Angelo rejects his bride on learning that her promised dowry has been lost at sea; Crosbie deserts the gentle resident of the Small House at Allington in favour of the dazzling riches and social advancement proffered at Courcy Castle; and the scheming groom pledged to Miss Havisham, we learn by the end of the novel, had disappeared as soon as he could extort from her no further pecuniary gain.[54]

Mammon, in these recurrent scenes of fallen and rejected women in the painting and literature of the mid-century, is depicted as the force ultimately responsible for destroying the home. At a time when the domestic hearth, presided over by its mistress, had come to symbolize the sacred enclave of Christian love and charity segregated from the sordid affairs of commerce, the obverse of that image, the defiled or deserted female, represented, we may suspect, a growing awareness on the part of the Victorian that such meretriciousness could no longer be so easily sequestered. It manifested an emergent recognition of a contemporary socioeconomic factor, the circulatory interchange between art and the pressure of current conditions to which New Historicism has sensitized us, that the noble ideal was itself being corrupted by the ruthless pursuit of worldly profit, a pursuit so intrinsic to the material prosperity of the age, yet so inimical to the ideals of selflessness, compassion and love to which the Victorians consciously subscribed.

3

Commodity Culture in Dickens and Browning

(i)

From early in his career, as evidenced by the title he created for *Sketches by Boz*, Dickens had perceived the kinship existing between his own literary vignettes and those of the draughtsman. His original assignment as author of *The Pickwick Papers* had been in a subordinate capacity, hired to provide, as he put it, '. . . a vehicle for certain plates to be executed by Mr Seymour'; but the immense popularity of his contribution reversed the priorities, the success of that work being largely responsible for introducing in nineteenth-century England the marriage between the serialized novel and the accompanying illustrations, a hybrid form resisted for some time by the more staid three-volume novels of the day.[1] Dickens took very seriously the nature of that marriage between the media, recognizing the delicate balance that needed to be maintained in what was now becoming an essential partnership in the fictional process. In negotiating his earliest commissioned work, he became at once involved in a dispute recurrent throughout his career; his insistence, in the face of all contrary pressures, that the illustrations must not be imposed upon the writing but should '. . . arise naturally out of the text', as an integral part of the developing story. For the most part he worked in contented co-operation with his various illustrators, praising Cruikshank as an 'incomparable artist', but he examined scrupulously all proposed illustrations before publication in order to ensure their fidelity to the text.[2]

Dickens' affinities to the visual arts of his time are in that respect sufficiently well-documented. To argue for broader synchronic relationships might also appear superfluous as comparisons have so frequently been drawn between his own depiction of urban living and the remarkable series of engravings produced by Gustave Doré on the latter's visit to England, including his *Over London* (Fig. 10). Those engravings grimly record in similar chiaroscuro terms the cramped living conditions prevailing in the slum areas, the soul-destroying repetitiousness of the structures in which Londoners lived, the smoke-filled atmosphere, and the oppressive plethora of brickwork, scenes so evocative of Dickens' verbal portrayal of nineteenth-century London and of the provincial towns spawned by an industrial age:

> It was a town of red brick, or of brick that would have been red if the smoke and ashes had allowed it; but as matters stood it was a town of unnatural red and black like the painted face of a savage. It was a town of machinery and tall chimneys, out of which interminable serpents of smoke trailed themselves for ever and ever, and never got uncoiled . . . It contained several large streets all very like one another, and many small streets still more like one another, inhabited by people equally like one another, who all went in and out at the same hours, with the same sound upon the same pavements, to do the same work, and to whom every day was the same as yesterday and tomorrow, and every year the counterpart of the last and the next. (*Hard Times*, Chapter 5)

Doré, in his depressing view of *Whitechapel*, captured no less disturbingly than Dickens in his fictional account the chilling poverty pervading such areas, its denizens dejectedly huddled together as if unsure why fate has brought them there, and apprehensive of the destiny awaiting them on the morrow. That parallel response of author and artist, so widely cited by historians, might appear perfect evidence for the validity of synchronic investigation. Peter Conrad, for example, has written eloquently of the phantasmagoria of dreams and fears animating both Dickens and Doré, the London fog becoming in the novels, as in the engravings, a medium both for blurring the sharp edges of reality into the mysterious, and for suggesting that each shuttered house encloses some dark enigma.[3] The shared artistic technique to which he alludes (without substantiating his point) can certainly be supported from the text, such as the scene in *Little Dorrit* when Arthur Clennam revisits his old home:

> As he went along, upon a dreary night, the dim streets by which he went, seemed all depositories of oppressive secrets. The deserted counting-houses, with their secrets of books and papers locked up in chests and safes; the banking-houses, with their secrets of strong rooms and wells, the keys of which were in a

very few secret pockets and a very few secret breasts . . . The shadow thickening and thickening as he approached its source, he thought of the secrets of the lonely church-vaults, where the people who had hoarded and secreted in iron coffers were in their turn similarly hoarded . . .[4]

Yet that widely acknowledged comparison between the artist and writer, justified as it is, has no bearing on the theme of our present investigation since it is, in fact, chronologically misleading. Doré's engravings were not only produced long after Dickens' novels had already established in people's minds that depressing and melancholy view of the city. Even more significantly, the drawings of London had been specifically commissioned as illustrations for a book aimed at recapturing and, indeed, trading upon the spirit of Dickens' novels. Blanchard Jerrold, whose father had been a close friend of Dickens, was, in his *London: a pilgrimage* published in 1872 with Doré's drawings, to a large extent exploiting the popularity of the author (Dickens had died two years before), and the scenes and characters of his novels were repeatedly invoked in the course of the work:

On the road, and at the Derby, it is Dickens' children you meet, rather than Thackeray's. All the company of Pickwick – Sam Weller and his father, a hundred times; Mr Pickwick benevolent and bibulous: Jingle at the top of many a coach and omnibus. Pushing through the crowd, nimble, silent, and unquiet-eyed, Mr Fagin's pupils are shadows moving in all directions . . .[5]

and so on, in a lengthy paragraph citing Dombey, Scrooge, and numerous other such figures familiar to Jerrold's readers. The areas of London, moreover, which he selected in planning the book and to which he escorted the commissioned artist in order to supply material for the drawings, were chosen because of their echoing of Dickensian scenes. The shared viewpoint of artist and writer thus emerges as an instance not of parallel synchronic response but of an acknowledged indebtedness, subsequent in time. As additional evidence, one may note that Doré's stylistic affinity to Dickens is not apparent in his other work. His impressive illustrations to Coleridge's *Ancient Mariner*, for example, produced in 1875 and therefore almost exactly contemporary with these London engravings, create an entirely different ambience, evoking, as successful text illustration should, the Romantic boundlessness, dreaminess, and neo-Gothic horror as conveyed by that visionary poem, in a manner remote from that of his scenes of the English metropolis.

There is, of course, a further link with the French lithographers, most evident in the element of caricature in Dickens' writing, namely the exaggeration of facial features or the highlighting of personal idiosyncrasies which proved so valuable for his serialized novels, enabling readers to remember more easily the eccentricities of the various characters from one issue to the next. It was a technique strongly evocative of the satirical drawings of Honoré Daumier. But without detracting from that shared characteristic, which undoubtedly plays a major part in the formation of Dickens' style, it deserves to be seen less as an artistic innovation on his part or on the part of his contemporaries than as the culmination of a process gradually developing in both England and France over the previous hundred years. Fielding may have dissociated himself from the genre of *Caricatura*, distinguishing in a well-known passage between his own striving for fidelity to nature even in his most comic scenes and the tendency in that latter genre to produce mere burlesque – 'for sure it is much easier, much less the subject of admiration, to paint a man with a nose, or any other feature, of a preposterous size, or to expose him in some absurd or monstrous attitude...' But his own boisterous descriptions of such characters as Squire Western helped nonetheless to inaugurate in the novel a line of comic portrayal, often hyperbolic, which Smollett was able to take further, crossing the border of the human and the realistic into the realm of true caricature. It was a development paralleled in the arts, where Hogarth's figures, although they may be eccentric, remain human, with the possibility, as it were, of emerging from the canvas into real life, while in the work of Gillray and Rowlandson, they become exaggerated beyond human proportions. I have compared elsewhere in this connection the central figure in Gillray's *Hero's Recruiting at Kelsey's* (Fig. 11) with Smollett's description of Count Lismahago, whose thighs, we are told,

> ... were long and slender, like those of a grasshopper; his face was at least half a yard in length, brown and shrivelled, with projecting cheek-bones, little grey eyes on the greenish hue, a large hook-nose, a pointed chin, a mouth from ear to ear...[6]

And that progression from a more restrained and moderate form of caricature to its fully-fledged, unabashed type at the end of the

century was closely reflected (at times with some degree of collu-
sion between the arts, and accompanied by expressions of mutual
admiration) as Hogarth's mordant but ultimately naturalistic sat-
ires led into the flamboyant drawings of Rowlandson and Gillray,
culminating during Dickens' day in the political and social cartoons
characteristic of *Punch* in England and of *Le Charivari* across the
Channel.

There can be no doubt, then, that in that regard Dickens inevitably
shared certain qualities with the French lithographers of his time,
including Daumier. The latter had been imprisoned for his disrespect
in depicting Louis Philippe as Gargantua, and on his release won
considerable popularity for his irreverent representations of other
dignitaries of state, as in his 1834 lithograph of the French legis-
lature, portrayed as a congregation of owlishly somnolent figures
(Fig. 12). David Copperfield's first visit to an English law-court provides Dickens with an opportunity for no less irreverent a description of bureaucratic authority, employing a similarly reductive
technique:

> . . . on the two sides of a raised platform of the horseshoe form,
> sitting on easy old-fashioned dining-room chairs, were sundry
> gentlemen in red gowns and grey wigs, whom I found to be the
> Doctors aforesaid. Blinking over a little desk like a pulpit-desk, in
> the curve of the horseshoe, was an old gentleman, whom, if I had
> seen him in an aviary, I should certainly have taken for an owl,
> but who, I learned, was the presiding judge. In the space within
> the horseshoe, lower than these, that is to say on about the level
> of the floor, were sundry other gentlemen of Mr Spenlow's rank,
> and dressed like him in black gowns with white fur upon them,
> sitting at a long green table . . . Altogether, I have never, on any
> occasion, made one at such a cosey, dosey, old-fashioned, time-
> forgotten, sleepy-headed little family-party in all my life; and I
> felt it would be quite a soothing opiate to belong to it in any
> character – except perhaps as a suitor.[7]

Dickens' illustrator, Hablot Browne or 'Phiz', was in fact greatly
influenced by Daumier, admiring the latter's 'La Garde Malade'
which had just appeared in *Le Charivari*, and adopting its lines for
his own depiction of Mrs Gamp. But that delight in caricature was,
as we have seen, the end-product of a gradually developing process well established by the end of the eighteenth century rather

than specific to the Victorian period. In defining the originality of Dickens' artistic style and his specific contribution to the novel, one would need to search beyond that element of caricature, his satirical or humorous exaggeration of the features or mannerisms of his characters, to discern subtler aspects of his imaginative creativity.

Some years ago, in a stimulating essay, Dorothy Van Ghent identified as a primary ingredient of Dickens' novels the principle of demonic animism. Objects there, she pointed out, fiendishly usurp the prerogatives of their owners. It is '. . . as if the life absorbed by things had been drained out of people, who have become incapable of their humanity'. In an era of growing materialism, the Victorian, she argued, felt engulfed or overwhelmed by the plethora of articles encroaching upon him, the products needed for the fast-moving existence dictated by the machine age or the possessions requisite for establishing social standing. Accordingly, people become transformed into objects, and objects, in that interchange, take over the role of people. As part of this loss of control over the inanimate, a four-poster bed in an inn where Pip spends a night is seen by him as straddling the room like some despotic monster, '. . . putting one of his arbitrary legs into the fireplace, and another into the doorway, and squeezing the wretched little washing-stand in quite a Divinely Righteous manner'. Neighbouring houses twist round in order to spy upon him through a skylight. Human impulses are appropriated by the non-human as the inanimate springs to life, even parts of the body seeming to possess an existence of their own, divorced from their owners. Wemmick's mouth becomes a grinning slot or letter-box at his place of work; Jaggers' forefinger is transformed into a detached symbol of the law as it thrusts itself menacingly at the accused; and, as part of this exchanging of roles between animate and inanimate, Miss Havisham, who exploits Estella and Pip as mere 'things' dedicated to her vengeful purpose, has in her turn become a mere thing, dead-in-life, awaiting the final decay of her wedding-cake before being laid out in its place, for her relatives to 'feast on'.[8]

That insight, applied by her to all his novels, has become a staple of Dickens' criticism into our own time, especially after J. Hillis Miller translated it into the terminology of semiotics, whereby the people in Dickens' novels have become signs to be deciphered, cryptograms represented by articles of clothing, gestures, or idiosyncrasies of speech which need to be 'read'. Stylistically, he perceives in this technique a masterly demonstration of what Roman

Jakobson had called earlier 'the metonymical texture of realistic prose', in which items adjacent to an object, or single attributes of a person are, by a process of synecdoche, linguistically substituted for the whole. Mrs Gamp's late husband is thus, in a sense, dislodged by his wooden leg; he becomes absorbed metaphorically into the appendage, while the piece of timber itself is imaged as instinct with life: 'And as to husbands, there's a wooden leg gone likeways home to its account, which in its constancy of walkin' into wine vaults, and never comin' out again 'till fetched by force, was quite as weak as flesh, if not weaker.'[9]

It may be helpful, in order to approach this interpretation of Dickens from a fresh angle, to examine more closely, through the plastic arts, the Victorians' attitude to those inanimate objects and personal possessions which surrounded them and which, it is alleged, had intimidated them, overwhelming them with a sense of their own insignificance and loss of control, usurping their prerogatives and accounting by that usurpation for the stylistic technique adopted by Dickens. In fact, the very reverse would seem to hold true, especially if one recalls an event which came to be recognized as among the most brilliant achievements of Victoria's reign and the climax of Prince Albert's contributions to his adoptive country.

Although, when the idea was first mooted, many had opposed the holding of the Great Exhibition of 1851 as liable to prove a financial fiasco, and had scoffed at Paxton's plans for the Crystal Palace as a piece of architectural adventurism likely to shatter on the heads of visitors,[10] its astounding success won over even its original opponents, for the very reason that it demonstrated to the pride of all Englishmen the splendid variety, quality and sheer quantity of the commodities being produced by both craftsmen and industry for the world at large. As the *Art Journal* catalogue announced with a fervour echoed throughout contemporary accounts of the exhibition, it symbolized the practicality of nineteenth-century designers in applying scientific knowledge to the creation of objects for daily use: 'We have long boasted of our age as a most remarkable one; the number of useful applications which we have made within a comparatively limited period, are no doubt more numerous than were ever before made within the same time...'[11] In a mood of self-congratulatory awe, the impressive statistics relating to the project were cited, discussed, and commented on again and again. The building itself had required 3,500 tons of cast iron, 550 tons of wrought iron, and nearly a million square feet of glass, the resulting structure roofing an area measuring over 19 acres, '. . . thus presenting an edifice about four times the size of St. Peter's, at Rome, and six times that of St. Paul's.' And the objects displayed within, lovingly described and illustrated in the catalogue, with essays appended on their design, composition, and methods of construction, covered the entire gamut of craftsmanship and manufacture, with sections devoted to ceramics, textiles, wallpaper, furniture, cut glass, musical instruments, lighting fixtures, carriages, statuary, clocks, beehives, and a host of other items. 'Never before', as a contemporary remarked of the crystal-glass fountain displayed in the centre of the transept, 'had a piece of glass-work been executed, involving the treatment in casting, cutting and polishing, of blocks of glass of a size so large and of a purity so uniformly faultless.'[12] If the range and variety of these exhibited commodities overwhelmed the visitor, they overwhelmed him, it would seem, with pride in the inventiveness and industry of nineteenth-century man rather than with a humiliating sense of the tyranny of material goods.

The response to the Exhibition, drawing vast crowds from all levels of society, was, as may be seen with the advantage of historical hindsight, no isolated phenomenon but the culmination and public demonstration of certain trends in the changing artistic tastes of the time. It represented the inception of a commodity culture, dependent upon the taste of purchaser rather than designer, fashion now being dictated by consumer demand. Domestic furniture, which occupied so prominent a place among the items displayed at the Exhibition, in the larger form of sideboards, beds, and sofas and in such smaller items as vases, candelabra, fruit-dishes, and statuary figures, had been undergoing at that time a radical change, a change especially notable because such furnishings both reflected and helped to create that cherished image, the Victorian home. And it marked a reaction to long-established traditions. Throughout the preceding centuries, on the European continent as well as in England, furniture design and production had been remarkably standardized, conforming to the predominant fashion of the day, which itself had remained singularly conservative, variations being introduced very slowly. Chests-of-drawers in the Baroque period were predominantly rectangular, in the Rococo serpentine, in the Neoclassical semi-circular. The individual craftsman may have designed the specific form of ormolu or carving, and local tradition may have dictated certain minor differences, but those variations occurred within the parameters of conformity to the dominant mode.

There was, indeed, a practical reason dictating the traditional-
ism prevailing until the nineteenth century, for until then artisans,
employed in small workshops each specializing in a very limited
type of furniture, had been taught to respect the traditions of their
trade. They learned the processes of their craft during the period of
their apprenticeship, the heritage being handed down from generation to generation. At the turn of the century, however, methods
both of production and of trade underwent radical transformation
in response to new social needs and new methods of production. A
doubling of the population, from nine million in 1800 to eighteen
million by 1850, created a demand for furniture which the traditional
small workshops could not possibly meet, while the growing prosperity of the upper and middle classes, as British exports rose in that
same period from £34,000,000 per annum to £197,000,000, ensured
a much broader clientele for domestic furnishings of better quality.
John Store Smith's *Social Aspects*, published in 1851, noted how
'. . . the middle-class family now possesses carpets and hangings
which would have excited great wonderment even at so recent a
period as the American War, and not a few of our London middle-
class tradesmen possess a better stock of family plate and linen than
many a country squire, even of the last generation.'
    Manufacturing firms began to expand accordingly in order to meet
the new demand. As we learn from the records of a fire which destroyed the workshops of George Seddon, as many as three hundred
journeymen would now be employed at one time. Yet even that
increased workforce was to prove insufficient, and to meet the new
demands, mass-production methods began to be introduced. They
did not, as a recent study has shown, displace the small workshops,
which continued to thrive side-by-side with the larger mechanized
centres, but even in the smaller workplace, either machines, or
furniture parts produced by them, began to be employed. In place
of the turner's lathe, the only mechanical tool in use until then,
steam-driven wood-carvers took over, such as the highly successful
version invented by T.J. Jordan in the 1840s. Its contribution was
not only in saving labour costs; for it affected also the very nature
of the art, providing unending possibilities for variety in design, a
variety such as could never have been provided by a conservatively
trained artisan.[13]
    There is always, of course, a close relationship between advances
in production methods and the changing demands of the consumer,
mechanical inventiveness only becoming practicable when supplying

the immediate needs of the manufacturer. For that reason, it is insufficient to point to the mass-production technique alone as the source of the enormous variety in design which now flooded the market. For it indicated in itself an increasing desire among potential customers for a wider choice of goods, the main competition among the numerous manufacturers now springing up in the various cities being not so much in quality as in their ability to offer a range of innovative styles from which the buyer could choose with a sense of personal propriety.[14] Where the eighteenth-century cabinet-maker had preserved a close relationship with his patron, readily travelling for five hours or more in order to obtain details of an order at first hand, the actual selling now moved out of the cabinet-maker's control into the hands of a retailer, often drawing upon a number of warehouses and demanding wide diversity in design lest the buyer should feel that he was merely purchasing a standardized product. As Richard Redgrave remarked in his *Supplementary Report on the Exhibition of 1851*, '. . . the hunger after novelty is quite insatiable; heaven and earth are racked for novel inventions . . .' The nineteenth-century purchaser, therefore, instead of displaying his taste, as had the patron of the past, by commissioning items made especially for him, now did so by a different process – the same process as pertains in our own day – by *selecting* from the wealth of variegated items available the specific items suited to his or her own character and resources, whether in furniture, ornaments, carriages, or clothing. As Prince Albert formulated this changed attitude to commodities in his speech at the opening of the Great Exhibition: '. . . the products of all quarters of the globe are placed at our disposal, and we have only to choose which is the best and cheapest for our purposes.'

It is, I suggest, that new quality of the age which Dickens grasped so shrewdly and incorporated into his fiction as a distinctive literary mode, seeing within the proprietary selection of goods a method of differentiating character. The traits of inner singularity are now seen as manifested in externals, in choice of dress, in verbal idiosyncrasies, or in those eccentric possessions which mark out their owners so individualistically:

> . . . a queer sort of fresh painted vehicle drove up, out of which there jumped with great agility . . . a queer sort of gentleman who seemed made for the vehicle, and the vehicle for him. The vehicle was not exactly a gig, neither was it a stanhope. It was not what

is currently denominated a dog-cart, neither was it a taxed-cart, nor a chaise-cart, nor a guillotined cabriolet; and yet it had something of the character of each and every of these machines. It was painted a bright yellow . . .[15]

While this commodity culture, as Thomas Richards has pointed out, primarily affected the middle class, since most of the goods offered for sale were well beyond the means of the poor – a manufactured cigarette, for example, still costing, until the end of the century, considerably more than the hand-rolled version[16] – the variety of clothing and other items discarded by the wealthier classes and passed on to their social inferiors increased the range from which the latter could choose. The distinctive green jacket of the impecunious Alfred Jingle, which '. . . had been a smart dress garment in the days of swallow-tails, but had evidently in those times adorned a much shorter man', and the weird second-hand dresses hanging in Mrs Gamp's room and on her person, together with her ever-present umbrella, allowed them a similar opportunity to express their individuality. If the working-class area of Coketown seems from the distance drearily composed of hundreds of identical people living in identical houses and performing identical tasks, Dickens' fictional genius, by this technique, makes his cities and urban dwellings come alive with people perceived upon closer view as sharply distinguished from each other by their eccentricities and personal prejudices, expressed in large part through their habiliments or other possessions.

Although histories of furniture duly note the introduction at this time of new materials and new processes of fabrication, the far-reaching effect those materials had upon the actual shape and structure of the products has attracted little attention. In many ways it produced a revolution in style no less significant than the invention of plastic goods in our present century, allowing a flexibility of design fundamentally altering traditional form.[17] Some of the materials were employed for only a short time, being discarded for reasons of price, of convenience, or of durability, their subsequent disappearance no doubt accounting for the brief notice they have received; but their impact on furniture design during the period of their adoption proved to be of major importance, leaving their impress upon the shapes and forms of the Victorian home long after they had ceased to be used.

Until the nineteenth century, whatever ingenuity a furniture designer might possess, his potential inventiveness had been bounded by the natural limitations of the wood from which the basic frame was to be constructed. Curved armrests demanded the skilful joining of two wooden pieces separately carved to meet exactly and to continue the curve, with the strength of the join again requiring expert craftsmanship. Now two changes occurred, simultaneously introduced, which obviated that need and opened up unending possibilities for variation in form. The 'bentwood' process, which became commercially viable around 1850 as developed at the workshop of Michael Thonet, made the wood malleable by means of steam-heating, the new shape being retained after it had cooled. The advantages accruing from that technique are self-evident. The second innovation was experimentation with a range of entirely new materials, often replacing wood altogether, even for the frame. *Papier mâché* had come into limited use earlier, in the eighteenth century, when wet paper-pulp was found suitable for being moulded into picture frames and other minor objects as substitutes for wood carving, its receptiveness to paint making it on completion almost indistinguishable from lacquered wood. But in the nineteenth century a more advanced process was introduced whereby it became strong enough to bear considerable weight and was accordingly available for larger items. The paper in that process was laid out in sheets, pasted together over a mould, and hardened by stove-heating. Easy to mass-produce and forming an even better surface for japanning, it was ideal for the new markets, providing not only a host of trays and ornaments but, more importantly, solid furniture too, including elaborately 'carved' tables and chairs. Although iron, recently improved to provide wrought-iron and cast-iron goods, was usually reserved for garden furniture, it too suggested possible shapes and forms to which wood had not been amenable, and the metal was sometimes itself incorporated into furniture for the home. In addition, a number of new substances such as *gutta-percha* (extracted from the sap of a Malayan tree, and first introduced in the 1840s), *carton-pierre*, and bamboo helped further release furniture manufacture from the earlier restrictions inherent in the exclusive use of wood, offering innumerable possibilities for freedom in design.

The resultant effect upon the furniture, both of the new materials and of the new competitive methods of production, was far-reaching. One of the characteristics of the earlier forms of furniture standardized throughout the previous centuries, with, as has been noted, very limited variation within the fashion of the day, was its tendency to preserve a basic uniformity of structure, clearly visible to the eye. The woodwork might, as in the Baroque period, be ornamented with a cornucopia, with cupids, or with other figures carved upon the surface, but such carving had rarely obscured the functional framework itself. Now, however, there entered an element of plasticity, of liberty from constraints which permitted the designer to twist, bend, and curl his pieces at will. Where upholstery had, on its introduction in the eighteenth century, generally formed only a superficial softening laid over the webbing of a seat or back but not interfering with the general line, it now thickened and deepened. Held in place by sunken buttons, it produced a ballooning effect which could entirely obscure the line of the sustaining framework.

As evidence of the extent of this change, it is instructive to compare a page of catalogue sketches advertising couches in the earlier part of the century with one offering selections from the mid-century onwards (Figs 13 and 14). The first of those pages testifies to only minor variations upon a standardized, front-facing, four-legged couch. The second sheet reveals the astonishing flexibility and malleability in design that had entered the manufacturing process, the cabinet-maker now being free to exploit his imaginative faculty at will – duplicating, tripling, quadruplicating seats in circular, oval, or rectangular shapes, the components facing whichever direction suited his fancy or, more important, would be likely to suit the individual preferences of his potential clients.[18] The result is so wide a freedom of choice that the very selection of one design over another now constitutes a mark of taste, and its introduction into the home a demonstration of individual choice.

The more personal relationship between owner and item that had entered the furnishing trade is evidenced in the attempt now being made by the designer to tailor his goods to suit the mood or traits of a particular buyer. The 'Day-dreamer' armchair, as it was named in the Great Exhibition catalogue (Fig. 15), produced by H. Fitz-Cook, employed a *papier mâché* frame to offer maximum versatility of design, with the new buttoned upholstery for comfort. It was richly ornamented with imitation carving, including two figures along the top of the backrest, one endowed with the wings of a bird to represent (as a note in the catalogue informs us) happy and joyous dreams, the other with leathery bat-like wings representing unpleasant or troubled ones. It was intended, therefore, not only to welcome its owner into its capacious and comfortable interior but to establish a more intimate, whimsical relationship with him, encouraging the day-dreams that occupied so central a place in Victorian sensibility.[19]

The chair, by the invitation it seems actively to extend and by the symbiotic relationship it establishes with the owner's moods, has, like so much furniture of the time, lost the formal impersonality of an object and become almost animate – animate not as usurper of the owner's spirit, but as an extension of his personal traits and whims. Another armchair in the Great Exhibition (Fig. 16), made in Dublin from Irish bog-wood, with chivalric busts of ancient Irish warriors, possesses arm-rests in the form of two carved wolf-dogs, one recumbent bearing the motto 'Gentle when stroked' and the other barking aggressively, with the comment 'Fierce when provoked'. The chair is not only designed to suit the moods and predispositions of a very specific purchaser – a dog-lover proud of his Irish ancestry – but seems itself to come alive as the wolf-dog on the left defiantly guards the recumbent owner.

That new aspect of Victorian furniture cannot be unconnected with such incidents in Dickens' writings as the Bagman's story. As the latter, resting in his room at the inn, gazes at a high-backed chair, it seems human to him even before the dream-vision begins – 'carved in the most fantastic manner, with . . . the round knobs at the bottom of the legs carefully tied up in red cloth, as if it had got the gout in its toes.' Then, as he watched, a further change seemed to come over it:

> The carving of the back gradually assumed the lineaments and expression of an old shrivelled human face; the damask cushion became an antique, flapped waistcoat; the round knobs grew into a couple of feet, encased in red cloth slippers; and the old chair looked like a very ugly old man, of the previous century, with his arms a-kimbo . . . and what was more, he was winking at Tom Smart.[20]

So far from representing, as Dorothy Van Ghent has argued for such objects in Dickens' fiction, the intimidating despotism of a materialistic age, the armchair in that tale offers some very friendly and helpful advice, leading to the Bagman's marrying the widowed inn-keeper and living in enviable comfort ever after.

The notorious bric-à-brac, which to modern eyes seems merely to clutter the Victorian room, functioned in much the same way, as a

means of personalizing the home, of transforming it into an extension of self and creating an air of intimacy. The innumerable anti-
macassars lovingly embroidered by spinster aunts, the souvenirs
of remembered visits, the samplers fashioned in girlhood, and the
family albums displayed about the room may appear, as they have
so often been described, merely to express a *horror vacui,* since we
ourselves see them impersonally, stripped of the sentimental associations they bore for the owner; but clothed in those associations,
their presence brought the room to life, each cherished object, by
arousing nostalgic reminiscence, creating a personal congeniality.
Queen Victoria's writing desk at Osborne House, preserved as it
was at the time of her death, with its crowded proliferation of framed
photographs, carved paperweights, and other paraphernalia, may
have left her little space for writing; but it provided her with a
personal enclave, serving as an optical barrier between her private
world and the formalities of her public life. Where Van Ghent was
undoubtedly correct was in recognizing the potential threat which
the Victorians felt in the face of this plethora of new products. But
instead of being engulfed, they responded characteristically by
asserting their identity through their possessions, which would seem
– like the mementoes on the royal desk – not to have detracted from
nor to have oppressed the individuality of the owner, but rather to
have sustained it.

The warm bond experienced in this period between the individual
and his belongings included a sense of muted dialogue, the mementoes speaking to him, as it were, of past experiences. Henry Tallis
commented in his *History and Description of the Crystal Palace* on the
Victorians' penchant for objects that told a story. The Englishman
of his day, he remarked, '. . . would have everything in a house
touched by the divining rod of the poet. An inkstand, instead of
being a literal glass bottle, or a fine piece of ormolu or bronze,
significant of nothing but costliness, might be fashioned to represent a fountain, with a Muse inspiring its flow.'[21] The elaborately-
carved Kenilworth side-board displayed at the same exhibition
aroused great interest among visitors not so much because of the
high quality of the carving. Its main attraction was the fact that it
had been carved from an oak which had stood in the grounds of the
castle and which had therefore itself witnessed the historic scene
depicted on its panels, the entertaining there of Queen Elizabeth by
the Earl of Leicester. The silent eloquence of the piece, the stimulus
it offered for dreamy thoughts, catered to this Victorian disposition

to instil objects with life, in much the same way as Lizzie Hexam in *Our Mutual Friend* gazed each evening into the hearth to conjure up from its glowing coals living shapes and figures redolent of past and future.

It was, it would seem, Dickens' sensitivity to this Victorian endowing of objects with life that prompted him to employ with such remarkable effect the possessions, environs, appendages, and habiliments of his characters as animated external emblems of their inner being. As he informs us of the oddments in the Old Curiosity Shop kept by Nell's father: 'There was nothing in the whole collection but was in keeping with himself; nothing that looked older or more worn than he.'[22] The celebrated description of the Veneerings' home in *Our Mutual Friend* is not only a powerful satire on the false pretensions and perverted values of the *nouveau riche* but a recognition too of this peculiarly Victorian predilection for displaying themselves through their possessions. Not only was everything about these 'bran-new people' new – 'all their furniture was new, all their friends were new, all their servants were new' – but, as the narrator informs us with a glance at their name, '. . . what was observable in their furniture, was observable in the Veneerings – the surface smelt a little too much of the workshop and was a trifle sticky.' In a passage too lengthy to quote here in full but no doubt familiar to the reader, the great looking-glass above the sideboard is depicted as it 'reflects' (in both the metaphorical and literal senses of that term) the weighty complacency of the home: 'Reflects the new Veneering crest, in gold and eke in silver . . . Reflects Veneering . . . Reflects Mrs Veneering . . . gorgeous in raiment and jewels . . .' And in the no less famous passage describing the Podsnaps' dinner, the heavy silver plate is itself represented as coming alive, 'speaking' with the self-satisfied and pompous voice of its owner, while in the process, like Podsnap himself, unwittingly betraying his least attractive qualities:

Hideous solidity was the characteristic of the Podsnap plate. Everything was made to look as heavy as it could, and to take up as much room as possible. Everything said boastfully, 'Here you have as much of me in my ugliness as if I were only lead; but I am so many ounces of precious metal worth so much an ounce; – wouldn't you like to melt me down?' . . . Four silver wine-coolers, each furnished with four staring heads, each head obtrusively carrying a big silver ring in each of its ears, conveyed the sentiment up and down the table, and handed it on to the pot-bellied silver salt-cellars. All the big silver spoons and forks widened the mouths of the company expressly for the purpose of thrusting the sentiment down their throats with every morsel they ate.[23]

Such is the intimate relationship between the owner and his chattels, the latter revealing by virtue of their acquisition the inner characteristics of their master. David Copperfield's first suspicion of the scatter-brained untidiness of his child-bride Dora is aroused by that very quality in one of her beloved possessions, her dog Jip, who he wishes '... had never been encouraged to walk about the table-cloth during dinner ... putting his foot in the salt or in the melted butter', a foretaste of the way his mistress spills ink over the household accounts, forgetting in the process entirely what she is about. Mr Dick's kite in that same novel is, as David vaguely senses, far more than a plaything. It is the surrogate for its owner's desire to escape from the perplexing realities about him, soaring into the skies as an extension of self:

I used to fancy, as I sat by him of an evening, on a green slope, and saw him watch the kite high in the quiet air, that it lifted his mind out of its confusion, and bore it (such was my boyish thought) into the skies ... [and afterwards] I remember to have seen him take it up, and look about him in a lost way, as if they had both come down together.[24]

It is not, as J. Hillis Miller claims, that people in *Our Mutual Friend* are 'turned into objects by money',[25] but the reverse, that the purchased objects by that act of selection eloquently articulate their owners' hidden traits for good as well as ill. Wegg in that novel, we are told, with imagery that cannot be missed, '... was a knotty man, and a close-grained, with a face carved out of very hard material ... he was so wooden a man that he seemed to have taken his wooden leg naturally.' The appendage, indeed, is seen with a touch of whimsy as complementing him so perfectly that its lack was somehow felt even when he possessed two legs. And in the same novel appears the room designed by that affectionate couple, the Boffins, in which they sit amicably together each evening. Divided precisely down the middle, it is, by mutual consent, furnished on the lady's side in conformity with current Fashion (for which she has recently developed a fondness) with flowered carpet, stuffed birds, and waxen fruits. But along the line where Fashion ends, a region of Comfort commences, the habitation of Mr Boffin being characterized by sawdust floor, shelves displaying a large veal-and-ham pie together with a cold-joint, and a table bearing a pipe ready for smoking. Each regards these surroundings as projections of self, not to be sacrificed even in the interests of matrimony but to be enjoyed with mutual tolerance, the dividing line liable to altera-tion in conformity with any future changes in the tastes of their occupants:

'If I get by degrees to be a highflyer at Fashion, then Mrs Boffin will by degrees come for'arder. If Mrs Boffin should ever be less of a dab at Fashion than she is at the present time, then Mrs Boffin's carpet would go back'arder. If we should both continny as we are, why then *here* we are, and give us a kiss, old lady.'[26]

This tendency to bestow upon one's possessions, upon the furni-ture, the dinner service, or one's favourite kite the emotional qual-ities of their owner was by no means identical with the 'pathetic fallacy' attacked by Ruskin in the third volume of his *Modern Painters*. In 1856, Ruskin had complained that the kind of imagery favoured not only by the Romantic poets but in verse-composition at large quite unjustifiably imposed upon the natural world the pass-ing moods of the viewer, endowing the vegetative or inanimate with qualities they do not actually possess, insentient daffodils being made to 'dance' and crocuses to 'shiver', the wind being described as 'lazy', or a ship's sails as 'nimble'. Such language, he suggested, is only justified in the speech of morbid or agonized characters who have lost their mental stability and discrimination, since true art demands accuracy of perception and an objective attention to detail. In contrast to such traditions, the Victorian proclivity for animating objects was not, in general, the temporary imposition of the viewer's emotions or mood upon the scene but the creation of a more permanent bond, the expression of a lasting and personal relationship between the owner and the object possessed.

The distinction is most clearly visible in the essentially new atti-tude to animals, an endowing of dumb creatures with human traits in a manner unprecedented in either art or literature. The principle itself was not new, Aesop's fables having long established the practice, to be echoed in England by Chaucer's Chanticleer and

Swift's Houyhnhnms. But in those works, the bestowing of speech upon the animals had been patently allegorical, an acknowledged literary pretence intended to convey a didactic or satiric message. In painting too, the canine had frequently served an allegorical function, heraldically representing Fidelity, as in Van Eyck's portrait of *Jan Arnolfini and his Wife.* The nineteenth century, however, broke with that tradition and, in line with the process of projecting one's self into one's possessions, it fostered the concept of a personal intimacy between owner and pet, an intimacy sometimes mawkish in its sentimentalism, at least to modern taste. There is Sir Edwin Landseer's enormously popular canvas, *The Old Shepherd's Chief Mourner* (Fig. 17) of 1837, depicting a sheepdog grieving beside the coffin of his master, revealing an emotional attachment quite absent from the eighteenth-century genre of animal painting. The work of George Stubbs had displayed meticulous attention to anatomical accuracy, but with no sense of empathy between man and beast;[27] and even when affection was suggested, as in Hogarth's *Self-portrait with Trump the Pug*, the emotion was one-directional, the dog itself displaying no interest in the portrait of its master – in contrast to its counterpart in the popular painting *His Master's Voice* of 1889 (a product of the movement we are examining), which gazes with earnest puzzlement at the gramophone from which the voice emanates. In earlier periods, that animal response is lacking. In Sir Joshua Reynolds' portrait of the young *Miss Bowles* hugging to her breast her favourite canine, the latter merely looks uncomfortably cramped in her embrace. And Constable's habitual inclusion of a horse or dog in such canvases as *Flatford Mill* and *The Haywain* implied only their reliability as co-workers in the setting of nature. The Victorian, on the other hand, was sensitive to the emotional reciprocity between man and animal, a bond of comradeship and mutual loyalty between owner and animal which lent the latter semi-human qualities. Hence the pathos implicit in Briton Riviere's *Fidelity* of 1869, in which the despair of a man cast into prison evokes the mournful commiseration of his dog, the latter sharing his master's grief, however unable to comprehend its cause, and sympathetically resting its head upon his knee.[28] This endowing of animals with human characteristics was to become an integral part of the art and literature of the time, both in a serious mood, as in these two paintings, and in more whimsical settings, such as Landseer's portrayal, at the request of his friend Jacob Bell, of the latter's labrador and Scotch terrier sharing a kennel, the painting titled *Dignity and Impudence* (Fig. 18).

It was this penchant to make the world of animals and objects come alive that motivated the work of Lewis Carroll. The waist-coated Rabbit gazing anxiously at his watch, the Caterpillar super-ciliously smoking his hookah, and the pompous Fish-Footman, although existing within Alice's dream-world, are in fact extra-polations of her humanizing attitude to animals in the real world, before she drifts off to sleep:

> 'Oh, you wicked, wicked little thing!' cried Alice, catching up the kitten, and giving it a little kiss to make it understand that it was in disgrace. 'Really, Dinah ought to have taught you better man-ners! You *ought*, Dinah, you know you ought!' she added, look-ing reproachfully at the old cat, and speaking in as cross a voice as she could manage . . .

Beneath the humour implicit in Carroll's animation of pets and household objects, there may be perceived a more serious theme, a projection, into such figures, of the anxieties and concerns of his own inner world – another form, indeed, of that extrapolation of self into one's environs that characterized Dickens' work. Charles Dodgson himself, though widely admired for the humour of his writings, was, in matters of Christian faith, one of the most extra-ordinarily solemn and unbending dogmatists of his age. He would not suffer the slightest hint of religious irreverence in his presence, sternly reprimanding a friend (in writing) for having repeated to him some amusingly ingenuous remarks of children concerning the deity. While such remarks might be forgivable in the young, Carroll austerely insisted, they could never be so when quoted by an adult. He did not hesitate to rebuke a bishop for a mildly humorous re-mark included in a sermon, on the grounds that it '. . . went far to undo, in the minds of many of your hearers, and especially among the young men, much of the good effect of the rest of the sermon.' Nor would he willingly enter into any discussion on matters of Christian belief, remarking: 'I have a deep dread of argument on religious topics; it has many risks and little chance of doing good.'[29]

It requires little knowledge of psychology to perceive that his dread of such discussion arose from a suppressed fear of exposing his own doubts. But the animated dream-world of his Alice books seems to have liberated him from such fears, allowing his sup-pressed anxieties and even his unorthodoxies to surface and find expression in these animal figures. The poem on the 'smiling' crocodile may appear light-hearted in tone:

How doth the little crocodile
Improve his shining tail,
And pour the waters of the Nile
On every golden scale!

How cheerfully he seems to grin,
How neatly spreads his claws,
And welcomes little fishes in
With gently smiling jaws.

But as a parody of Isaac Watts's well-known hymn for children ('How doth the little busy bee/ Improve each shining hour,/ And gather honey all the day/ From every opening flower . . .'), the poem had grimmer implications. The Christian vision of nature under a benevolent deity, suffused with moral messages for the pious, and employing that didactic use of animistic allegory traditional to art, is subverted here by the crueller vision implicit in the new concept of Nature, red in tooth and claw. It is, in its way, as damning as Clough's famed *Decalogue*, achieving in that animal setting a questioning of traditional religious faith which, as we have seen, Dodgson would never have permitted himself in real life.

Indeed, throughout his nonsense world can be perceived a similar grappling with problems shrouded in his subconscious. His *Hunting of the Snark*, however frivolous in tone, was in fact composed at a time when he was both spiritually exhausted and deeply distressed after a night spent nursing his dying godchild. The flippancy of 'serving the Snark with greens' may provide a temporary comic diversion from the seriousness of the underlying theme, but visible through the disguise is the genuine throb of fear, the Victorian dread of Death as a possible dying into nothingness:

I engage with the Snark – every night after dark –
    In a dreamy delirious fight:
I serve it with greens in those shadowy scenes,
    And I use it for striking a light.

But if ever I meet with a Boojum, that day,
    In a moment (of this I am sure),
I shall softly and suddenly vanish away –
    And the notion I cannot endure![30]

Rabbits, crocodiles, playing-cards, lobsters, and walruses take on in such writings the cheerful, irate, or mournful traits of the Victorian in both his lighter and graver moments, becoming repositories or reflections of their author's sentiments in much the same way as the purchased armchair reflected the characteristics of its owner. And for Dodgson himself, the imposition of his own traits upon those creatures served a profoundly liberating function.

The commodity culture manifested in the arts and furnishings of the time, and so impressively absorbed into the novel, was not only an aesthetic factor but found expression too in terms of economic theory, in the work of Stanley Jevons in England, Carl Menger in Austria, and Leon Walras in Switzerland. Jevons, in his *Theory of Political Economy* (1871), argued (less as an initiator than as a theorist perceiving the emerging changes in the commerce of his day) that economics must no longer be based upon such financial factors as the cost of material, of labour, and of transport, but on the principle of supply and demand. His subjectivist economics arose from the perception that man and woman, once their basic needs have been satisfied, crave *variety* in their dress, furnishings, and possessions, and that competition among manufacturers in satisfying these customer needs would determine, to a major degree, the final costing. In economic theory too, therefore, the whims of the consumer had attained new prominence as the primary determinants of trade, creating a need on the part of the supplier to offer a wider selection of goods to suit individual choices.[31] More recently, Lucien Goldmann's *Towards a Sociology of the Novel* has distinguished between the traditional appropriation of objects for their usefulness and the new sense of profiteering, of concern with the exchange or saleable value which entered society at this time and, by extension, the novel too. In Dickens' writings, acquisition for the latter purpose, for profiteering, is anathema, and it is that which he generally identifies with commerce. Major Pawkins in *Martin Chuzzlewit* he describes sarcastically as 'an admirable man of business', adding in explanation that he '. . . had a most distinguished genius for swindling . . .'; and he despised the kind of possessiveness or utilization of others exemplified by Dombey or by Arthur Clennam's parents, who '. . . weighed, measured, and priced everything; for whom what could not be weighed, measured, and priced, had no existence . . .' One notes how the philanthropists in his novels, such as the benevolent Pickwick and Mr Brownell, have all obtained their wealth from unnamed sources before the novel begins, and are never depicted in the act of obtaining it. The reverse of this process was, for Dickens as for so many of his age, the valuing of objects not for their saleable value but as intimate extensions of self, representing nostalgic memories or affectionate associations.

This element of personal subjectivity permeating the bric-à-brac and decorative arts of the time has implications for the buildings too. Despite the more sympathetic assessment of Victorian architecture in recent years, notably through the revisionist approach of John Betjeman, one aspect that has not undergone any serious change is the view that its architecture is a sad story of pastiche, a pot-pourri of imitations without, it is charged, any style that could legitimately be called its own. It may be argued, however, that the very eclecticism prompting this hybrid combination of styles, instead of denoting a lack of imaginative creativity, should be seen as representing, by this same process of personal selectivity, the type of creative act most befitting the period and in itself constituting its distinctive character.

Georgian architecture of the eighteenth century had undoubtedly been *sui generis*. It may have derived from classical forms but it had adapted them to produce an identifiable style appropriate to the needs of its time, incorporating the newly invented sash-windows of the day as essential components of its rectilinear forms. But whatever praise may be accorded to that style, even its most fervent admirers will admit to an element of sameness – a repetitiveness of square symmetrical structures usually in grey stone, except where, as at Bath, the houses were formed into a graceful crescent or circle in order to relieve the rectilinear forms. In contrast, Victorian architecture offered a wealth of diversity as each architect or proprietor chose from whatever style pleased them those elements suited to their particular taste, combining their selections, often with disdainful disregard for historical accuracy, to produce something essentially their own. In 1864, Robert Kerr recorded how the country-house builder was offered by the architect an often bewildering choice of styles which he was invited to tailor to his own tastes:

'Sir, you are the paymaster, and must therefore be pattern-master; you choose the style of your house just as you choose the build of your hat; – you can have *Classical*, columnar or non-columnar, arcuated or trabeated, rural or civil, or indeed palatial; you can have *Elizabethan* in equal variety; *Renaissance* ditto; or, not to notice minor modes, *Mediaeval* in any one of many periods and many phases, – old English, French, German, Belgium, Italian, and more.'[32]

The transformation of Georgian regularity of design into more elaborate Victorian forms is exemplified in Shadwell House, Norfolk (Fig. 19). The original rectilinear structure from the 1720s was successively remodelled and imaginatively expanded between the years 1840 and 1860, first under the direction of Edward Blore and, during further renovation, under the direction of Samuel Teulon, to become a characteristically Victorian country home, its charming asymmetrical medley of Gothic and Jacobean elements embodying the personal fantasies of its designer.[33]

For all Pugin's insistence on purity in neo-Gothic architecture and his demand for fidelity to what he regarded as the noblest elements of ancient medieval buildings, what really characterizes that style upon the Victorian scene is a polychrome *adaptation* of it such as had never existed in the medieval world. The Lady Chapel of Pugin's St. Giles' Church at Cheadle, richly endowed with decorative crowns, crosses, and trellises covering every inch of visible surface, is a paradigm of Victorian inventiveness, with the introduction of Minton's tiles and Hardman's metal-work unparalleled in medieval sources. Similarly, William Butterfield introduced as a matter of principle into his All Saints' Church in Margaret Street – the model building of the Camden Society, supposedly exemplifying its medieval ideals – such contemporary materials as glazed brick, which he believed, because of its availability, should be pressed into service for the glory of God even though such bricks had no counterpart in any medieval church. His Keble College Chapel is a monument of Victorian Gothic revivalism, whose two-coloured brickwork façade, ornamented by diamond patterns and checker-board designs, frankly acknowledges its nineteenth-century origin.

Perhaps, then, the most impressive aspect of the Victorian Gothic revival is the independence it displayed in the very process of imitation, employing the revered models of the medieval era, despite the strictures of the Ecclesiological Society, not for the production of Victorian 'clones' but rather as reference points, as evocations to be flexibly adapted to the needs, tastes, and whims of each designer or house owner. The Ecclesiological Society itself was, incidentally, not always as inflexible in its rulings as might have been expected from the severity of tone predominant in its publications or from the principles its founders had laid down so categorically. They approved, for example, somewhat surprisingly, William Slater's plan for a church constructed of cast-iron, for which, of course, no possible precedent could be found in antiquity, even publishing the design in the 1856 issue of their *Instrumenta Ecclesiastica.*[34]

Within the sphere of church building itself, therefore, where the sacerdotalism of the Oxford Movement and the revalidation of ancient Christian symbolism had imposed powerful theological constraints, the urge to indulge personal preferences and to adapt the model to individual taste frequently broke through the limitations. But outside ecclesiastical architecture, in the design of secular buildings, such as Scott's stately St. Pancras Hotel or the host of country houses now being erected or refurbished, eclecticism functioned as a primary and very positive force, not least in the uninhibited transfer of genres from their traditional contexts to an entirely new setting. There was, for example, the impressive carpet factory in Glasgow designed by William Leiper in 1889 for the firm of Templeton (Fig. 20). No expense was spared by the manufacturer in transforming the building into a Venetian palace, with the one signal difference that, where the wealthy Venetian of the Renaissance had invested the profits of his mercantile activities in creating an impressive residence for his social and familial activities, here it was the source of that wealth, the factory itself, that was dignified instead. Its elaborate neo-Gothic windows, its mosaics in brilliant turquoise, blue, and gold, set against the glazed brickwork of patterned yellow and roseate hue, constituted a personal statement of the owner's pride in his industrial enterprise and his conviction of the respect to be accorded to commerce and industry.

The Victorian refusal to be limited by the dictates of traditional architectural genres is amply illustrated by the work of William Burges. He had, in his younger years, been an enthusiastic disciple of Pugin, but when he came to re-design Cardiff Castle and its adjacent Castell Coch, in close collaboration with their owner Lord Bute – both buildings in recent years admirably restored to their pristine splendour – he did so with a playfulness and casual permissiveness in his use of sources that showed his main aim to have been the subordination of that style to his and his patron's caprice, rather than any serious attempt at revivalism. While the Gothic was the acknowledged model for both reconstructions, with turrets, spires, finials, and battlements reminiscent of medieval fortress or palace, and with a fully functional drawbridge for entering Castell

Coch, equipped with a portcullis and even including apertures in the walls through which burning oil could be poured on besiegers, Burges did not hesitate to transform one room within the Castle into an exotic evocation of the Moorish Alhambra, another into a nineteenth-century memorial to Chaucer, while he dispersed throughout the building riddles, surprises, puns, and jokes reflecting his own delight, well-known to his friends, in light-hearted jests and facetiousness.[35] In the Castle dining-room, the bell-push is disguised as an acorn held in a monkey's mouth, while the monkey's tail incongruously thrusts through the ornamental framework. And many of the animal figures decorating the rooms in a manner evocative of the medieval gargoyles and 'babooneries' in fact are intended as sources of amusement, such as a crocodile which, from lower down the staircase, can be seen to be gazing hungrily at the figure of a baby seated upon a rail below.

In the eighteenth century, such fantasies had been indulged outside the home. Uncle Toby's idiosyncratic pastime in *Tristram Shandy*, his 'hobby-horse' of reconstructing in model form the pallisadoes, ditches, batteries, saps, and bastions of a famous battle-siege, was executed at the bottom of the kitchen garden, well away from the house; while the 'follies', consisting of Doric temples, obelisks, and Gothic hermitages, had been similarly relegated to the landscaped grounds outside, inappropriate to the seriousness of the main building, except when, as at Strawberry Hill or Fonthill Abbey, the building had itself been intended for display purposes rather than as a residence.[36] But now it was the house itself which both absorbed and displayed the traits of its owner, in order to surround him during his leisure hours with extrapolations of his own eccentricities and to endow his home with his distinctive characteristics.

Dickens' novels partake of that same principle, the personality of each fictional owner flowing outward into the building and permeating it with his or her essential qualities. Just as the armchair, judiciously selected by the Victorian from the host of models available, betrays by that act of selection something of the nature of his own set of values, so Dickens interpeted the paraphernalia now accruing to nineteenth-century man, including his front door, as insignia of their owners' temperaments. In one of his early sketches, he remarked:

Whenever we visit a man for the first time, we contemplate the features of his knocker with the greatest curiosity, for we well know, that between the man and his knocker, there will inevitably be a greater or less degree of resemblance and sympathy.[37]

This principle applies not only to such minor features but to the house in its entirety. Miss Wade in *Little Dorrit* is, like his earlier creation Miss Havisham, a cold creature, her spirit already defunct; and the house she selects for tenancy inevitably reflects those same qualities: 'A dead sort of house, with a dead wall over the way and a dead gateway at the side, where a pendant bell-handle produced two dead tinkles, and a knocker produced a dead, flat, surface-tapping . . .'[38] That instance, in isolation, might appear to justify Van Ghent's view of animism as representing the dehumanization of man, when '. . . objects actually usurp human essences; beginning as fetishes they tend to – and sometimes quite literally do – devour and take over the powers of the fetish-worshipper.'[39] But, as so many other examples from Dickens' work confirm, this element arises not because the inanimate tyrannizes over the animate but because of a reverse process, whereby the spiritual *rigor mortis* of the human inhabitant freezes all objects around her, imbuing them with her own mortality, a process shared with opposite effect by the more attractive and amiable characters in his novels.

Dickens, indeed, is the very last of novelists to be accused of dehumanizing his characters, which emerge from his fiction with such irresistible vitality – not drained of their humanity but vibrant with life, overflowing with the vigour of their own being. The mainstream of his fictional figures, whether virtuous, comic, or villainous – the Pumblechooks and Wopsles, the Wemmicks and Drummles whom he moves in and out of his novels with such exuberance – consistently infuse their environment with the spirit of their own amusing or deplorable traits. The charming home Wemmick has constructed possesses, like Burges' Castell Coch, its own miniature drawbridge and moat, its flag hoisted regularly every Sunday, and its gun fired at precisely nine each evening to the joy of his Aged P. And again like Castell Coch, it is filled with ingenious gadgets and witticisms, the arrival of its owner at the drawbridge outside being announced '. . . by a sudden click in the wall on one side of the chimney and the ghostly tumbling open of a little wooden flap with "John" upon it.' The objects with which he delightedly surrounds himself constitute for him a refuge from the soul-destroying obsequiousness and bureaucratic anonymity required at his place of work. It is a home of which he is the master, and to which he can impart the mischievousness and lively inventiveness so stifled outside, his filial affection and his prank-ishness. The privacy of that home he guards jealously from his employer for the very reason that it reveals so much of his true inner self. 'No; the office is one thing, and private life is another', he explains to Pip. 'When I go into the office, I leave the Castle behind me, and when I come into the Castle, I leave the office behind me. If it's not in any way disagreeable to you, you'll oblige me by doing the same.'[40]

Houses throughout Dickens' novels possess this quality, the select neighbourhoods of London deriving their cold air of superiority and condescension from their socially pretentious inhabitants:

> Like unexceptionable Society, the opposing rows of houses in Harley Street were very grim with one another. Indeed, the mansions and their inhabitants were so much like in that respect, that the people were often to be found drawn up on opposite sides of dinner-tables, in the shade of their own loftiness, staring at the other side of the way with the dulness of the houses.[41]

If Dickens was among the earliest to perceive this kinship between the Victorian and his possessions in a society becoming increasingly stratified – and increasingly conscious of the distinctions between those strata which such acquisitions could represent – it formed for him part of a broader relationship between human and inanimate. The urban scene created by industrialism represented to him the crushed individualism of its inhabitants. The chiaroscuro mystery which Doré so admired in Dickens' work and which he evoked in his own engravings of the metropolis, arose, as Dickens recorded in his memorandum book, not from any attempt at realism but from a deliberate clothing of the metropolis in the emotional mood of its denizens, a projection upon it of their inner selves: 'Representing London – or Paris, or any other great place – in the new light of being actually unknown to all the people in the story, and only *taking the colour of their fears and fancies and opinions* – so getting a new aspect, and being unlike itself. An odd unlikeness of itself' (my italics).[42]

Dickens, as we know, trusted in fantasy to relieve the harshness and monotony of a utilitarian age, arguing that '. . . the imagination, with all its innumerable graces and charities, should be tenderly nourished' in order to preserve the humanity of the individual.[43]

To interpet Dickens' characteristic use of metonymy as representing the usurpation by material goods of human prerogatives – a sense on his part that people '. . . were being de-animated, robbed of their souls'[44] – is, I think, to miss the richness his technique lent to the characters he portrayed, the investing of belongings or appendages with the foibles, eccentricities, and spiritual aura of their owner, an intimacy delightfully projected by Dickens into his imaginary world. If that vital spirit is withdrawn in his novels, the objects collapse into anonymity, losing their independent life. The moment that Pecksniff's hypocrisy is exposed towards the end of *Martin Chuzzlewit* and his pomposity deflated, the author informs us, 'Not only did his figure appear to have shrunk, but his discomfiture seemed to have extended itself even to his dress. His clothes seemed to have got shabbier, his linen to have turned yellow, his hair to have become lank and frowsy; his very boots looked villainous and dim, as if their gloss had departed with his own.'[45] Even when objects do appear to overwhelm the human, as in the instance of the four-poster bed cited by Van Ghent, the situation needs to be interpreted in reverse. For the bed's suffocating encroachment upon Pip is in fact a projection upon the room of Pip's own emotional condition at that moment, his sense of being utterly crushed by Estella's rejection of his love just before he entered the room itself.

In the same way, James Carker, we are told in *Dombey and Son*, infused the objects about him with his own spirit: '. . . there issues forth some subtle portion of himself, which gives a vague expression of himself to everything about him.'[46] Objects participate exuberantly in the life of the characters Dickens created, like the utensils of the well-meaning maidservant Charley in *Bleak House*, '. . . in whose hand every pen appeared to become perversely animated, and to go wrong and crooked, and to stop, and splash, and sidle into corners, like a saddle-donkey.'[47] There is the chimneyed, superannuated boat-house of Mr Peggotty seen from afar 'smoking very cosily' like its owner; and, in contrast, the filthy, rat-infested, wharf where Quigley feels most at home, or the clawing, snarling cat seated perpetually on Mr Krook's shoulder. The gigs, kites, wooden legs, and other appurtenances appropriated by Dickens' characters, if they also served as a narrative device wonderfully appropriate for the newly serialized novel, helping readers at each issue to identify them afresh by their owners' distinctive turns of phrase, dress, or accoutrements, succeeded no less in expressing a quality specific to Dickens' time, the Victorian's personal, often sentimental attachment to his possessions as expressions of self by virtue of their having been selected by him from the enormous range of products made available to him by England's industrial power, an eclecticism expressed at the architectural level in his individualistic mingling of styles and traditions to suit his own tastes. The armchairs and other furnishings may have become more animate in this process, but it was still, as Dickens informs us in his *Sketches by Boz*, the human who initiated the process, who constituted the source of that animation by projecting his own moods upon them:

> ... we should have gone dreaming on, until the pewter-pot on the table, or the little beer-chiller on the fire, had started into life, and addressed to us a long story of days gone by. But, by some means or other, we were not in a romantic humour; and although we tried very hard to invest the furniture with vitality, it remained perfectly unmoved, obstinate, and sullen.[48]

Conversely, when he *was* in a 'romantic' humour, such investing of furniture with vitality was to constitute a major ingredient of his art.

(ii)

Browning's first published poem, his *Pauline*, of 1833, leaned heavily upon the Romantic tradition, the autobiographical style whereby Byron, Keats, and Shelley bared their souls before the reader, reliving in intensely personal terms some emotional experience from the past:

> Pauline, mine own, bend o'er me – thy soft breast
> Shall pant to mine – bend o'er me – thy sweet eyes,
> And loosened hair and breathing lips, and arms
> Drawing me to thee ...

But his first venture in that tradition was also his last. A critical review by John Stuart Mill, beginning with the scathing comment that the author '... seems to me possessed with a more intense and morbid self-consciousness than I ever knew in any sane human being', changed, we are told, the course of his poetic creativity. The ridicule and censure included in that review, as he was to recall in later years, stung him 'into quite another style of writing', the new style of the dramatic monologue. In that genre, the poet, instead of exposing his inner being to the withering gaze of the public, creates a fictitious *persona*, with whom the reader only partially sympathizes and who could not be confused with the personality of the poet himself in the way, for example, that Byron invites us to identify him with the figures of Childe Harold or Don Juan.[49]

Such, indeed, is the accepted account of Browning's adoption of that genre. In its essentials it is historically correct. Yet, just as the unexpected birth of a twin brother weakens the claims of the first-born, the fact that the identical sequence of events is related also of Tennyson suggests that there may be something more behind this shared experience than biographers have claimed. We learn of Tennyson that, depressed by the unfriendly criticism with which his 1832 volume of poems had been received, he was impelled to venture upon a new experiment and accordingly fashioned (at the same time, yet independently of Browning) his own version of the dramatic monologue in *Ulysses* and *St. Simeon Stylites*. Wordsworth, we should recall, had also been exposed to critical ridicule on the initial appearance of his poems, charged with adopting 'childish' diction and nursery-rhyme patterns in his contributions to the *Lyrical Ballads*; but he had not immediately deserted that style in consequence. And the fact that both Victorian poets, when attacked, resorted to the dramatic monologue, a genre previously employed only rarely in English poetry, suggests a convergence in some way dictated by the cultural configuration of the time.[50] Behind their prompt change of direction was, we may presume, some germinating prior suspicion on their part, exposed rather than created by the adverse criticism (and hence, perhaps, more painful to them), that the poetic patterns of the previous generation could no longer serve their needs.

The theme of this present chapter, the Victorian's interest in acquiring possessions and the concomitant bond existing between owner and object, has, it would seem, a peculiar relevance to the emergence of the dramatic monologue as a prominent genre in this period, a relevance both to the content of such poems and to the literary form they adopted. Self-reflexivity attains there a new prominence as the focus shifts from the acquired artefact as a projection of its owner to the owner himself as a creative entity, with the fictional or semi-fictional artist representing vicariously the poet's own process of generation. The art-collector too is invested with a more actively imaginative function not only as an acquirer of objects but as employing his aesthetic discrimination to commission new works, to display them creatively, or to recombine them constructively in a manner approximating to the task of the poet, especially in the manner of Browning's monologues, where historical or semi-historical figures are 'acquired', imported, and refashioned to express aspects of his own inventive struggles. The poem as artefact thereby becomes simultaneously internalized and externalized, itself an object to be 'acquired' and interpreted by the reader in the way that the inner artefacts are acquired and interpreted by the fictional characters themselves, the reader being stimulated either to adopt or reject the criteria employed by the fictional figure in accordance with the approbational or pejorative implications of the author's representation. To apply the terms with which Harold Bloom describes such process, the poet, challenged by a powerful predecessor, in this instance the Renaissance artist, is impelled to 'misread' or rework that material into a new form, while at the same time recognizing that he too is subject to the interpretive misprision of his reader, and must therefore, as far as lies within his power, direct the latter into a response compatible with the poet's own reading.[51]

Browning seldom discoursed upon the nature of poetry as he conceived it, nor commented on general principles of critical theory. One of the rare instances that has been preserved occurs in his *Essay on Shelley*, commissioned by Moxon in 1851 to introduce a volume of letters attributed to that poet, although they were discovered soon after to be spurious. His comments there have an important bearing on his own verse, especially in the distinction he draws between subjective and objective poetry. At the time he wrote that essay, the terms 'subjective' and 'objective' had become fashionable in literary circles, imported from German criticism in part through Madame de Staël's *L'Allemagne*. But as such terms will, they had acquired an imprecise and elusive quality, sometimes applied sweepingly to differences of genre (the 'subjective' lyric versus the 'objective' epic), and sometimes with arbitrary looseness to individual works, so that Ruskin declared in despair that as literary distinctions no words had become '. . . more exquisitely, and in all points, useless.'[52] Browning chose now to apply them more specifically and more cogently, discriminating in his essay between two types of poet. The subjective poet at best, he remarked, focuses, as did Shelley, upon his inner self, employing his spiritual condition as a means of appealing to the absolute Divine mind, and dwelling only upon those external scenic appearances '. . . which strike out most abundantly and uninterruptedly his own inner light and power'. While he praised such poetic activity as excellent in itself, Browning complained that, for his own period, such subjectivity had spawned a progeny of minor poets subsisting on no more than the shadowy reflection of such authentic pursuits, offering merely the convention of a moral, what he termed 'the straw of last year's harvest'. For his own generation he saw as imperative the emergence, in their place, of the 'objective' poet focusing away from internalized experience to the visible and tactile world, producing verse '. . . prodigal of objects for men's outer and not inner sight'.

Hence the actuality of Browning's own monologues, anchored in specific temporal and physical settings, and dramatic in the sense that the speaker seems to be standing visibly before us in a scene conjured up with vivid realism. Moreover, as in drama, there is no authoritative voice to encourage uniformity of response. Where the Wordsworthian sonnet, the Byronic stanza, and the Keatsian ode had imposed the mood of the poet upon the scene so that the first-person flow of speech constituted the single voice to which credence was due, in contrast a tension is now created between the speaker's convictions or moral assumptions and those induced in the reader through the poet's strategy, counter-responses evoked by unintentional revelations on the part of the fictional *persona*, by incidents, gestures, or the implied comments of others alluded to in his speech, which undercut the speaker's conscious attempts to persuade. Andrea del Sarto furtively 'corrects' the Raphael painting:

> . . . indeed the arm is wrong.
> I hardly dare . . . yet, only you to see,
> Give the chalk here – quick, thus the line should go!

Such acts perform a double function in the process of misprision, discrediting, or refashioning in less admirable form, the figure of the Renaissance artist, patron, or citizen, now adopted as the paradigm of vigorous creativity, by unmasking their frustrated ambitions, envious rivalry, twisted animosities, or perverted morality, while at the same time they suggest defensively to the reader the integrity of the new creative artist, the poet himself. As Robert Langbaum has revealed in a penetrating and wide-ranging study of the genre (which preceded Bloom's theory), the result is a bifurcation of the

reader's sympathy; at one level, the aesthetic sensibility, the single-
ness of purpose, or the courteous magnanimity of the monologuer
fascinates and attracts, while at another level the licentiousness,
hypocrisy, or ruthlessness unconsciously betrayed in the course
of the recital repels and disenchants.[53] Such tension confirms the
poet's own distancing from his characters, shielding his privacy in
a manner which contrasted with the uninhibited confessionalism of
the Romantic tradition. That aspect of the genre no doubt proved
a major attraction for these two Victorian poets, charged by critics
with indulgence in morbid subjectivity at a time when such self-
revelatory writing was moving out of vogue. It offered them the
possibility of retreating behind their fictional inventions, while at
the same time offering by implication a vindication of themselves
as artists.

The psychological exploration of character which the technique
of dramatic monologue invited and the inner contradictions demanded for their speakers encouraged on the part of both poetic
experimenters the creation of soliloquists marked by eccentricity,
by weird modes of thought, by inverted moral assumptions, or by
sheer violence of emotion, manifesting even in that aspect alone a
certain affinity to the idiosyncratic figures peopling Dickens' novels.
There is Tennyson's ascetic St. Simeon, denigrating himself with
due Christian humility as being 'From scalp to sole one slough and
crust of sin', yet at the same time clutching greedily at the crown
of sainthood which he believes to be so rightfully his. Browning's
Caliban wallows happily in the mud as he ponders a deity projected
in his own image; a jealous woman gloats over the poison to be
administered to her rival; a tyrant evocative of Cesare Borgia is
appalled that his unbridled covetousness and cruelty have failed to
crush a subject's spirit – all these revealing not just an inventive
ingenuity on the part of these poets but a burgeoning sense of the
infinite variety of human character, and offering to the reader the
privilege of experiencing that wonderful range vicariously through
the medium of verse. And as Dickens, sensitive to the new acquisitive impulses of his generation, employed the objects in their
possession as a means of revealing their anomalous or grotesque
qualities, so Browning adopts time after time the speaker's relationship to his possessions as the means of disclosing his hidden
traits, of divulging to the reader the value judgements, moral and
aesthetic, upon which the eccentric, enviable, or warped conceptions of his characters are based.

The type of acquisitiveness which held a special attraction for Browning – a more refined version of the crude bourgeois possessiveness caricatured in Dickens' Podsnaps and Veneerings – reflected the increasingly popular avocation of the art collector. The hobby of procuring *objets d'art*, although entering England much later than the continent, had become well established as an aristocratic pastime by the time of Charles I, an interest which was pursued with friendly rivalry by the Earl of Arundel. After a pause for the Puritan interregnum, with its deplorable dispersal of Charles I's magnificent collection, only a small portion of which could be later retrieved, the practice had been revived by his son at the time of the Restoration, to be adopted more widely during the following century. Palladian mansions, such as Lord Burlington's Chiswick House and the Earl of Leicester's Holkham Hall, were often designed to serve primarily as display centres for their owner's extensive art collections, in which emphasis had shifted from the rich variety of paintings drawn from international schools, such as that assembled by Charles I, to concentrate primarily on classical antiquities, statuary, and other artefacts purchased during the requisite Grand Tour and exhibited, in large part, as a means of testifying to the cultivated interests of their owner. As the Grand Tour became mandatory for the sons of the upper middle class too, the practice began to be adopted by them, with the twofold purpose of displaying newly acquired wealth and of testifying to the eligibility of their owners for acceptance into the upper class on grounds of their artistic sensitivity.

The mid-nineteenth century, however, marked a displacement of aesthetic sympathies producing a change in the nature of those collections, as concentration on the classical world of Greece and Rome was edged aside by the growing interest in the Renaissance, fostered by contemporary concerns, a personal identification with both the artist and patron of that period in terms of their dedication to art as the exquisite consummation of human achievement. As the eighteenth-century search for universal rules of art, its advocacy of classical principles valid for all generations, gave way to a conception of the artist as an individualist, attention was transferred to such painters as Giotto and Filippo Lippi who had introduced unconventional, often revolutionary elements into their work. The surge of interest during the Victorian era in Italian art of the fourteenth to sixteenth centuries, popularized by Ruskin, warmly supported by Prince Albert, and more recently documented by John Hale and

Hilary Fraser, constituted a nineteenth-century projection upon the past, whether historically justified or not, of its own advocacy of robust individualism, an advocacy furthered by the somewhat tendentious studies of Jacob Burckhardt.[54]

Browning within his own poetry focused frequently and with considerable fascination upon this aspect of art, interpreting it as arising from the response of individual genius to immediate pressures within his own life, often from the artist's urgent need for money as he struggled for recognition or deriving from some chance interaction between a painter and the idiosyncratic whims of his patron. Art had become intensely personalized, and the desire of the Renaissance patron to foster some indigent painter of genius, or to acquire an outstanding work left mouldering by others became the model for his Victorian counterpart. Browning, when in Florence, himself adopted that role, being constantly on the alert to discover forgotten masterpieces. In a letter dated 4 May, 1850, his wife reported: 'Robert has been picking up pictures at a few pauls each, "hole and corner" pictures which the "dealers" had not found out; and the other day he covered himself with glory by discovering and seizing on (in a corn shop a mile from Florence) five pictures among heaps of trash; and one of the best judges in Florence (Mr Kirkup) throws out such names for them as Cimabue, Ghirlandajo, Giottino . . .'[55]

Such vigorous search for artworks formed part of a wider movement. The National Gallery in London altered its policy at this time, no longer relying as in the past upon chance bequests but, under the energetic directorship of Sir Charles Eastlake, competing at public auctions and sending emissaries overseas to acquire works which would (as the public was constantly urging through the Press) raise the status of the gallery to a level worthy of the imperial power that England had become. And prominent among its acquisitions were now the works of such Early Renaissance artists as Gentile da Fabriano, Fra Angelico and Gozzoli. By 1861, its new policy had been considerably advanced, the enlarged and improved collection it boasted evoking from Trollope a glow of patriotic contentment: 'I conceive that our National Gallery should be a subject of self-congratulation to every Englishman who sees it; that every Englishman should say, in the pride of his heart, that, in collecting it in so short a time, his country has done what no other country could achieve.'[56]

With an immediacy that only a dramatic monologue can achieve, the intensity of that acquisitive passion, projected on to a Renaissance setting, was brilliantly captured in such poems as *The Bishop Orders his Tomb at St. Praxed's*. The dying, feverish cleric, fearful lest his plans be posthumously frustrated by his heirs, gradually reveals with grotesque frankness the complex impulses motivating his plan for the tomb. At one level, the prepared tomb will serve, like the Podsnaps' silver plate, as proud testimony to the wealth and status of its owner. But a new element has entered, contrasting with the Podsnaps and, indeed, with all such Dickensian counterparts, the recognition that the Bishop, whatever his other foibles, is a genuine, dedicated, and gifted connoisseur, endowed with sensitivity and a deep love of beauty. The marble columns, the bronze bas-relief, the costly agate urns so cunningly procured and stored away over the years have been selected with the judicious eye not only of an expert but of an aesthete exhilarated and intoxicated by their wine-like beauty, and that, of course, in direct contradiction to the asceticism incumbent upon an ordained priest of the Catholic church:

> I shall fill my slab of basalt there,
> And 'neath my tabernacle take my rest,
> With those nine columns round me, two and two,
> The odd one at my feet where Anselm stands:
> Peach-blossom marble all, the rare, the ripe
> As fresh-poured red wine of a mighty pulse.
> – Old Gandolf with his paltry onion-stone,
> Put me where I may look at him! True peach,
> Rosy and flawless . . . [57]

Whatever antipathy may be aroused in the reader by the deviousness and stealth whereby he has obtained these materials, by the glaring conflict with the abstemiousness due to his calling, or by the mania that grips him at a time when, as he well knows, he should be preparing his soul for eternity, such antipathy is countered in large part by the very spontaneity of his aesthetic joy in the surpassing beauty of his possessions. His expertise in discriminating between the gradations in hue of each precious stone and his proficiency in evaluating them become in themselves admirable traits, creating the positive aspects of reader response and thereby heightening the dramatic appeal of the vignette. Respect for artistic sensitivity or for the passion of the true collector functions in this poem as what Wolfgang Iser has termed a 'code', a communicative pattern semiotically recognized and endorsed by the reader, which we are here compelled, nevertheless, to re-assess and adjust in the course of the poem. The underlying tension of the monologue as that positive code is offset by a negating counter-code, the Bishop's slyness and moral hypocrisy, produces, moreover, what Roland Barthes would call a 'pulverizing' of the original assumptions or, as Bakhtin would describe it more generously, the creation of a dynamic interplay between two contrary elements, an interplay resulting in the enriching dialogue which Bakhtin sees as the hallmark of all great literature.[58]

No less significant is the way in which the metonymy of possessions, which we examined in the work of his contemporary Dickens, functions here, especially the projection into those possessions of the owner's personality. For the sepulchral effigy, to be executed in purest jasper, is gradually conceived by the Bishop as an *alter ego*. It will take over from him posthumously, permitting him, as it were, to continue rejoicing beyond death in the richness of his basalt slab and marble columns. As he lies dying, within the cleric's mind he and the statue exchange roles. While his soul enters into his marble tomb to animate it and survive there beyond death, his failing body settles into the cold sculpted lines of the stone effigy:

> And then how I shall lie through centuries,
> And hear the blessed mutter of the mass,
> And see God made and eaten all day long,
> And feel the steady candle-flame and taste
> Good strong thick stupefying incense-smoke!
> For as I lie here, hours of the dead night,
> Dying in state and by such slow degrees,
> I fold my arms as if they clasped a crook,
> And stretch my feet forth straight as stone can point,
> And let the bedclothes, for a mortcloth, drop
> Into great laps and folds of sculptor's work . . .

The proposed tomb, moreover, functions not only as an extension of self in that regard, but as a preserver of his own duality, a surrogate for the complexities and contradictions of his inner being, expressing for eternity the polarized elements co-existing with such dramatic credibility within his character. It is manifested in the artwork itself that will adorn his sepulchre, with the sacred and the erotic, as in his own life, inextricably mingled, as the bronze bas-relief wonderfully depicts

> The Saviour at his sermon on the mount,
> Saint Praxed in a glory, and one Pan
> Ready to twitch the Nymph's last garment off . . .

For the *cognoscenti* among his readers, such mingling of religious devotion with titillating eroticism was no mere figment of a fevered imagination nor a hypothetical fantasy of Browning's, but a staple ingredient of Renaissance and Baroque painting, marking the strange merger there of pagan and religious impulses. Ribera's *St. Agnes in Prison* may depict a scene of pious dedication as the female saint, stripped by her captors, is rewarded by the miraculous appearance of a shining white garment; but both the choice of that theme and the method of its presentation betray an erotic interest too, the *putto* seeming about to twitch aside the sole garment precariously covering the naked female saint.

The Bishop's tomb reflects that fundamental change in the conception of the *objet d'art* which we have been following, no longer a work learnedly exhibited like the antique statuary displayed at Holkham Hall, but now taking on a life of its own as an extension of its owner's being, in his longing for eternal Christian rest incongruously coupled with an un-Christian jealousy, pride, and lust:

> . . . leave me in my church, the church for peace,
> That I may watch at leisure if he leers –
> Old Gandolf, at me, from his onion-stone,
> As still he envied me, so fair she was!

In *My Last Duchess*, the acquired work of art serves again as the surrogate for a human being, in this instance not of the speaker himself but of the source of his aesthetic pleasure. The living, breathing figure of beauty which the Duchess had been to him in life has been translated by the Duke into the safer, frozen form of art, a painting preserving her vital spirit beyond death – 'There she stands / As if alive' – but controlled and subjugated into a form no longer capable of arousing his jealousy. As the Bishop's obsession was in large part inspired by the art-collector's passion, that new avocation of the Victorian connoisseur modelled on Renaissance patronage, so it functions as the motivating force of this poem. For intrinsic in the activity of art collection is an element of jealousy and rivalry, the desire to out-do all others in the quality of the works acquired. Even during her life, the Duchess had been in essence only a collector's item, added to the Duke's property for the splendour her beauty reflected upon her purchaser, and valued by him as a rare possession, like the Count's fair daughter whose acquisition he is in the process of negotiating.

The fascination of that situation for Browning is not merely the Duke's callousness in disposing of his wife but, even more so, the hierarchy of values which that action implied, a hierarchy on whose scale the perfect work of art holds far higher rank than the life of a mere mortal sacrificed in so splendid a cause. Paradoxical as it may seem – and literature does function by such contrary impulses – the aversion aroused by his ruthlessness was, for the Victorian reader as it is for us as long as we remain under the spell of the poem, accompanied by a degree of admiration for such total dedication to perfection, a dedication that, the poem implies, could only have existed in the court of a Renaissance autocrat, exemplifying a period devoted to the supremacy of art. Alive, the Duchess had been an imperfect possession, graciously bestowing smiles on others in a manner offensive to that desire for exclusive ownership motivating the dedicated collector and patron. Transferred from the living form to the eternalized, she is a commodity placed totally within his power, the 'depth and passion' of her earnest glance now gratifying others only at its owner's whim,

> . . . (since none puts by
> The curtain I have drawn for you, but I)

The portrait will be revealed to such privileged visitors as the Count's plenipotentiary and, by extension, to the reader. And yet by that tension of opposites inherent in the new dramatic monologue, in a sense it is the Duchess who triumphs beyond death, revealing through her artistic representation each time the Duke proudly relates this instance of his power the very aspects of his own character to which he is so blind, his unworthiness of her as both husband and lover, his insufferable pride in disdaining to correct her supposed failing by a timely word – 'E'en then would be some stooping' – and (quite apart from the horror of his act) the insensitiveness to true beauty which could allow him to destroy it in its natural form in order to preserved it as artefact.

The gratification of his masculine prerogatives through the taming of his wife's feminine intractability is echoed by the other works in his gallery. Like Dickens' inanimate objects, they represent the qualities on which their owner prides himself, his god-like subduing of the recalcitrant:

> Nay, we'll go
> Together down, sir. Notice Neptune, though,
> Taming a sea-horse, thought a rarity,
> Which Claus of Innsbruck cast in bronze for me!

Post-modernism has sensitized us to the conception of art as being intentionally representational, a recognition that, in semiotic terms, the 'healthy' signifier is one betraying a self-reflexive awareness of its own arbitrariness.[59] Richard Wollheim, in a treatise accepting the receptor's ever-present awareness that he or she is gazing not through some magic casement on to an imagined world but at a solid, material object, a piece of canvas, a block of stone, or a printed page, deduces that a work of art demands from the viewer, in place of normal perception, a specific form of seeing appropriate to such representational forms. The 'artifactuality' of the work is never mentally suppressed in such acts of perception, and that specific type of seeing, he suggests, fulfils the artist's original intention in creating the work.[60] It is a theory especially relevant to this poem which, in a sense, adopts 'artifactuality' as its central theme, allowing it to eddy outward from the inner symbol and to impinge upon the art-work created by Browning, the poem itself. The portrait commissioned by the Duke constitutes, as we have seen, not so much an attempt at mimetic illusionism, intended to deceive by its verisimilitude, but rather the replacement of a breathing, living being by an acknowledgedly inanimate substitute, a process deliberately exploiting the non-mimetic quality of art – its frozen and unchanging quality. The warm glance is thereby confined and isolated from the vital, quotidian world, and shorn of the reprehensible freedoms enjoyed by its charming original in real life. The Duke's act, therefore, is of a patron (and, through Frà Pandolf, of a painter too) cherishing the artefact as inanimate representation distinguished from the real. The irony of the poem, the Bakhtinian counter-thrust, is, as we have seen, in the reader's partial dissociation from the sense of triumph induced by that translation. But the argument needs to be taken a stage further. For the implications of that twofold response ripple outward, reminding us that the monologue in which they appear, vivid as it may seem in its dramatic recapturing of the scene, is also in itself a frozen artefact. It is a poetic construct in which the historical distancing from the recounted event compels readers, as so often in Victorian poetry, to sense a certain ambiguity, to contrast the moral and aesthetic assumptions prevalent in that past era with the standards predominating in nineteenth-century society, and to draw from that comparison – not least, from the Duke's admirable dedication to art, however misguided its application – conclusions appropriate for their own time.

If, as I have suggested, a dominant theme of the dramatic monologue was this contemporary interest in the often idiosyncratic relationship between people and their possessions – witness Porphyria's lover derangedly ensuring eternal possession of his mistress's devotion by strangling her at the moment of their embrace – it is evidenced also in the nature of the verse which it produced. In a manner unprecedented in earlier eras, the poem as artefact becomes moulded by the character of the speaker, taking on the unique and eccentric traits of the fictitious *persona* supposedly producing it.[61] In the same way as Victorian architecture deserted formal stylistic genres to absorb and represent the personal whims of the designer, and the furniture of that period accepted the impress of its owner, with an armchair displaying the chauvinism and love of dogs of its Irish purchaser, so there emerges a heightened correlation between the temperament of Browning's speakers and the convoluted, mellow, or terse verse-forms distinguishing each specific poem. The broken rhythms, the alliterative cacophonies, the exclamatory ejaculations varying the poetic timbre of Browning's verse produced innovative metrical forms essentially different from earlier practice. Even Shakespeare as a consummate dramatist, brilliantly varying the speech of his characters to suit their traits, remained within the formal parameters of blank verse, while most other poetry, whatever its theme, conveys primarily the personality of the poet, as in the prophetic tones of *Paradise Lost*, the urbane wit of *The Rape of the Lock*, the meditational musings of Wordsworth or, to return to dramatic poetry, the Cain or Prometheus figures which function as the scarcely disguised mouthpieces of Byron and Shelley. Browning's fictional characters, however, not only attract us by the contrast they afford to their author's personality, often being placed in situations remote from anything that could possibly be related to him – the fury of a woman tricked by the Inquisition into betraying her lover, the bland theologizing of a nineteenth-century bishop, a deathbed confessor exulting in the sin he is being urged to repent – but they intrigue us also by the way in which their weird passions and convictions mould and impress themselves upon the form of the verse:

> Gr-r-r – there go, my heart's abhorrence!
>   Water your damn flower-pots, do!
> If hate killed men, Brother Lawrence,
>   God's blood, would not mine kill you! . . .

The traditional poetic genres of heroic couplet, ballad, blank verse, or sonnet, within whose framework poets had previously been content to express their thoughts and emotions, are in Browning's *Dramatic Lyrics* or his *Men and Women* continually deserted in favour of innovative configurations designed to reflect the emotional pulsation of his speakers, the grateful sob of a reconciled mistress, the venom of a cuckolded husband, or the deep pain of a rejected paramour. There is the magically hushed:

> Let's contend no more, Love,
>   Strive nor weep:
> All be as before, Love,
>   – Only sleep!

the rasping whisper of the reluctant church-goer, mocking at the farce of religious coercion:

> Higgledy piggledy, packed we lie,
> Rats in a hamper, swine in a stye,
> Wasps in a bottle, frogs in a sieve,
> Worms in a carcass, fleas in a sleeve.
> Hist! square shoulders, settle your thumbs
> And buzz for the Bishop – here he comes.

or the suppressed, throbbing passion of an unrequited lover:

> Yet I will but say what mere friends say,
>   Or only a thought stronger;
> I will hold your hand but as long as all may,
>   Or so very little longer.[62]

All verse, of course, by its very nature exploits the nuances and rhythmical stresses of metre, but in Browning's usage the poetic construct has become more malleable, taking upon itself the impress of the speaker's concerns, reflecting the eclecticism of Victorian architecture and the new bond between owner and object, as in the inkstand from the Crystal Palace Exhibition (Fig. 21) whimsically displaying the angling interests of its owner.

One striking instance of such projection of the speaker's personality on to the verse-form is the poem *Saul*, published originally in 1845, which derives much of its emotional impact from the powerful, forward momentum of its rhythms, as the young David approaches the distraught King:

> And first I saw nought but the blackness;
> But soon I descried
> A something more black than the blackness
> – The vast, the upright
> Main-prop which sustains the pavilion, –
> And slow into sight
> Grew a figure, gigantic, against it,
> And blackest of all; –
> Then a sunbeam, that burst thro' the tent-roof,
> Showed Saul.[63]

That irresistible progressive movement derives, one may suspect, from the syncopated rhythm – still novel to Victorian ears – of the railway train moving forcefully along its tracks. We may recall that it was, in the very year of this poem's composition, incorporated into painting as a source of artistic inspiration in Turner's *Rain, Steam, and Speed* (cf. Fig. 4). Prosaic as the source may seem for the biblical theme of this poem, its appropriateness becomes more comprehensible in the light of Charles Kingsley's mid-century movement advocating 'muscular Christianity', with its attempt to de-emphasize the traditional virtues of humility, submissiveness, and suffering in favour of a robust and virile version of the faith, more in keeping with the imperial pride of the Englishman of the day. It was that muscular view of religion to which Millais subscribed, and which conjured up the vision of biblical prowess in his *Victory, O Lord!* depicting Moses courageously overcoming the immense physical weariness of holding his arms aloft for so many hours in order to ensure that the battle of the Hebrews against the Amalekites would be duly won. By this more vigorous conception of religion, the Victorian was urged to resist the Amalekites of his own era, to combat the challenges of the real world, including those posed by science and industry, and to face them with valour and self-reliance.

This poem by Browning, like his *Prospice,* is charged with that same sense of stalwart, spiritual fortitude, the rhythms moulded by the speaker's determined forward movement, climaxing in the dramatic vision of King Saul as a prefiguration of Christ upon the Cross, not in meekness or surrender but as *agonistes.* He embodies in his personal struggle both Christ and the serpent, gathering his strength for the mighty thrust towards his soul's deliverance, in the same way as the Victorian was called upon to wrestle manfully against the powerful religious doubts which beset him:

> He stood as erect as that tent-prop;
>   Both arms stretched out wide
> On the great cross-support in the centre
>   That goes to each side:
> So he bent not a muscle but hung there
>   As, caught in his pangs
> And waiting his change the king-serpent
>   All heavily hangs,
> Far away from his kind, in the Pine,
>   Till deliverance come
> With the Spring-time, – so agonized Saul . . .

That deep yearning for restored faith, a yearning which must overcome all opposition, imposes itself upon the metrical form of the artefact to create the irresistible forward-moving rhythm from which so much of its force derives.

Such innovations are thus facets of this more general propensity to extrapolate character into objects. In his *Pictor Ignotus,* an anonymous painter wearily produces the tediously repetitive canvases on which he must subsist:

> My heart sinks, as monotonous I paint
> These endless cloisters and eternal aisles
>   . . . blackening in the daily candle-smoke,
> They moulder on the damp wall's travertine,
>   'Mid echoes the light footstep never woke.
> So die my pictures! surely gently die!

The decaying canvases darkening on the wall are again artefacts reflecting the painter's own character; they are doomed to the same neglect and ephemerality in art as their creator has been destined to experience in life. And the weary notes of the poem itself, with the echoing of the final line, provide the twofold projection of character typifying Browning's verse, from the *persona* on to the object and, internally, from the *persona* on to the poetic form.

The symbiotic relationship of animate and inanimate peculiar to the Victorian era would seem, therefore, not to have symbolized, as has so long been assumed, a contemporary sense that the proliferating objects produced by industry had usurped human authority, and that man had surrendered his vitality to them. The animation of objects has a more positive source and more positive implications, reflecting the proprietary mode of a thriving society which proudly regarded the articles it had created or had acquired as projections of personality, absorbing their owner's tastes, traits, and quirks.

Both Dickens and Browning had sensitively perceived the centrality of that element in Victorian culture, incorporating it into their works both thematically and stylistically. Within their art, those objects enjoy a life of their own as surrogates for the self, helping to create the boisterous quality of Dickens' fictional world, where the eccentric homes, the soaring kite, the wooden leg, and the myopic spectacles of his fictional characters function, as did the Victorian country house and its furnishings, as metonyms of self. So too, in Browning's lyrics and dramatic monologues the personal eccentricities of his diverse characters, the jealous rivals, the embittered clerics, the Renaissance tyrants, and the frustrated artists peopling his verse, are presented primarily through their acquisitive or proprietary motivations, impressing their personalities not only upon their possessions but upon the form of the poem itself, which, in a manner unique to Browning's art, is moulded by the contours of each idiosyncratic speaker.

4

George Eliot and the Horizons of Expectation

Eliot's penchant for realism in her early novels has little bearing on the important post-modern distinction between mimesis and representation.[1] Her primary purpose in choosing scenes from daily life was not to achieve a credible fictional illusionism – that, she admitted, had already been accomplished by others – but to combat a current fashion of which she disapproved. She wished to create an essentially innovative form of narrative opposed to the heroic tradition of Scott's Waverley Novels, to the romantic mystery of the Brontës, and to the Gothicism that had continued to permeate Dickens' work even when exposing social injustice. While admiring Dickens' ability to render urban scenes with remarkable vividness, she complained of his tendency to sentimentalize the poor, arguing that it is the function of painter or novelist to make us feel '. . . not for the heroic artisan or the sentimental peasant, but for the peasant in all his coarse apathy, and the artisan in all his suspicious selfishness.'[2] Accordingly, in her first published story issued in the same year as that comment, she warned her readers that, '. . . being unable to invent thrilling incidents for your amusement, my only merit must lie in the truth with which I represent to you the humble experience of ordinary fellow-mortals.' That initial tale focused therefore upon a commonplace clergyman, the Reverend Amos Barton, whose very faults, she assures us, were middling, who was not by nature superlative in anything, '. . . unless, indeed, he was superlatively middling'.[3]

In interdisciplinary studies, the source of her interest in depicting unpretentious scenes drawn from common life has long been attributed to her admiration of seventeenth-century Dutch art, to the inspiration it provided for depicting unheroic domestic interiors, or scenes of the common people at play, in the canvases of Vermeer, Metsu, Ter Borch, Steen, and De Hooch. Mario Praz noted some years ago the sociological parallels between the two periods which would seem to substantiate that attribution. Literature, he pointed out, was in the nineteenth century no longer addressed (even if only ostensibly) to persons of 'polite learning' as in the days of Fielding but to a wider, predominantly middle-class public immersed in the social activities and preoccupations of its own world. The altered character of the Victorian reading public he saw as mirroring the earlier emergence in the Netherlands of a new type of patron for the arts, patrons drawn not from the aristocracy but from the mercantile class rooted in their mundane activities.[4] Hence the Dutch painters' provision of vignettes familiar to the prospective buyer – music lessons, a maidservant cleaning the courtyard under the watchful supervision of her mistress, a game of skittles outside an inn – in place of the grand mythological, heroic, or devotional scenes occupying the canvases of the High Baroque.

Hugh Witemeyer's perceptive study *George Eliot and the Visual Arts*, with its detailed exploration of her indebtedness to the great painters of the past, has corroborated this traditional attribution. He notes rightly that her knowledge of artists and her employment of their stylistic techniques was much wider in range and in variety than has been thought, and that in such later novels as *Romola* and *Middlemarch*, she drew primarily upon the painters of the High Renaissance for the portraiture of her fictional characters, notably upon Raphael and Titian for whom she possessed an especial fondness. And Joseph Wiesenfarth has strengthened that reading by noting how Dorothea's maturing discrimination in her response to painting, under the guidance of Ladislaw, reflects the authoress's own developing tastes. But in analysing the realism of her early novels, Witemeyer subscribes to the accepted view, that Dutch genre painting was the primary source for her naturalistic depictions of common life.[5]

Indeed, to question that attribution would appear to defy George Eliot's own unhesitating acknowledgment of her model. In a passage in *Adam Bede* which must form the starting-point for any such enquiry, it was to the realism of the Dutch school that she turned as precedent for her own refusal to '. . . straighten the noses of her characters', to brighten their wit, or to rectify their dispositions, seeing in those earlier depictions a paradigm for her own determination to write of commonplace people, whose conversation might not be brilliant but who harboured within their dim and narrow existence joys and sorrows worthy of regard, and to present her fictional figures as breathing men and women drawn from the world of actuality. To do otherwise would, she maintained, be falsehood, offending against that precious quality of truthfulness which delighted her in so many of the Netherlandish paintings:

> I find a source of delicious sympathy in these faithful pictures of a monotonous, homely existence, which has been the fate of so many more among my fellow-mortals than a life of pomp or of absolute indigence, of tragic suffering or of world-stirring actions. I turn, without shrinking, from cloud-borne angels, from prophets, sibyls, and heroic warriors, to an old woman bending over her flower-pot or eating her solitary dinner, while the noonday light, softened perhaps by a screen of leaves, falls on her mob-cap, and just touches the rim of her spinning-wheel, and her stone jug, and all those cheap common things which are the precious necessaries of life to her; – or I turn to that village wedding, kept between four brown walls, where an awkward bridegroom opens the dance with a high-shouldered, broad-faced bride, while elderly and middle-aged friends look on, with very irregular noses and lips, and probably with quart-pots in their hands, but with an expression of unmistakable contentment and good-will. 'Foh!' says my idealistic friend, 'what vulgar details! What good is there in taking all these pains to give an exact likeness of old women and clowns? What a low phase of life! – what clumsy, ugly people!' But, bless us, things may be lovable that are not altogether handsome, I hope . . .[6]

There is, however, a substantial danger in this traditional attribution, the danger of confusing sequential influence with literary strategy, of ignoring the possibility that she was merely employing the Dutch painters of an earlier generation to add the weight of past authority to her own pre-existent proclivity, her personal response to a cultural shift occurring within her generation. In synchronic investigation, as has been noted elsewhere in this present study, such identification of earlier sources, even when publicly proclaimed by the author, is of very limited value unless it includes an enquiry into the fluctuations within the current scene which led to the selection of that specific model above all others, perhaps as an aegis under which the innovative elements within his or her own work could be developed, and which could offer some degree of validation for the writer's resistance to established traditions.

A post-modern strategy which may prove particularly relevant in analysing this aspect of her work is that of Hans Robert Jauss.

Where the dynamics of exchange within each text, the underlying tension to which contemporary criticism has been so responsive, has been identified by most critics primarily in terms of an inner conflict – in the writings of Bakhtin and Derrida as a disharmony between text and sub-text, in Harold Bloom's writings as the author's Oedipal resistance to preceding writers – Jauss has focused upon the conflict between author and reader, between the writer and the 'horizons of expectation' which the reader brings to the work. In contrast to reader-reception critics such as Wolfgang Iser and Stanley Fish who downplay the authority of the text, placing major emphasis upon the personal interpretations brought to the work by each reader, Jauss has perceived a two-sided discourse. His theory was derived to some extent from Karl Popper's illuminating insight concerning the processes of discovery. Scientific and scholarly hypotheses, Popper had maintained, are generally not the result of planned research but of false premises. They arise from the disappointment of certain anticipations on the part of the discoverer, those setbacks constituting the revelation of a new truth, a process he compared to '. . . the experience of a blind man running into an obstacle and thereby learning of its existence. We gain contact with "reality" by disproving our assumptions.'[7] In the same way, Jauss argues for literature, each reader brings to a literary work an intertextual referential framework derived from the established codes or values embedded within contemporary culture and reinforced by previous reading. The author, he suggests, wary of the body of contemporary assumptions which would predispose the reader to interpret signals received from the text in accordance with the semiotic matrix of the time, whether moral, philosophical, social, or aesthetic, is obligated, when desirous of innovation, to wean the reader away from them, constructing a new set of values as their replacement. The result is a covert contest between author and reader, a process of seduction, in which the writer employs a strategy of manipulation to lure the reader from such preconditioning, from the 'horizons of expectation' brought to the work.[8] This concept of the dynamics of exchange within literary texts would seem especially appropriate to a study of George Eliot's writing and of the tactics she employed in order to encourage the reader to adopt new criteria for fiction more suited to the changing times, including that focusing-down from the heroic to the commonplace which engages us here.

In searching for the contemporary impulse prompting her to look

back to Dutch painting for support, it is surely relevant that across
the Channel, at precisely this time, there occurred a shift in artistic
direction of major aesthetic significance, a re-routing of art to which
her own innovations have, one may suspect, much closer affinities
than to the Dutch school some two hundred years earlier. The indebtedness was not direct – there is not attempt to suggest here that
she learned the principles from that continental movement – but it
would indeed seem that she was, within the medium of literature,
providing an independent, parallel expression of a trend manifesting
itself simultaneously in France. For in the same year that George
Eliot was warning her readers of the unheroic subject-matter that
she intended to adopt for her fiction, Courbet was, in 1855, defiantly
opening his own pavilion near the Exposition Universelle, whose
jury had rejected both his *Burial at Ornans* and his *Artist's Studio*, and
was issuing there his provocative 'Realist Manifesto' inaugurating
a new era in art. Each generation, he argued, must begin its work
afresh; and, with echoes of the insistence upon clear and objective
scrutiny necessary in the contemporary sciences, he urged those
students who had left the Ecole des Beaux-Arts in order to register
at his own *atelier* that only through fidelity to truth would they
achieve their purpose. Painting, he maintained, '. . . is an essentially
concrete art and can only consist of the representation of *real and
existing* things'.[9] And central to that search for realism was his
desertion of the mythological, historically stirring, or ennobling
themes current in art in favour of scenes drawn from the unpretentious activities of the lower classes and the rustic, the latter no
longer viewed idealistically as 'noble savages', nor with the condescension implicit in the genre of Theocritan and Virgilian pastoral,
but as subjects for artistic depiction valid in their own right. His
Burial at Ornans – in contrast to El Greco's *Burial of Count Orgaz*,
with its miraculous vision of the Count's soul being received into
heaven, or Poussin's *Funeral of Phocis* fraught with classical and
Stoical allusions – depicts the simple interment of an anonymous
peasant in the artist's own village of Ornans, the ceremony attended
by relatives and fellow-labourers, for whose portraits Courbet
conscripted the villagers themselves as models. Free from sentimentality and from allegorical elevation, it was impressive primarily
in its uncompromising depiction of truth, as in the rough, gaping
hole in the foreground in which the body is about to be deposited.

How close to this new continental orientation George Eliot's
own work came may be seen from the aesthetic doctrines she was

promulgating at the same time, partly under the influence of Ruskin, even though one important deviation from Ruskin's views is apparent. As Gillian Beer has shown, she admired and adopted the latter's demand for scrupulous accuracy of detail in depicting the *minutiae* of nature, as in her description of '. . . the level sunlight lying like transparent gold among the gently-curving stems of the feathered grass and the tall red sorrel, and the white umbels of the hemlocks lining the busy hedgerows'.[10] But she did not adopt in her own work his preference for the Grand Style and for elevated themes in art. In that regard, she followed a path closer to that of the continental movement. In her 1856 review of the third volume of Ruskin's *Modern Painters*, she advocated, in language remarkably similar to Courbet's, the principle '. . . that all truth and beauty are to be attained by a humble and faithful study of nature, and not by substituting vague forms, bred by imagination on the mists of feeling, in place of definite, substantial reality'.[11] It was a sentiment she shared with George Lewes who, during that period, was enunciating the dogma that 'Art always aims at the representation of Reality, i.e. of Truth; and no departure from truth is permissible, except such as inevitably lies in the nature of the medium itself. Realism is thus the basis of all Art, and its antithesis is not Idealism, but Falsism.' More specifically, he condemned the depiction of milk-maids in picturesque garb, never old or dirty, concluding: 'Either give us true peasants, or leave them untouched . . .'[12]

The composition of George Eliot's *Scenes from Clerical Life* provided her with an opportunity to translate into practice the theories being formulated by Lewes and herself. The commonplace, tawdry settings of these stories did not arouse a public furore in the same degree as Courbet's work, but did indeed produce consternation on their original appearance – confirming the existence of those horizons of expectation in her readers which she would need to modify and which she repeatedly confronted by means of authorial comments within her own work. Her publisher, John Blackwood, circulating the manuscript among his advisers, was especially disturbed by the strongly negative response of W.G. Hamley, an editorial colleague whose views he greatly respected and with whom he could not recollect having experienced any previous difference of opinion. Hamley was firmly against publishing the work on the grounds that the story of Amos Barton contained too much 'sniffing and dirty noses'. Blackwood himself, schooled by Lewes to be especially gentle in offering suggestions to so sensitive an authoress, invariably couched his criticisms in very hesitant terms. Yet on this occasion he felt so convinced that readers would object to the harsh depiction of the religious conflict in 'Janet's Repentance' that he took the risk of urging her to replace that aspect by a more sympathetic picture, such as the portrayal of '. . . a really good active working clergyman, neither absurdly evangelical nor absurdly High Church'. In her reply to him dated 11 June, 1857, Eliot was unequivocal. She insisted that her sketches both of clergymen and of dissenters in that story had been drawn not from hearsay but from close personal observation of them in real life, and that the fictional versions had already been accommodated to readers' expectations as far as she was prepared to go. The actual town on which she had based the tale, she added pointedly, '. . . was more vicious than my Milby; the real Dempster was far more disgusting than mine; the real Janet alas! had a far sadder end than mine'. Accordingly, she stood firm in her refusal to alter the work.[13]

The negative response of her publisher had not been unexpected on her part, and was to characterize reader reaction for many years, the appearance of *The Mill on the Floss,* for example, being greeted in the *Quarterly Review* with marked distaste for its portrayal of mere 'uncultured provincials'. But she was determined to win support for her interest in depicting the apparently humdrum world of the poorer classes. She therefore inserted passages into her novels and stories, particularly during the earlier phase, intended both to anticipate and to deflect opposition – the kind of objections that were then being bestowed on Courbet's work across the Channel, where his *Les Demoiselles au bord de la Seine* of 1856 had been condemned as vulgar because the two women portrayed there did not belong to the higher echelons of society.[14] In 'Amos Barton', anticipating Roland Barthes' statement that '. . . the *I* that approaches the text is itself already a plurality of other texts, of infinite or, more precisely, lost codes',[15] she acknowledged to her readers, nurtured on historical novels of valour or dark tales of Gothic suspense, that to them the choice of so banal and unexceptional a character would no doubt prove disturbing:

> . . . perhaps I am doing a bold thing to bespeak your sympathy on behalf of a man who was so very far from remarkable, – a man whose virtues were not heroic, and who had no undetected crime within his breast; who had not the slightest mystery hanging about him, but was palpably and unmistakably commonplace.

Her pungent account of the sermon her cleric delivers at the work-
house as part of his weekly duties is unswerving in its veracity, a
truer portrayal of the real denizens of a country poorhouse than the
public may have liked to acknowledge. The unenviable curate's
audience, she points out, consisted of a stone-deaf nonagenarian
seated in the front row '... with protruded chin, and munch-
ing mouth, and eyes that seemed to look at emptiness', a defiant
harridan resenting all representatives of authority including the
preacher, a young man sadly afflicted with hydrocephalus, and an
ex-footman with a tendency to doze off under spiritual instruction.
To that group of reluctant auditors he must try to convey some
message of religious comfort and faith; but the Reverend Amos
Barton, we are informed, possessed neither the flexible imagination
nor the adroit tongue appropriate for such a task and incongruously
'... talked of Israel and its sins, of chosen vessels, of the Paschal
Lamb ...', failing to produce any salutary effect upon his listeners.[16]

The clergyman's conscientiousness in fulfilling his duties within
his own humble limitations mutes the potential comedy of the scene,
but the hopelessness of the task and the spiritual gulf separating
the curate from his flock result in a masterpiece of realistic narrative. In that respect it constituted, as is evidenced by her authorial
apologies, a daring departure from the conventions of contemporary
fiction; and it was as a means of buttressing her work against negative criticism that, both in her correspondence with Blackwood
and in her first novel *Adam Bede*, she resorted to the Dutch school
of genre painters. She employed them not as the source of her
inspiration but as sanction for her own experimentation with a new
form of art, as part of her strategy for combating reader anticipation
and justifying the uncompromising truthfulness of her depiction.

If, then, George Eliot's choice of supposedly humdrum themes
was prompted by contemporary aesthetic tendencies rather than
some supposed 'influence' bridging two centuries, it should be possible to discern significant divergences from the traditions of Dutch
art, which would reveal her as more closely aligned with the trends
of her own time. And indeed, beyond the 'bourgeois' or democratic
tendency which she did find in that earlier school, there may be
descried a quality in her work which held no place in the paintings
of Vermeer or Jan Steen. In marked contrast to those seventeenth-
century painters, Eliot, like other artists and writers of her era, was
sensitive to the transformations taking place in her own generation and anxious to identify and to record them.[17] Well-established

traditions were being replaced, often at a bewildering rate, by new and often disquieting modes. As Daniel Cottom has pointed out, while expressing at times a nostalgic longing for the supposed stability of the past, she reveals in her writings an increasing recognition that the changes taking place were often ultimately beneficial, although she combined with that awareness a sense of the urgent need to improve the lot of the poor.[18] In that regard she diverged from the essentially conservative domesticity of Dutch painting in favour of social remonstration intrinsic to the new movement in art, in this respect too, reflecting the motivation of the painters emerging into prominence across the Channel.

Courbet's *The Stone-breakers* of 1849 (Fig. 22), for example, has often been interpreted, particularly in our own day, as a vaguely sentimental depiction of labourers at work. But in its time, it was both intended by the artist and understood by his viewers and critics as an act of social protest arising directly out of the 1848 Revolution. Pierre-Joseph Proudhon, the socialist philosopher with whom Courbet worked closely, in his *Du principe de l'art et de sa destination sociale* of 1865 (a treatise which had originally been planned as a joint enterprise together with Courbet but which the author eventually issued under his own name) described the painting explicitly as an attack upon the evils of industrialization. It was intended, he points out, to condemn the advent of mechanization which, robbing man of his craftsmanship, was now leaving to the poor only those soul-destroying tasks that machinery was unable to handle. As a result, the portion of society required to fulfil those tasks was being subjected to a servitude worse than that of the black slaves, a servitude against which all enlightened men should vehemently protest:

> *The Stone-breakers* is an irony addressed to our industrial civilization which every day invents marvelous machines to work, sow, mow, harvest, thresh the grain, grind it, knead, spin, weave, sew, manufacture nails, paper, pins, cards; to execute, in short, all kinds of jobs, often very complicated and delicate, and which is incapable of freeing man from the heaviest, most difficult, most unpleasant tasks, the eternal lot of the poor.[19]

Courbet himself, in a letter to his friend Francis Wey, described the feelings of compassion originally aroused in him by the scene he witnessed and subsequently painted, his encounter with '. . . the most complete expression of misery . . .' The worker, in both his suffering and in the more fulfilling aspects of his labour, was to become a dominant image in Realist art, the many paintings on that theme including Millet's *The Sower*, Legros' *The Tinker*, Breton's *The Return of the Gleaners* and Henry Wallis's *The Stone-breaker* of 1857 (with an impassioned quotation from Carlyle appended to the latter). That was the year in which George Eliot, while granting the right of painters and writers to portray elevated scenes of noble, celestial Madonnas, added the plea in *Adam Bede*:

> . . . but do not impose on us any aesthetic rules which shall banish from the region of Art those old women scraping carrots with their work-torn hands, those heavy clowns taking holiday in a dingy pot-house, those rounded backs and stupid weather-beaten faces that have bent over the spade and done the rough work of the world – those homes with their tin pans, their brown pitchers, their rough curs, and their clusters of onions.[20]

For all her empathy with the working class, George Eliot was no militant socialist, and it is not there that the similarity lies. The primary interest which she shared with the nineteenth-century Realists and which distinguished them from the Dutch school was her focus upon the contemporary scene in terms of a continuing social flux, the waves of permutation introducing far-reaching changes in the human condition. The painters of the seventeenth-century Dutch school were indeed bourgeois in their choice of subjects, recording the daily life of the comfortably established middle class, portraying with a charming accuracy of detail their social and recreational activities, their supervision of sometimes troublesome servants and, with condescension, the vulgar but amusing relaxations of the peasant labourers tippling within the inns. But the most striking innovation of that genre in its shift from the heroic to the everyday was its reflection of the new rationalism and objectivity demanded from the artist as observer. The dazzling light of divine power in the chiaroscuro paintings of High Baroque art, as in Rubens' splendid *Fall of the Damned*, was replaced in such paintings by the calm, evenly-spread light of reason, representing a desire for the depiction of non-miraculous truths, which found its counterpart in poetry, as Marjorie Nicolson revealed many years ago in her *Newton Demands the Muse*.[21] Gabriel Metsu's *The Music Lesson* may portray a seventeenth-century scene – the figures wearing the clothes and adopting the hairstyles of the day, as well as seated beside instruments such as would have been in general use at that time. But there is nothing intrinsically contemporary about the scene itself, nor the activity depicted, in terms of an attempt to identify or chronicle some interestingly new manifestation. Instead, it aims at recording, with a certain distancing, human scenes universal in their application, the belief in such universality suggesting a social as well as intellectual stability. Metsu's painting differed little in that regard from a Renaissance painting such as Lorenzo Costa's *The Concert*, portraying four singers harmonizing companionably.

In contrast, Courbet and Proudhon were responding to ominous changes in the world around them. They saw industrialization as threatening the livelihood of the worker; and Eliot herself, while less militant in her response, displayed in all her writings an extraordinary sensitivity to and concern with the fluctuations, both major and minor, occurring within a wide range of human activities, in medical research, in religious sectarianism, in the identification of mythological archetypes, even in such apparently abstruse themes as the first hints of modern Zionism, before the Jewish people themselves had consciously responded to European nationalist tendencies.[22] The description of the carpentry shop in *Adam Bede* not only serves to advocate Carlyle's work-ethic but moves at once into a discussion of the current conflict between the Dissenters' call for total dedication to the spiritual life and the urgent financial need of labourers to participate in the advances of industrialization. There is such a thing, Adam urges his brother Seth, as being over-spiritual: '. . . we must have something beside Gospel i' this world. Look at the canals, an' th' aqueducs, an' th' coal-pit engines, and Arkwright's mills there at Cromford; a man must learn summat beside Gospel to make them things . . .'[23] While her novels are often set back some thirty to forty years before the time of writing, her purpose in adopting that past setting is never to avoid the present. The chronological discrepancy allows her to evaluate the change with the privilege of hindsight, offering authorial animadversions on the advantages or disadvantages that have accrued.

She possessed, indeed, an extraordinary sensitivity to the changes in social and religious patterns occurring in her day, sometimes portraying them in their initial stages a few decades before the time of writing, sometimes in their current form, but in all instances offering a scrupulously accurate representation of such scenes. Her interest in the attempts of the more intelligent labourer to better himself at night school, studying mathematics and allied subjects, forms a sub-theme of *Adam Bede*, as does the contribution of Evangelicalism to the sense of individual dignity among such labourers. But essential for the exploration of those topics was a faithful rendering of the day-to-day activities of contemporary rural life, as in the opening scene of the novel, portraying carpenters in the village workshop engaged in their various tasks as the day's work draws to its close, making fun of an absent-minded workman who has forgotten to complete his assignment, and in their rough dialect discussing local village affairs as the beams of the setting sun shine through 'the transparent shavings that flew before the steady plane, and lit up the fine grain of the oak panelling which stood propped against the wall'.[24] Courbet's *The Wheat Sifters* of 1855 (Fig. 23) in the same way strips the rural scene of the romantic mysticism with which Edward Calvert or Samuel Palmer might have elevated it, offering instead a canvas which, like the other paintings of country life defiantly exhibited in his Realist pavilion, puzzled contemporaries by its banality, by the awkward pose of the central figure, her feet splayed out and one shoe slipping off, while her companion somnolently picks out by hand the chaff which has slipped through the sieve. *Felix Holt* opens with the observation that five and thirty years ago the glory had not yet departed from the countryside of England with its roadside inns, jocose ostlers, and the tinkling bells of the pack-horses:

> In those days there were pocket boroughs, a Birmingham unrepresented in Parliament and compelled to make strong representations out of it, unrepealed corn-laws, three-and-sixpenny letters, a brawny and many-breeding pauperism, and other departed evils; but there were some pleasant things too, which have also departed . . .

And this account of the changes forms the spring-board for a novel which takes as one of its central themes the movement in favour of political suffrage, and the enormous difficulty, inherent within that programme, of persuading the common people to refuse the electoral bribes to which they had become so accustomed.

In this respect, too, she belonged within the current trends of painting. One facet of that nineteenth-century Realist school long recognized by art historians was its interest in regionalism, in aspects of local life which were beginning to disappear as the countryside became opened up to faster means of communication.

Not least among such consideration was a focus upon Christian
observance in the country villages, as yet largely untouched by the
ferment of theological dispute, together with a delight in the simple
faith of country people far removed from the centres of ecclesiastical authority but soon likely to be swept up in such controversies.
In painting, Thomas Webster's *A Village Choir* of 1847 (Fig. 24) captured the informality still prevailing in parish churches in the generation prior to that of the artist but beginning to disappear even
then as the strict demands of the non-conformist sects burgeoning
among the lower classes – the Unitarians, Methodists, and Baptists
– replaced those more relaxed eighteenth-century traditions. It was,
indeed, a broader European phenomenon, represented in Germany
by William Leibl's *Three Women in Church*, wearing the traditional
costumes of their locality, in France by Millet's *The Angelus* of 1859
depicting country labourers pausing to pray as the evening church
bell sounds across the field, and in England by Alphonse Legros'
painting of the same name, also from 1859.[25] The latter was praised
by Baudelaire for its Courbet-like characteristics, its realistic portrayal, free from the miraculous or sacred elements associated with
previous religious painting, of rustic worshippers within a country
church, '. . . the little community clothed in corduroy, cotton and
home-spun . . . simple people with their sabots and their umbrellas,
all bowed by work'. As Legros' fellow-painter, Jules Breton, remarked in terms similar to Eliot's: 'We associated ourselves with
the passions and feelings of the humble, and art was to do them the
honour formerly reserved exclusively for the gods and the mighty'.[26]
These works mark an attempt not to elevate or ennoble peasant
experience but to find validity in the local and the particular, and
the English painter James Lobley devoted much of his work to such
rural religious scenes, including *The Free Seat* of 1869, depicting with
sympathetic veracity the variegated occupants of the bench at the
back of the church, a bench reserved for those too poor to afford a
pew, here including a young man surreptitiously peering over his
prayer-book at the pretty girl beside him.

It is in the setting of that contemporary interest that one should
view George Eliot's own depiction of the unpretentious services in
the village church. Based upon memories of her childhood, they
again reveal a perception of changes recently inaugurated by the
ecclesiastical authorities, perhaps to the detriment of the traditional,
uncomplicated pieties of the village as she recalled them from those
earlier years:

Mine, I fear, is not a well-regulated mind: it has an occasional tenderness for old abuses; it lingers with a certain fondness over the days of nasal clerks and top-booted parsons, and has a sigh for the departed shades of vulgar errors. So it is not surprising that I recall with a fond sadness Shepperton Church as it was in the old days, with its outer coat of rough stucco, its red-tiled roof, its heterogeneous windows patched with desultory bits of painted glass . . .[27]

For the perceptive contemporary reader that passage was more than mere indulgence in nostalgia. Its veiled sarcasm marked a protest against the spate of church restoration and reconstruction which England was experiencing at that time, the extensive alterations often necessitated by crumbling structures but frequently exploited, under the stern supervision of the Camden Society and its organ *The Ecclesiologist*, as a means of removing the 'vulgar errors' of church ritual to which she refers here. The supposed improvements were in part prompted by a fervour for theological purism, often based upon symbolic readings of architectural elements in church structure derived from medieval sources no longer part of the consciousness of the English worshipper, such as the recommendation that the west window should have two lights to represent the dual nature of Christ. On doctrinal grounds, the familiar three-storeyed pulpit was to be replaced by an 'eagle' lectern, high pews were condemned and the new low pews made to face east, while the altar was to be raised on steps. But the changes also arose from a desire for architectural 'amelioration', often resulting in the dismantling of the genuinely medieval in favour of what were believed to be 'superior' Gothic forms – as George Gilbert Scott was to deplore in his *Plea for the Faithful Restoration of our Ancient Churches*. It was a failing of which Scott himself was not innocent. In 1849, Ruskin had attacked, in his *Seven Lamps of Architecture*, the irresponsibility of such contemporary architectural restorations, and Scott dutifully joined the growing chorus of protest. But it was, ironically, Scott's own proposal for the restoration of Tewkesbury Abbey that produced practical results. The plan so horrified William Morris that in 1877 the latter founded, together with Philip Webb, the Society for the Protection of Ancient Buildings, a movement eventually responsible for persuading Parliament to pass the Ancient Monuments Protection Act.[28] Neither of the impulses for restoration, theological nor architectural, held in any respect the local practices

which had over the years taken so firm a hold on the unsophistic-
ated worshippers in village churches, and whose forcible removal
served only to bewilder the country parishioner cherishing the
familiar and the traditional.

The anchoring of religion in its regional forms and the resistance
to ecclesiastically imposed change themselves formed part of a new
theological tendency closely related to the movement of Realism –
the inclination, with which Eliot herself sympathized, to see Jesus
not in terms of a divine figure miraculously sent to earth but as a
man of flesh and blood dedicated to spiritual concerns, as in David
Strauss's *Leben Jesu*, which had so powerful an impact on her own
faith and which she was soon, in 1846, to translate. Its portrayal of
Jesus in humble domestic surroundings, as a child growing into
manhood in the small village of Nazareth, infected by the religious
fervour prevailing at that time but conceiving of himself as teacher
rather than divine saviour, encouraged the naturalism motivating
Millais' *Christ in the House of His Parents* of 1849. The mystically
adumbrative elements of the Christian story, although present in
the painting – the water carried by John symbolizing the Baptism,
the blood on Jesus's hand and foot prefiguring the Crucifixion, the
ladder against the wall representing the Resurrection – are offered
there in disarmingly mundane terms, requiring no faith in the
miraculous, a setting of such unelevated, everyday realism that it
evoked Dickens' notorious attack upon it as being offensive to every
Christian believer.[29]

In this regard, as in other aspects of her realism, Eliot was both
inaugurating and reflecting the changing interests of her time. If the
present chapter has, in the context of this interdisciplinary study,
been concerned with George Eliot's relationship to the visual arts,
questioning the traditional attribution of her changed focus to
seventeenth-century Dutch painting, the suggestion that her true
affinity was with Courbet may prompt us to re-think an additional
relationship to which comparatively little attention has been paid in
criticism; that is her affinity to such continental novelists as Stendhal,
Balzac, and Flaubert. Her instinctive response to French realistic
fiction had, indeed, been strongly negative, thereby discouraging
further critical investigation of a possible relationship; for she found
its frank depiction of immorality offensive to her innate sense of
decorum. But that response, one should note, had been only her
initial reaction. After her instantaneous recoil from the indelicacies
of such writings, she did come to acknowledge that a forthright

treatment of social and moral affairs was justified. In a letter written in 1857, she records how, on first reading *Madame Bovary*: 'We flung the book to the four corners of the room . . .' But, as she herself recounts, she soon took the book up again, and, by the time she had finished reading it, had reached a different conclusion, that in a novel on the theme of adultery that aspect must be laid out boldly in all its ugliness and '. . . not tricked out in meretricious allurements'.[30] A distinguishing quality of the French realistic novel, moreover, as Erich Auerbach pointed out many years ago, was its responsiveness to the incessant change in social forms and manners, as well as to political fluidity – those very elements which were central to the realism of Courbet and of Eliot.[31] With her membership in that nineteenth-century mode re-established in the context of the visual arts, there would be room for a re-assessment of her literary connection with the French realistic novel too, especially in her steering of English fiction towards a depiction of 'uncultured provincials', of unheroic characters possessing only 'middling' qualities, and presented with the same uncompromising honesty as characterised Flaubert's writings. Here too, however, that connection should be seen not as an influence upon her writing but as a parallel manifestation, as writers and artists in neighbouring countries responded to a fundamental shift in the cultural perceptions of their time. And it offers for her own work an insight into the need she felt to counter her readers' horizons of expectation, to wean them away from the literary matrix established by her predecessors towards a set of values more suited to her day, a realism for which the Dutch painting of the past served not as model but as sanction, as a means of endorsing innovations motivated by current trends which were emerging simultaneously across the Channel, independently of that supposed artistic source.

5

Hopkins as Poetic Innovator

The crisis of language underlying literary Modernism has been rightly identified by Roland Barthes as having arisen in large part from the writer's growing belief that there should exist a disjunction between social dialogue and literary discourse. Poets felt impelled to dismantle the structures of conventional communication and to create a new verbal icon, a language more compressed and allusive than that of everyday speech.[1] Hopkins' *Wreck of the Deutschland*, composed in 1875, marked, as has long been recognized, the inauguration of Modernist poetry in England, of verse stubbornly refusing to conform to conventional modes of language. Within his poems, disused and forgotten words of Anglo-Saxon origin mingle with unexpectedly disparate images in sentence structures violating normative syntax, to produce a poetry remote from normal speech patterns, challenging, as well as richly rewarding in its cryptic, intellectual vigour:

> I am sóft síft
> In an hourglass – at the wall
> Fast, but mined with a motion, a drift,
> And it crowds and it combs to the fall;
> I steady as a water in a well, to a poise, to a pane,
> But roped with, always, all the way down from the tall
> Fells or flanks of the voel, a vein
> Of the gospel proffer, a pressure, a principle, Christ's gift.[2]

Across the Channel an aesthetic revolution in painting was occurring during that same period which has, correspondingly, been acknowledged as marking the inception of Modernism in that medium. Marking in the 1880s a break-away from Impressionism, it was initiated by a generation of artists who also sought a new 'language' for art, a language deserting the faithful representation of reality which had dominated so much of Western art.[3] No longer

130

attempting to capture on canvas the brilliant, evanescent play of sunlight upon buildings, objects, and landscapes, Cézanne, Seurat, Signac, Gauguin, and Van Gogh conceived of art as *metamorphosis*, a translation of the visible scene into hieratic patterning. They strove, indeed, to produce acknowledged artefacts rather than simulacra.[4] While Hopkins was deserting the Romantic tradition of poetry with its characterized *persona* speaking in the language '. . . really used by men', a language that closely resembled that of life and nature,[5] and was constructing instead a compressed, unnatural-istic style demanding from the reader the effort of decipherment, optical verisimilitude was being replaced in France by a contrived or coded form of art. In Cézanne's landscapes, traditional mimesis was being supplanted by a schematic restructuring of the scene which eschewed normative perspective and volumetric fidelity. Similarly, Gauguin's canvases introduced a consciously stylized 'cloisonism' distancing his scenes from reality, a technique which Van Gogh eagerly adopted. And in the paintings of Seurat, Signac, and Pissarro, objects were being scientifically dismantled into an amalgam of variegated dots. Yet the relationship between these two inaugurative Modernist modes has never been seriously investigated.

One reason for the disinclination of historians to relate these contemporary manifestations may well be the patent disparity be-tween the austere, ascetic scholar of Oxford undertaking the vows of celibate priesthood and the popular image of the French painters (not always based on fact) as bohemian in their style of life, fre-quenting the cafés, bars, and often the brothels of Paris in search of their subject-matter, and for the most part casual in their sexual liaisons.[6] It is, however, the concept of art itself which concerns us here, the aesthetic response to cultural change as expressed in the works produced, rather than the personal behaviour of the artists. The techniques they introduced into their respective media, which will form the major theme of this chapter, transcended religious, social, and national barriers to introduce a new concept of art itself.

In fact, Hopkins was far from inimical to the world of painting. He grew up in a family deeply involved in its practice, two of his brothers becoming full-time professional artists, while he himself, as he recorded in an early diary, had originally planned to pursue the same career. Even after his decision, under the influence of Newman and the Oxford movement, to join the Jesuit order, he retained a strong interest in the medium. But it is not there that the parallels we shall be pursuing are to be discerned. As so often

– witness Henry James's failure as an art-critic to appreciate contemporary trends in painting despite his own remarkable, and often
similar innovations in the art of the novel[7] – Hopkins' sensitivity to
change found expression only in his poetic creativity. One searches
in vain within the artistically undistinguished drawings by his hand
for hints of the stylistic originality he introduced into his verse. His
reproductions of fauna and flora in meticulous detail, in the manner advocated by his mentor Ruskin, merely followed the procedure
standard among Victorian amateurs. His taste in painters was no
less conservative, the school of artists he most admired being the
Pre-Raphaelites. In a letter written in 1863, he described Millais not
only as the greatest English painter but as 'one of the greatest of the
world', a view that he seems never to have altered.[8] But no-one could
accuse him of conservatism in his poetry.

Before exploring the suggested link, it may be worth noting the
extraordinary time-lag that occurred in both media before these
Modernist modes achieved public appreciation. Opposition to artistic
innovation is endemic in all generations, but it does not usually
appear in so virulent a form nor last for so lengthy a period. The
English Romantic poets were as revolutionary in their own time
as the Modernists in this later generation, but the animosity of re-
viewers had then been of comparatively brief duration, Wordsworth
and Coleridge enjoying public veneration from their middle years
onward, and such younger colleagues as Keats and Shelley being
deprived of their accolades only through early death. In contrast,
the Neo- and Post-Impressionist painters have the dubious distinction of becoming paradigms for the public neglect of genius,
and for the hostility to innovation predominating throughout their
lifetime. John Rewald's detailed account of the successive phases of
the movement, largely reliant upon the surviving correspondence
of the painters themselves, provides a moving record of their abject
poverty when not supported by other sources of income, and their
despair of attaining recognition. Cézanne had to wait some thirty
years for appreciation outside his small circle of fellow-artists, until
1904, shortly before his death, when a room was at last assigned to
his work in the *Salon d'Automne*. Van Gogh had the rare benefit of
an affectionate and supportive brother who was a professional art-
dealer, eager to publicize and sell his work. Yet, in the course of
his entire career, he succeeded in selling only one small painting
and a few drawings, the sale of that one painting occurring in the
same year as he was publicly labelled an ignoramus and an artistic

charlatan.[9] Even Roger Fry, soon to be the leading advocate of the Post-Impressionists in England, was, as late as 1906, responding negatively to Cézanne's work as touching '. . . none of the finer issues of the imaginative life'.[10] And if the Grafton Gallery Exhibition of 1910 which he organized in England, and the Armory Show of 1913 arranged in New York were to mark the beginning of their acceptance by the public, the hostility continued for some twenty years, before those artists became legitimized by public esteem.

The same held true of Hopkins. His poems, known only to a few select friends, remained unpublished for over forty years, until 1918, when Robert Bridges hesitantly issued them, apologizing in an introductory note for '. . . the rude shocks of his purely artistic wantonness'. Although they were coolly received at first – a review in the *Spectator* dismissed the poetry as 'needlessly obscure, harsh and perverse' – the poems began slowly to win respect. By the second edition of 1930, they had achieved wide regard, a Hopkins 'cult' emerging as admirers found in his work a new model of artistic compression and challenging intellectual allusiveness more to its taste and closer to the new modes introduced by Ezra Pound and T.S. Eliot than to the traditionalists represented by Bridges himself. For many in the 1930s, it came as a shock to realize that the poems in fact dated from so long before – that the work of a poet who had been dead for nearly half a century was achieving recognition not in terms of an antiquarian discovery but as Modernist poetry of immediate relevance for their own time. As Hopkins' nephew recorded, speaking for his own generation, it had been strange '. . . to find that a writer so often hailed as "modern" should in the prosaic annals of chronology, turn out to be so ancient.'[11] Were that time-lag the only basis for comparison, it would scarcely justify this present chapter. But the similarity in time-lapse does at least suggest a link, that, like the painters of the 1880s, Hopkins may have been responding to a complex cultural shift as yet only perceptible to the sensitive artist, and hence due to achieve broader recognition after a far longer delay than is customary in such historical processes.

One element Hopkins shared with contemporary painters was an extraordinary concern with technical experimentation. Methods of palette preparation had always been integral to the work of painters; but at this period, innovations in brush-work and experiments with new ways of placing pigment upon the canvas began to fascinate artists to a degree exceeding that of previous generations.

In an article in 1887 which was to serve as a manifesto defending the Neo-Impressionist art of Seurat and Signac, it was upon that aspect of their innovative practice that Félix Fénéon focused:

> ... instead of triturating the pigment on the palette in order to come as close as possible to the tint of the surface to be represented, the painter places directly on the canvas brushstrokes setting out the local color – that is to say, the color that the surface in question would take on in white light (obviously the color of the object seen from close up). This color, which he has not achromatized on the palette he achromatizes on the canvas, by virtue of the laws of simultaneous contrast...[12]

A year later, in 1888, Van Gogh wrote to Emile Bernard:

> I hit the canvas with irregular touches of the brush, which I leave as they are. Patches of thickly laid-on color, spots of canvas left uncovered here and there, portions that are left absolutely unfinished ...

Similarly, Gauguin, inspired by the tradition of medieval enamels (*cloisonné*) and stained-glass, where shaped pieces composed of a single, unvaried colour were held in place by metal surrounds, introduced into his own paintings boldly-outlined areas of unmodulated colour, deserting the delicate shading traditionally employed from the time of the Renaissance to create an illusion of solidity and depth. It was a process reinforced for him by the discovery that Japanese painting employed a comparable technique, with simple areas of colour demarcated by dark contours. In *Ta Matete – The Market* of 1892, he created, as he did throughout his Tahitian paintings, an Eden mythic in quality, removed from actuality, with figures in the stylized pose of Egyptian frescoes, blue tree-trunks never existent in nature, or splashes of red and green vaguely indicative of shrub or lawn in the dream-world of his art. The bright colours which characterized his canvases contributed to their distancing from the mimetic, suggesting the cryptic quality of the scene, its enchanting indeterminacy: 'One does not use colour to draw but always to give the musical sensations which flow from itself, from its own nature, from its mysterious and enigmatic interior force.' Strindberg was among the first to perceive this non-naturalistic quality in Gauguin's paintings, initially with some antagonism but, as he admitted in the course of a letter to the artist, with a growing recognition of its persuasive originality:

> ... I saw on the walls of your studio that confusion of sun-flooded paintings which pursued me this night in my sleep. I saw trees that no botanist would ever discover, animals that Cuvier never suspected the existence of, and men that you alone have been able to create. A sea that might flow from a volcano, a sky in which no god could live. Monsieur (said I in my dream), you have created a new earth and a new heaven...[13]

His adaptation of cloisonism and of the stylization of Egyptian and Japanese art provided an essentially new artistic approach which his friend Van Gogh admiringly imported into his own canvases, to be adopted before long as a primary ingredient of Post-Impressionist painting. The latter's *Bedroom at Arles*, a canvas distinguished for subsequent generations by the endowing of an otherwise ordinary room with a vivid, intensely subjective vision, evoked from the artist himself, while engaged in painting it, a comment on the sense of restfulness he hoped to achieve by the use of colour; but the main innovation for him, as he informed his brother, was his experimentation there with a new form of applying pigment, that the canvas was '... painted in free flat tints like the Japanese prints ... No stippling, no hatching, nothing, only flat colours in harmony.'[14] The pointillism of Seurat and Signac similarly rejected the traditional concept of art as providing a window on to reality, rejecting conventional depth-perspective and illusionism.

If these artists wrote very rarely of the changed concept of art that animated their work, almost invariably discussing instead details concerning their palette or brush-technique, Hopkins too seemed virtually indifferent to those aspects of his poetry which we today see as marking his major break with tradition and as inaugurating a new era, focusing instead, with a certain obsessiveness, upon the technical aspects of his verse. Those serious difficulties in comprehension which his verse posed for the contemporary reader he ignored. Robert Bridges, although eventually to become the leading advocate of Hopkins' verse, on receiving a first copy of *The Wreck of the Deutschland* very hesitantly submitted to him by Hopkins in 1877, was, like most readers on their first encounter, bewildered by its cramped allusiveness. He read it through once, dismissed it out of hand as 'presumptious [sic] jugglery', and refused to re-read it on the grounds of its obscurity.[15] Of especial interest is Hopkins' reply, entreating him to try reading it again. In that entreaty, he offered no hint of assistance in elucidating the many obscure passages, nor provided aid in deciphering the often tortuous and esoteric allusions, of which stanza eight may be regarded as representative:

> ... Oh,
> We lash with the best or worst
> Word last! How a lush-kept plush-capped sloe
> Will, mouthed to flesh-burst,
> Gush! – flush the man, the being with it, sour or sweet,
> Brim, in a flash, full! – Hither then, last or first,
> To hero of Calvary, Christ's feet –
> Never ask if meaning it, wanting it, warned of it – men go.

He might have explained to Bridges the general gist of the passage, how only under the lash of disaster, the imminent threat of death, do men turn with their dying word to the Saviour, sourly or sweetly as with fruit crushed upon the palate, when their final gush of penitence delivers them to the foot of the Cross. Instead, Hopkins' reply was restricted to a highly detailed defence of the metrical principles on which the poem had been composed:

> There are no outriding feet in the *Deutschland*. An outriding foot is, by a sort of contradiction, a recognized extra-metrical effect; it is and it is not part of the metre; not part of it, not being counted, but part of it by producing a calculated effect which tells in the general success. But the long, e.g. seven-syllabled, feet of the *Deutschland*, are strictly metrical. Outriding feet belong to counterpointed verse ...

and so on, for some four pages. A similar letter, sent to R.W. Dixon to accompany the poem, records briefly the circumstances which inspired it, and then moves at once to a complicated analysis of the new rhythm it employs, which '... consists in scanning by accents or stresses alone, without any account of the number of syllables, so that a foot may be one strong syllable or it may be many light and one strong ...' The 'Preface' he prepared for a proposed, but aborted, publication of his poems was again devoted exclusively to a discourse on the subtle distinctions between rising feet, slack feet, falling feet, and the variegated stress patterns resulting from their relationships:

If however the reversal is repeated in two feet running, especially so as to include the sensitive second foot, it must be due either to great want of ear or else is a calculated effect, the superinducing or mounting of a new rhythm upon the old; and since the new or mounted rhythm is actually heard and at the same time the mind naturally supplies the natural or standard foregoing rhythm, for we do not forget what the rhythm is that by rights we should be hearing, two rhythms are in some manner running at once . . .

The difficulty of comprehension for the reader, an obstacle about which Hopkins himself seemed so unconcerned, arose primarily from his apparently cavalier treatment of sentence structure, the words, images, and compound modifiers being offered either in a manner grammatically unrelated to each other or in a sequence inverting or distorting normal syntactical order:

> The jading and jar of the cart,
> Time's tásking, it is fathers that asking for ease
> Of the sodden-with-its-sorrowing heart,
> Not danger, electrical horror . . .[16]

The omission of the relative pronoun in the phrase 'it is, which fathers . . .' leaves the reader momentarily confused, assuming *fathers* to be a noun. The verbal units are, in fact, arranged with a freedom one would expect only in an inflected language, where word-endings assist in distinguishing subject from object, noun from adjective and, by such identifiable forms, highlight their structural relationship. Clement Barraud, S.J., who studied with Hopkins at St. Beuno's, shrewdly commented:

> The wildest of all his wild freaks is that, with a notably pure Saxon vocabulary, he chooses to cast his sentences and phrases into Latin order, the fanciful order of Latin verse.[17]

The result in his poetry is frequently a disturbing reversal of expected sequence. He describes Andromeda, who

> . . . on this rock rude,
> With not her either beauty's equal or
> Her injury's, looks off by both horns of shore . . .

Another poem opens with the lines:

> When will you ever, Peace, wild wooddove, shy wings shut,
> Your round me roaming end, and under be my boughs?

That last phrase, 'under be my boughs', is not poetic licence in any conventional sense, the prerogative often adopted by poets to make slight inversions unallowable in prose. It marks instead a disregard for normal sentence-order as impeding the creation of valid sound patterns, the latter to be achieved even at the expense of lucidity. He admitted that at times his verse 'errs on the side of oddness', explaining elsewhere that, while epic, drama, and ballad must, by their nature, be immediately comprehensible to the reader, in more subtle and recondite poetry such as his own, '... something must be sacrificed, with so trying a task, in the process, and this may be the being at once, nay perhaps even the being without explanation at all, intelligible'. He went so far as to claim on one occasion that poetry employs 'an order of sounds *independent of meaning*', thereby assigning to the sense of the passage a markedly subordinate position.[18] Thus, in the lines to *Peace* quoted above, in order to achieve the phonic pattern so important to him, he delays the word *be* to create an alliterative echo with *boughs*, an echo which a normal placing would weaken or lose. It was a principle which was to characterize his verse, as in the lines addressed *To his Watch*:

>   ... shall I
>   Earlier or you fail at our force and lie
>   The ruins of, rifled, once a world of art?

where *fail* is transposed from its normal position after *I* in order to resonate with *force*. This alliterative concern, although intrinsic to all forms of verse, does not accord with accepted practice; for such cumulative sound effect is normally made to emerge naturally from the sense reading, as in Milton's climactic

>   ... and with new-spangled ore
>   Flames in the forehead of the morning sky.

In Hopkins' poetry, in contrast, assonance, internal rhyme, alliteration, and stress distort and over-ride the traditional forms of speech sequence.

His practice, in fact, rested upon deeper foundations than mere wilfulness; for if, as he believed, words had originated onomatopoeically, then alliteration and assonance should by right be privileged above everyday speech-patterns which had, by his day, lost the pristine force of those sounds; and the rhythms should, where necessary, subjugate socially-accepted forms in order to restore the vitality of the earlier patterns. 'Why do I employ sprung rhythm at all?' he asked Bridges rhetorically. 'Because it is the nearest to the rhythm of prose, that is the native and natural rhythm of speech.'[19] By the 'natural rhythm of speech' he meant not the syntactical order of contemporary prose but the primary forms of natural discourse at a time when sound had still echoed meaning, a form of discourse preserved in the writings of earlier poets but ignored or forgotten in subsequent years. His reintroduction of sprung rhythm he saw, therefore, as bringing verse genuinely closer to those unformulated pristine impulses of thought which – as stream-of-consciousness writings were soon to demonstrate – tend to thrust the emotionally charged word to the forefront, allowing the remainder of the sentence to form somewhat lamely around it, regardless of normal order. Hence the extraordinarily elliptical form of Hopkins' verse, the suppression of subordinate words, the omission of conjunctions and prepositions as details which merely distract, a technique stylistically exemplified in his brilliant portrait of Harry Ploughman:

> Hard as hurdle arms, with a broth of goldish flue
> Breathed round; the rack of ribs; the scooped flank; lank
> Rope-over thigh; knee-nave; and barrelled shank –
>   Head and foot, shoulder and shank –
> By a grey eye's heed steered well, one crew, fall to;
> Stand at stress . . .

He admitted that the main difficulties posed by the poem derived from its convoluted syntax, but added: 'I want Harry Ploughman to be a vivid figure before the mind's eye; if he is not that the sonnet fails.'[20]

The affinity of this aspect of his verse to the new school of French painting is, I would suggest, fundamental; but, as it will require a brief explanatory detour in order to make the connection apparent, we may merely note at this point that the crucial element in the poetic technique he introduced was his focusing upon the dynamic interaction of adjacent phrases, of contiguous words or images in a manner quite different from his predecessors, often allowing the contrasting proximity to function in place of a syntactically ordered sentence. The reciprocal interplay resulting from such proximity, he maintained, functions even at the level of adjacent syllables, which are always pitched 'one against another', a strong stress affecting the accent which follows. No two weak accents in a word are exactly equal, he pointed out, those next to the strong accent becoming by their positioning the weakest.[21] That concern for the careful patterning of his verse Hopkins himself perceived to be close to the design of painting (without indicating a specific style), as well as to that of music, commenting of his own aims that, just as what is '. . . melody strikes me most of all in music, and design in painting, so design, pattern, or what I am in the habit of calling "inscape" is what I above all aim at in poetry.'[22] How closely his concern with the juxtaposition of words paralleled one of the primary innovations of the post-1880 French painters may be perceived, even before we examine it more closely, in Gauguin's contrast between the principles adopted by his generation and those assumed by earlier painters. In their use of colour, he wrote, the Impressionists '. . . retain the shackles of verisimilitude', whereas he and his contemporaries were concerned with a new factor, the dynamic interaction of adjacent colours: 'A green next to a red does not produce a reddish brown, like the mixture [of pigments], but two vibrating tones. If you put chrome yellow next to this red, you have three tones complementing each other and augmenting the intensity of the first tone, the green. Replace the yellow by a blue, you will find three different tones, though still vibrating through one another.'[23]

Although I shall be arguing that there was a more profound reason behind this interest in the interaction of colours, it should be noted that this innovative practice in painting has been traditionally attributed by historians to certain scientific discoveries in the area of optics; and there can be no doubt that Seurat particularly was profoundly interested in those discoveries. Michel-Eugène Chevreul, a chemist by profession specializing in the use of dyes at the Gobelin tapestry factory, had revealed the surprising fact that areas of colour physically affect by their proximity the tone of those adjacent to them, each tinting its surrounding space with what was termed its 'complementary', the lighter colour appearing lighter, and the darker of the two darker, so that '. . . under simultaneous contrast of colors are included all the modifications which differently coloured objects appear to undergo in their physical composition, and in the height of tone of their respective colours, when seen simultaneously.'[24] On the basis of that principle, further developed by such researchers as Bunsen, Kirchoff, and Rood, these painters, it is argued, deserted the long-established practice of mixing colours upon the palette before applying them, restricting their palette instead to the primary colours and intermediary hues, the mingling to be obtained not in that preparatory stage before putting paint to canvas, but by the juxtaposing of the colours upon the canvas itself.[25] It was, indeed, on the basis of such experimentation that Seurat prepared a disc consisting of radiating hues, intermediate to the colours of the spectrum and in progressively fading tones, in order to establish the precise 'complementary' of each colour variant. And before long, he and Signac, later joined by Pissarro, evolved the innovative technique of 'pointillism' (or 'divisionism', as they preferred to call it), the application of tiny brush-strokes or dots, unprecedented in the history of painting, as in Signac's *Quay at Clichy* of 1887 (Fig. 25). Their purpose was to produce in minuscule form a breakdown of colour into its primary categories and complementaries, and thereby to ensure maximal interplay of cross-tonal effect.

What tends to be overlooked – and is especially relevant to our present concerns – is the time factor; that when Seurat, at the height of his enthusiasm over the new process in 1884, arranged to visit Chevreul himself in the hope of discussing these principles with him in further detail, he discovered that the latter was by then an elderly gentleman of ninety-eight, hard of hearing and of failing memory, whose theories had been published some forty-five years earlier, in 1839.[26] As so often in synchronic study, our attention should be directed not only to the possibility of sequential cause and effect but also – and perhaps more importantly – to the contemporary changes in sensibility which motivate artists and writers to seek support in the past for innovative practices on which they have already embarked. What, we shall need to enquire, was the contemporary impulse which made artists of this later generation amenable to the implications of the theory, and which had had so little effect upon the Impressionists themselves, even though they seem to have been aware of it?

There is no need to elaborate here on the impact of evolutionary theories upon nineteenth-century ideas, theories which had been disturbing and stimulating thinkers well before the appearance of Darwin's work in 1859 through such provocative studies as Lyell's

Principles of Geology, published in 1831. Jerome Buckley has traced, for example, the far-reaching effect of those theories upon the concept of time in the Victorian era, the growing perception of history not as a series of separate, recorded events but as a continually evolving process. Most frequently such historical change was apprehended in terms of progress, a development from the primitive to the highly sophisticated, whether socially, philosophically, or technologically, while at other times it became viewed less comfortingly in terms of an irreversible decadence. The new view affected even arcane areas of scholarship, resulting, as O.B. Hardison revealed comparatively recently, in the incorrect assumption of E.K. Chambers and others that the simpler playlets of the surviving mystery cycles must, on the progressive, evolutionary principle, have preceded the more sophisticated versions. In contrast, for those espousing at that time the idea of evolution in terms of decadence, the formulation of the second law of thermodynamics in 1852, positing a gradual reduction in the energy of the universe, was seized upon as evidence that the cosmos was moving towards an eventual state of entropy when the earth would no longer be habitable by man.[27]

But one further aspect needs to be recognized, an aspect so familiar to our generation that it is difficult to comprehend how fundamental was the revolution in thinking it involved at that time – the contradiction it posed to the long-established notion of the Great Chain of Being structuring the universe. That concept of an established hierarchy, reaching from the Supreme Creator down to the lowest forms of life, was a paradigm that had dominated western thought for centuries, ending its reign only in the nineteenth century, as evolutionism began to assert itself. It had included as axiomatic the assumption that, in a universe designed by an omniscient and hence prescient Deity, everything requisite for the earth's future had been created during the first six days in its final and perfected form. With the possible exception of barren crags, deserts, and oceans, considered by certain theologians, such as Thomas Burnet, to have emerged at the time of the Deluge as a punishment for human sin and corruption, each form of life and each element in nature was held to be fixed for perpetuity.[28] 'The earth is the Lord's and the fulness thereof', the Psalmist had declared; and that scriptural description of terrestrial 'fulness' was seen as confirmation of the theory of 'plenitude', of a universe already containing everything necessary to it until the end of days, with all possibilities of generative action having already been fulfilled.[29]

The most startling element implicit in the new evolutionary theories for those confronting them at the time was the challenge they posed to this tradition, the suggestion that geological formations, animal species, and, in fact, all forms of nature, so far from being biologically, botanically, or geologically static in form, exist in a process of dynamic interaction with their surroundings, responding to environmental change in each generation, adapting themselves or being altered in accordance with the influence exerted upon them by their location. Lyell's geological theory, with detailed evidence to support its claim, argued that a series of separate, often individual 'creations' had occurred at different periods of history and in various areas, each resulting not from a divine *Fiat*, but from responses to local atmospheric or physical changes, the mountains having at diverse times been '. . . produced by subterranean fire in former ages at great depths in the bowels of the earth . . . upraised by gradual movements, and exposed to the light of heaven . . . indefinite ages before the creation of our race.' This conflict between the established view of a one-time plenitudinous creation and Darwin's idea of continuous responsiveness to surroundings was seen by Darwin himself as the most innovative aspect of his theory, the origin of species being attributable not to a prescient Creator but to 'secondary causes' to be sought in the environment: 'Authors of the highest eminence seem to be fully satisfied with the view that each species has been independently created. To my mind it accords better with what we know of the laws impressed on matter by the Creator, that the production and extinction of the past and present inhabitants of the world should have been due to secondary causes', largely, that is, to '. . . indirect and direct action of the external conditions of life' which had dictated at various stages in their development a necessary reaction on their part.[30]

The nineteenth-century thinker might accept or reject the implications of evolutionary theory, welcoming it as marking the end of age-long superstition or seeing it as a dreadful subversion of religious faith – witness Ruskin's pathetic cry, quoted in an earlier chapter: 'If only the Geologists would let me alone, I could do very well, but those dreadful Hammers. I hear the clink of them at the end of every cadence of the Bible verses.'[31] He could attempt to ignore the hammers and the theories associated with them, he could perhaps adjust his conception of the Bible to absorb the suggested changes, or he could embrace the implications unreservedly. But whatever his response, one element inevitably entering the consciousness of the period and moulding its cultural perceptions was this new idea of symbiosis and mutual interaction operating in all aspects of nature, with both animate and inanimate forms participating in this process of continuously influencing and being influenced by neighbouring objects.

It was that new conception which, I would suggest, lay behind the innovative approach to colour so central to the theory and practice of these painters. In the same way as Kepler's startling discovery of the elliptical orbits of the planets in 1611 so permeated contemporary ideas of the universe that Bernini instinctively produced his sun images in St. Peter's and in S. Andrea al Quirinale as ovals,[32] so artists began to regard colours in an essentially new way, not as fixed attributes of specific objects – blue for water, white for snow, brown for wood – with the painter mixing his pigments to the requisite hue on the palette before application to the canvas, but in more dynamic terms, as chameleon-like elements actively and individually responsive to the conditions of their environment, each exerting an effect upon a neighbouring area of colour and being in its turn subject to change through that proximity. For Cézanne, little-known outside the circle of the Post-Impressionists but acknowledged within it as the leading experimenter and innovator, this process of discerning the interaction between both colour-elements and shapes in a landscape, still-life, or portrait became a major factor. If the Impressionists had also begun to perceive the interrelationship of colour, noting how shadows, snow, and water absorb certain hues from objects around them (as Monet and Renoir demonstrated in the paintings that resulted from their joint outings to *La Grenouillère* in 1869),[33] Cézanne was concerned essentially with the *patterning* of his scenes, investigating the way adjacent objects as well as colours affect each other, and being prepared in pursuit of that aim to sacrifice unhesitatingly illusionist depth-perspective and mimetic fidelity in order to obtain the results he desired. In his *Sainte-Victoire Viewed from Bibémus Quarry* of 1898, the juxtaposing of the patches of colour and their reciprocity serve, in fact, as substitutes for traditional perspective. In painting the trees in the foreground and the yellow cliffs behind, he eschewed the subtle shadowing previously employed to give the effect of volumetric space; and, even more significantly, he provided no natural diminution in colour-intensity as the eye moves into the distance, the trees beyond the cliffs being painted in the same bright green as those in the foreground. Instead, spatial relations are defined by adjacency, the paleness of the mountain contiguous to those further trees 'influencing' them optically, reducing their vividness, and thereby producing a compensatory effect of distance. This reliance upon colour juxtaposition he undertook even though he knew (paralleling Hopkins) that he was thereby risking the charge of incomprehensibility, and Richard Shiff has confirmed in a recent study the artist's conscious decision to sacrifice depth-intelligibility to such patterning.[34] Cézanne was extraordinarily reluctant to discuss his artistic creed, but among the few comments he did offer, as usual extracted from him with some difficulty by his friend Emile Bernard, was the statement that in his work '... there is no line, there is no modelling, there are only contrasts. These contrasts are not given by black and white, but by the sensation of colour.'[35]

The new principle affected all genres of painting, not only landscapes. Cézanne's still-life canvases appeared merely perverse to most contemporary viewers, the objects malformed, the table slanting away from the horizontal; but, as we know from his own writings, he would spend an inordinate amount of time attempting to overcome his natural tendency to reproduce objects conventionally or mimetically, insisting instead upon recording the distortions which the proximity of other items imposed optically, at times exaggerating the abnormalities in order to draw attention to them. The curves of a bottle, he noticed, become diminished when it is placed beside a circular dish, as in his *Still-Life with Peppermint Bottle* (Fig. 26); it will seem to swell when close to a cube-shaped object; and areas of light colour appear larger than areas of dark. Certain of these distortions had been known to painters in earlier generations, but their purpose then had been to compensate for them as optical aberrations detracting from the mimetic effect, while Cézanne's aim was the opposite, to emphasize the dynamic interplay created by proximity. The resulting canvas may be ineffective in terms of verisimilitude, but it captures in a remarkable way the interaction of cylindrical and spherical forms responding to the conditions of their locality and to interlocking spatial planes. The apple in the centre, for example, lacks the rotundity of form normally achieved by subtle shading or reflected light but its rotundity is conveyed equally effectively by the sense that it is about to roll down the sloping plane on which it is precariously placed. The location itself thus substitutes for optical illusionism, thereby creating an essentially new perception on the part of the viewer, the recognition that each object would be fundamentally different were it placed in a different setting.

Seurat went further than Cézanne in this respect, consciously searching in this phase of his art for a basically new system of painting, an 'optical formula' scientifically dependent upon the reciprocal effects of adjacency. From Chevreul he learned that a colour reaches its maximum intensity when placed next to its complementary colour. When juxtaposed upon the canvas, they enhance each other, whereas when mixed on the palate, they destroy each other. Ogden N. Rood's important study of 1879, *Modern Chromatics*, which Seurat read in a French translation, had taken up Chevreul's ideas and added an important factor, the recognition that the human eye retains an after-image of any shape or colour it receives, which mingles with the next colour the retina absorbs. The result is a new conception of colours as not merely contrasting or complementing each other as they lie side-by-side on the canvas but as blending, reacting, or interacting as a dynamic sequential process within the viewer's eye. Where the Impressionists had striven, often with wonderful effect, to capture the transmutation of objects in altered sunlight, Seurat and Signac insisted upon a methodical 'separation of elements', a physical separation of the object's own or local colour from the sunlight shining upon it. Thus, in his first major experiment in this mode, *Une Baignade* of 1883–4, Seurat painted the grass in its natural colour as a green underbody, and applied over that basis orange brush-strokes representing the sun's illumination, allowing the two elements to interact, coalescing to form a vibrant yellow-green, tinged with orange. Had they been pre-mixed on the palette, they would, as William Homer has pointed out, have resulted in a duller, desaturated olive-green.[36] The most significant advance, however, was in his major work, *Un Dimanche à la Grande Jatte* of 1884–6, where he deserted brush strokes in favour of myriads of dots which could, in their minuscule form, resonate and interact more effectively on the eye. Signac described how, in the act of painting one of the early *croquetons* preparatory to this work, Seurat,

> ... before placing a touch of paint on his little panel, looks, compares, and squints to see the play of light and shadow, perceives contrasts, distinguishes reflections, plays for a long time with the box-lid which serves as his palette, struggling with matter as he struggles with nature: then, he picks from the little piles of

prismatically arranged pigments the diverse colored elements which constitute the hue destined best to express the mystery which he has discovered.[37]

In the final work, the same principle of separation was applied, the shadows, for example, consisting of blue dots applied over the 'local' colour, with dots of solar-orange added, though more sparingly, to indicate how even the shadows respond to the sunny areas around. It was the same technique as Signac was to adopt in such paintings as his *Quay at Clichy* of 1887, and Pissarro in his *Springtime in Eragny* of 1886. As Fénéon described the process:

> A pigmentary hue is weak and drab compared to a hue born of optical mixture; the latter, mysteriously vivified by a perpetual process of recombination, shimmers, elastic, opulent, and lustrous. . . . All the constituent colored elements will combine without muddying. Their polychrome mass of small dots is ordered according to the play of light and dark: justifying the perspective, making the air quiver over the scenes.[38]

Van Gogh was deeply impressed by his meeting with Seurat and Signac, and although he did not adopt pointillism as such, he recognized the importance of its innovative theory and incorporated into his own work its fascination with the interplay of adjacent colours and forms.[39] A painting such as his famed *Self-Portrait* of 1887 (Fig. 27) can leave no doubt on that score. The face is compounded not of dots but of lines or brush-strokes of variegated colours – yellow, brown, green, and orange, laid side-by-side in a manner remote from reality, which combine and interact by their adjacency to produce the effect of vigorous intensity and emotional force. Again in defiance of literalism, the same technique is extended to the background, where the red brush-strokes on the blue setting are arranged in a circular form around the head to echo and hence to emphasize the sense of vitality conveyed in the portrait itself.

Before examining the use of such mutual interplay and reciprocity in further detail, we may already perceive how closely Hopkins' concern with the design of his poetry reflected this contemporary interest; for its innovative quality arose from his fascination with the patterns emanating from the dynamic relationship of adjacent words, each influencing and being influenced by proximate members through alliteration, stress, connotation and association, in a

manner going far beyond the practice of his predecessors. Hopkins'
intense concern with diatonic and chromatic elements in poetry and
with verbal pitch and stress not only parallels the experimentation
with technique characterizing the empirical sciences but, like the
work of Signac and others, consciously draws its inspiration from
such scientific experimentation, employed by him to illustrate his
poetic principles and the nature of syllabic stress as he had come to
conceive it:

> Now every visible palpable body has a centre of gravity round
> which it is in balance and a centre of illumination or highspot or
> quickspot up to which it is lighted and down from which it is
> shaded. The centre of gravity is like the accent of stress, the
> highspot like the accent of pitch, for pitch is like light and colour,
> stress like weight, and as in some things as air and water the
> centre of gravity is either unnoticeable or changeable so there
> may be languages in a fluid state in which there is little difference
> of weight or stress between syllables . . .[40]

Hopkins' preference for 'primary' Anglo-Saxon words in his
poetry derived, as has long been known, from his ardent interest
in etymology, whose findings he repeatedly incorporated into his
own poetic practice. But that new discipline, one should note, was
itself a direct offshoot of evolutionary theory, language now being
viewed for the first time not as a fixed entity indigenous to local
areas, implanted there according to biblical tradition at the time of
the Tower of Babel, but as an organic element undergoing a continuing process of developmental change in response to altered contemporary conditions, its syntactical and lexical forms responding
to such pressures as regional requirements, convenience in communication, or ease in pronunciation. Whether or not such interest in
incremental philology would have manifested itself even without
the appearance of Darwin's work, Max Müller's *Lectures on the Science
of Language*, published in 1864 and well-known to Hopkins, had
highlighted this Darwinian aspect as a main justification for the
new science, claiming that, in its emphasis upon developmental
process, etymology had more in common with geology and biology
than with the humanities to which language study had previously
been affiliated.[41] Hopkins himself frequently notes such organic linguistic changes, often in connection with his theory of sprung rhythm
and his belief in the onomatopoeic origin of primary words. His

diaries and journals abound with such references, a note on the verb to *hawk*, in the sense of selling commodities, typifying his curiosity as to the original source and subsequent development of such terms:

I had imagined this to be derived from the bawling or screeching the hawkers made in proclaiming their wares, to *hawk* meaning to make a noise in the throat, as before spitting. But Kingsley uses the word to *hawk* of birds in sense of to move up and down in a place, to haunt . . .[42]

It was this conception of words as responding to changing associations and surroundings, therefore, that made him so sensitive to their placement within his own verse, leading to his determination that verbal interaction and juxtaposition should take precedence there over conventional word-order and even over ease of comprehension.

A further bond between Hopkins and this school of painters, integral to these new theories, was the nature of the ingredients for art. Axiomatic for the French painters (and in this they were in part indebted to the Impressionists) was their preference for 'pure' or 'primary' colours derived from the spectrum. Seurat eliminated earth-colours and black from his palette and, like Signac, used only colours derived from the solar spectrum, with white alone permitted as an additive. As Fénéon records:

Only prismatic colors play a role in the make-up of the paintings of Signac and Seurat. That is to say, given that the colors from the tube are spread out on the palette in the order of the prism, one would never combine any other than consecutive colors . . .[43]

The vividness of the resultant paintings derives to no small extent from this decision and, with due allowance for differences in media, a remarkably similar process may be perceived in Hopkins' poetry. Central to his poetic creed was a return to a purer, pristine Anglo-Saxon vocabulary. As he explained to Bridges, foreshadowing in many ways the priority which Wittgenstein and subsequent linguists would accord to speech discourse, language he believed to have evolved from words originally echoing sound associations, and he constructed his own poetry out of such elemental relationships: '*Grind, gride, gird, grid, groat, grate* . . . I believe these words to be onomatopoetic, *Gr* common to them all representing a particular sound.'[44] His sense of *inscape*, derived from the medieval philosopher Duns Scotus – the belief that every entity in the world, animate and inanimate, was characterized by a distinctive design or identity – led him to seek a similar specificity in the word employed to convey that inner essence, often unfamiliar to the reader, in order to create a greater immediacy of impact.

His etymological interest in tracing the origins of words became a vital part of his poetry and, on the rare occasions when he did explain a strange word or phrase, it was in order to demonstrate the rudimentary quality of its usage. On his introduction of the term *sake* in his sonnet to *Henry Purcell*:

> . . . only I'll
> Have an eye to the sakes of him, quaint moonmarks . . .

and in the lines from *The Wreck of the Deutschland*:

> . . . the finding and sake
> And cipher of suffering Christ.

he noted that its early Anglo-Saxon use had indeed disappeared from current English, surviving only in a kindred form in German, but that it was essentially the same usage as *for the sake of, forsake, namesake,* and *keepsake* – 'I mean by it the being a thing has outside itself, as a voice by its echo, a face by its reflection, a body by its shadow, a man by his name, fame, or memory.' It was the pristine or primary usage that he constantly sought, however queer the word might appear to his reader. For that reason, he objected to the poetic diction employed by his contemporaries – such as, *o'er* or *wellnigh* in the poetry of Tennyson and others – as being an artificialization of language, an attempt to achieve an elevation of tone by resorting to words that had never formed part of normal speech. The words that he himself re-introduced, as a means of revitalizing the language of poetry – a vocabulary that became characteristic of his verse – were such forgotten but well-used Anglo-Saxon words as *fettle, pash, mammocks, rivel, shive,* and *burl,* which reproduce by their sound the sense they convey ('to burl', for example, meaning, to *spin* or *whirl*).[45] In the way that nineteenth-century painters disdained the venerable gloom so often applied to new paintings in order to associate them with the Old Masters, so Hopkins abhorred the archaisms of

17. (*above*) Edwin Landseer, *The Old Shepherd's Chief Mourner*

18. (*right*) Edwin Landseer, *Dignity and Impudence*

19. (*above*) Shadwell Park, Norfolk, after its enlargement in 1860

20. (*left*) William Leiper, Templeton Carpet Factory, Glasgow

21. M. Odiot, inkstand from the 1851 Exhibition

22. Gustave Courbet, *The Stone-breakers*, formerly Dresden Museum (destroyed)

23. Gustave Courbet, *The Grain Sifters*

24. Thomas Webster, *A Village Choir*

25. Paul Signac, *Quay at Clichy*

26.   Paul Cézanne, *Still Life with Peppermint Bottle*

27. (*left*) Vincent Van Gogh, *Self-Portrait with Grey Felt Hat*

28. (*below*) Vincent Van Gogh, *The Starry Night,* pen drawing

29. (*right*) Louis C. Tiffany, Lamp

30. (*left*) Aubrey Beardsley, book cover for *Morte d'Arthur*

31. Carl Fabergé, opal carving of parrot in a gold cage

32. Carl Fabergé, *Coronation Egg*, containing a replica of the coronation coach

poetry employed to echo Shakespeare, arguing that they merely reproduce a '. . . diction which in him was modern and in them is obsolete.'

His return to pristine forms of speech is not only evocative of the French painters' use of primary colours and, if my suggestion is correct, derived from essentially the same desire to juxtapose elemental communicators, but reveals filaments connecting it with the allied principle of *plein air*, one of those principles which the painters had inherited from the Impressionists and continued to develop. In their work, that egress into the open air represented a desire to move away from formal groupings, classical conventions, and the artificiality of the studio, where the preparatory sketches of outside scenes had, even for so naturalistic a painter as Constable, served only as *aides-mémoires*, requiring transformation into finished canvases before they could be submitted.[46] Hopkins, similarly, saw the reintroduction of 'primary' words as a means of achieving emotional immediacy, or what he termed *haecitas*, in language unvarnished by its repetitive use in poetry and stripped of the associations that had accrued in literary settings:

> Left hand, off land, I hear the lark ascend,
> His rash-fresh re-winded new-skein'd score
> In crisps of curl off wild winch whirl, and pour
> And pelt music, till none's to spill nor spend.[47]

Although a distinguished Balliol classicist, later appointed Professor of Classics at University College, Dublin, and continuing to produce scholarly studies of Greek literature until his final years, he nonetheless eschewed all such learned references in poetry as numbing and deadening, in much the same way as painting was now eschewing scenes drawn from mythology. He returned Bridges' poetic drama *Ulysses* with the mordant comment: 'Believe me, the Greek gods are a totally unworkable material; the merest frigidity, which must chill and kill every living work of art they are brought into.'[48] And his own poems strove constantly for first-hand vitality, the capturing of an undiluted, and unconventionalized personal experience. Nor was he alone in the literary sphere, as his concern with the technical aspects of word patterns and of alliterative forms, often functioning as 'sounds independent of meaning', was being paralleled at this time on the continent in the writings both of Mallarmé and of his disciple Valéry, suggesting how integral this concern was to the broader aesthetic movements of the day. Indeed, Valéry came upon Hopkins' work many years later with a shock of recognition, amazed, as he expressed it, that the two men '. . . unknown to each other, at different times and in different places, with no contact, literary or other, arrive at the same idea.'[49]

If we may return for a moment to Chevreul and the belief that his discoveries concerning the physiology of colour influenced these painters, the unexpressed assumption behind that traditional reading may itself need questioning, the belief that the impact of scientific discoveries upon the art and literature of the time is a one-directional phenomenon. Since Marjorie Nicolson began exploring that indebtedness many years ago, she and subsequent historians have conceived the arts as essentially malleable phenomena, responding necessitously to the factual discoveries of empirical research.[50] But scientific research should be seen as itself no less responsive to the broad cultural changes of its time; for its major discoveries are rarely serendipitous, the attention of the experimenter being directed, consciously or not, to those problems which are of immediate concern to him. It was scarcely fortuitous that, at a time when, within Baroque art and literature, the newly-discovered materiality of the cosmos and the dazzling splendour of light were conceived as the two principal symbols of divine power, Newton's mind should have turned its attention to those elements, producing as two of his most outstanding discoveries the mechanistic principle of gravity and the analysis of light into the colours of the spectrum. It may well be that, in the same way, Chevreul's researches had themselves been prompted by the changing ideas we have been tracing, by this evolutionary sense of natural objects responding to the conditions of their environment epitomized in the work of Lyell, which led him to search for a similar mutability and interaction in the area of colour optics. The artists themselves would thus be seen as responding independently to that cultural change, and eventually, on discovering Chevreul's work, adopting its theory of 'complementary' influence as a means of authorizing their own practice. Within painting, the result is characterized by Van Gogh's comment that he longed one day '. . . to express the love of two lovers by the marriage of two complementary colours, their mingling and their opposition, the mysterious vibration of kindred tones.'

In Hopkins' verse, this concern with the interaction of words is heightened by the innovative use of compound adjectives, so characteristic of his poetry. Words apparently disparate are alliteratively combined to intensify each other by their even closer proximity and interconnection. A complex theological concept could thereby be compressed into one verbal unit, conveying more effectively its paradoxical validity:

> Now burn, new born to the world,
> Double natur'd name,
> The heaven-flung, heart-fleshed, maiden-furled
> Miracle-in-Mary-of-flame,
> Mid-numberèd he in three of the thunder-throne![51]

All poetry employs juxtaposition as an ingredient in its literary processes, and in that respect Hopkins' usage is not inaugurative – just as the interest in colour juxtaposition was not in itself original, with Cézanne and Gauguin acknowledging the leadership of Delacroix in this regard. But for the latter artists, as for Hopkins, their originality consisted in the heightened intensity and centrality of that usage in their work, as well as in the way they allowed the effects such adjacency produced to usurp the function of volumetric fidelity or literal statement. As Geoffrey Hartman has noted, Hopkins' verse relies upon a multiplication of the sound of one word in the next, like a series of accelerating explosions.[52] The *inscape* that Hopkins sought to convey in his verse was a quintessential element existing within the literal or factual; and one method he employed to convey that inner quality was this process of crystallizing an idea into a compressed phrase composed of different verbal units, whose interplay of sound and connotative associations stimulate the reader to discover the meaning unaided, to recompose them into a deeper, often unexpressed theme, existing, as it were, beyond the literal. Like a canvas by Seurat, Signac, or Pissarro, which left to the viewer the task of combining the separate dots or brush-strokes into meaning, so Hopkins characteristically transmits his theme – in the following instance, the idea of ephemerality – by a swift succession of separate, apparently disconnected images, which the reader's imagination, with no authorially-supplied linkage and relying solely upon the interacting proximity of the words, must connect into intelligible relationship:

> Cloud-puffball, torn tufts, tossed pillows | flaunt forth,
>   then chevy on an air-
> Built thoroughfare: heaven-roysterers, in gay-gangs | they

throng; they glitter in marches.
Down roughcast, down dazzling whitewash, | wherever
    an elm arches,
Shivelights and shadowtackle in long | lashes lace, lance,
    and pair.[53]

As Fénéon wrote of the pointillists, they let:

> ... the colours arise, vibrate in abrupt contacts, and recompose
> themselves at a distance, they enveloped their subjects with light
> and air, modelling them in luminous tones, sometimes even dar-
> ing to sacrifice all modelling.[54]

It was, in fact, a principle adopted not only in pointillism. Cézanne's
Bridge and Pool of 1888 consists, at first glance, of a jumble of apparently arbitrary brush-strokes, until the eye, viewing them from the
distance and perceiving the overall relationship, translates them into
significant design. So Hopkins offers only minimal hints of meaning, leaving the main effect to be suggested by the juxtaposed images
or adjectives, as in his vision of a sombre evening prefiguring the
Day of Judgement:

Earnest, earthless, equal, attuneable, | vaulty, voluminous,
    ... stupendous
Evening strains to be time's vást, | womb-of-all, home-of-all,
    hearse-of-all night.
Her fond yellow hornlight wound to the west, | her wild
    hollow hoarlight hung to the height
Waste; her earliest stars, earlstars, | stars principal,
    overbend us,
Fíre-féaturing héaven. For éarth | her béing has unbóund;
    her dápple is at énd, as –
Tray or aswarm, all throughther, in throngs; | self in self
    stéepèd and páshed – qúite
Disremembering, dismembering | all now ...[55]

That technique in poetry was, as Hopkins employed it, a major
adumbration of Modernism. It represented what was to become
one of the most distinctive qualities of twentieth-century verse, where
metaphor or symbol stand in place of logical discourse, suggesting

meaning solely by their mutual interaction or juxtaposition, as in Ezra Pound's moving description of old age:

> A blown husk that is finished
>   but the light sings eternal
> a pale flare over marshes
>   where the salt hay whispers to tide's change[56]

Yet whatever impulses Hopkins may share with the Neo-Impressionist and Post-Impressionist painters, there is one central quality in his poetry which may appear to divorce him from them – the fact that it is permeated throughout by deep religious devotion, a resonant sense of the presence of the divine in all nature, in all human activity, even in objects themselves:

> Summer ends now; now, barbarous in beauty, the stooks rise
> Around; up above, what wind-walks! what lovely behaviour
> Of silk-sack clouds! has wilder, wilful-wavier
> Meal-drift moulded ever and melted across skies?
>
> I wálk, I líft up, lift úp heart, éyes,
> Down all that glory in the heavens to glean our Saviour;
> And, éyes, héart, what looks, what lips yet gáve you a
> Rapturous love's greeting of realer, of rounder replies? . . .[57]

Such Christian orientation, however, should not be seen as isolating him. Religious experience, as recorded by the Christian poet, uniform as it may be in certain theological fundamentals, is individualized in all eras both by the personality of the writer and by modes of apprehension reflecting contemporary impulses. The Bible, as a store-house of archetypal figures, has in each generation attracted writers to those personages which appealed to their specific or local interests, Milton finding in Samson the paradigm of spiritual and physical wrestling appropriate for the inner agony he wished to portray, Byron sensing a Romantic affinity with the guilt-ridden Cain, and T.S. Eliot retelling his own hesitant, intellectual progression towards faith in terms of the doubting journey of the Magi as they wander through alien territory towards Bethlehem. As a facet of this eclectic reading of the Scriptures, the emphases and focuses within religious faith shift in accordance with the changing aesthetic patterns of the time. There is the dissatisfied transcendence of logic in Donne's poetry as in the phosphorescent mystery of a Tintoretto painting, there is Addison demonstrating to a rationalist age the calm fortitude of the Christian-Stoic; the prophetic denunciations of Blake, passionately refashioning God in his own image; and in our own day, the irony of a Graham Greene, substituting for the pietistic martyr of Catholic tradition a bumbling *prêtre manqué*, a self-deprecating anti-hero embodying a blending of Christian faith with the principles of twentieth-century existentialism.[58]

Within the parameters of Christian faith, there is room for a wide range of responses, appropriate to the exigencies of the time. Hopkins is no different in that respect. He may have admired the seventeenth-century poetry of George Herbert, revealing in his own verse echoes of that regard, an 'ah my dear', recalling the sweet intimacy of his mentor's relationship with God. But the differences in poetic conception are fundamental. Herbert saw the world about him – the flowers of the field, the anagrams of words, the structure of the church – as a divine book filled with moral instruction which it was his task to decipher to the reader, conveying the lessons with a simplicity and gentleness that should make them pleasing and palatable. From the stained-glass windows of the church he deduced the comforting lesson that the priest, however lowly or absurd he may be in person, is validated by the divine light of which he is the transmitter:

> Lord, how can man preach thy eternal word?
> He is a brittle, crazy glass,
> Yet in thy temple thou dost him afford
> This glorious and transcendent place,
> To be a window through thy grace.[59]

Hopkins esteemed the sincere faith apparent in Herbert's verse and consciously imitated it in some of his earlier poems, but it was not the style of his mature phase. There, in the verse he composed subsequent to the long silence attendant upon his ordination – as in *The Windhover, Pied Beauty, The Caged Skylark,* or *Felix Randal* – his purpose is not a didactic elucidation of divine hieroglyphics concealed within the natural world, nor, as with the Romantic poets, the transmission of a sense of pantheistic immanence. Instead, he aims at a vivid metamorphosing of the natural scene through his personal, imaginative apprehension of it, an emotional capturing of fugitive reality in sharply juxtaposed words and images, as in one of his most famous stanzas:

> I caught this morning morning's minion, king-
> dom of daylight's dauphin, dapple-dáwn-drawn Falcon,
> in his riding
> Of the rólling level úndernéath him steady áir, and striding
> High there, how he rung upon the rein of a wimpling wing
> In his ecstacy! then off, off forth on swing . . .[60]

A passing moment of intense beauty has been 'caught' here, the thrill of the experience ensconced in the excitement of the lines. In place of mimetic fidelity, a series of compressed, allusive images, highly personal in their associations, transform the scene into an individually conceived vision. Both in its technique and in the brilliance of its effect the poem is close to Van Gogh's *Wheat Field and Cypresses* of 1889 in which the landscape seems to vibrate with emotional force. The scene there may be different from Hopkins' dappled dawn, but it is animated by an impulse similar to the poet's. Both offer a new way of seeing the world, a vicariously-experienced visual discovery. After having once gazed at Van Gogh's trees, seeming to flame upwards in joyful participation in the vigour of nature, the viewer can never view a cypress tree again in quite the same manner, just as one can never regard nature in quite the same way after reading Hopkins'

> Glory be to God for dappled things –
> For skies of couple-colour as a brinded cow;
> For rose-moles all in stipple upon trout that swim;
> Fresh-firecoal chestnut-falls; finches' wings;
> Landscape plotted and pieced – fold, fallow, and plough . . .[61]

As Hopkins declared: 'All things therefore are charged with love, are charged with God, and if we know how to touch them give off sparks and take fire, yield drops and flow, ring, and tell of him.'[62]

Both of them sought to portray the distinctive *inscape* of things rather than externals, and were sensitive to the ways in which that inner essence was to be perceived. Hopkins believed that human beings, the most highly 'selved' or individualized creatures in this universe, apprehended the inner essence of objects (including the spiritual bond with the divine) through a consciously energized

act which he termed *instress*; and Van Gogh similarly sought for
methods of penetrating the outer appearance of objects to distinguish their inner quality. He developed for himself a process now
part of normal studio technique, discovering that one method of
excluding visual detail in order to perceive the inner character of a
scene was to half-close his eyes: '. . . in these studies I believe there
is something of that mysteriousness one gets by looking at nature
through the eyelashes, so that the outlines are simplified to blots
of colour', adding that '. . . everything is difficult to do if one wants
to get at its *inner character*.'[63] In his poetry, Hopkins conveyed the
act of *instress*, of penetrating to the *inscape* of a scene, by blurring
the outward factual elements, either through a series of dazzling
images as in his *Windhover* or, as in *The Candle Indoors*, by responding to the play of light upon his half-shut eyes in the night air,
evoking by that misty luminosity the personal, inner response which
gives the scene its true validity:

> Some candle clear burns somewhere I come by.
> I muse at how its being puts blissful back
> With yellowy moisture mild night's blear-all black
> Or to-fro tender trambeams truckle at the eye.
>
> By that window what task what fingers ply,
> I plod wondering, a-wanting, just for lack
> Of answer the eagerer a-wanting Jessy or Jack
> There/God to aggrándise, God to glorify . . .[64]

Were this response shared only with Van Gogh, the underlying
connection might be thought to reside in their religious suscept-
ibilities rather than in any broader, emergent style of the time. Van
Gogh was, as we know, initially bent on a career as an evangelical
preacher, and only on his failure at that vocation did he subsequently
transfer his religious fervour to painting.[65] But there is behind both
impulses a principle arising out of the larger aesthetic configuration we have been examining. For Hopkins' attempt to capture the
essence of objects rather than their outward form, leading to his
disdain for the demands of syntax and conventional word-usage in
pursuit of that transcendent quality, was one he shared with the
Post-Impressionists, with their discarding of volumetric fidelity and
their adoption of a hieratic concept of art, striving to apprehend
what Gauguin termed the 'inner meaning' of objects.[66]

Hopkins was not concerned with optical theory, but his conception of *instress* reflected that same desire to see nature afresh through the prism of imaginative experience, to record in similar fashion not literally what the eye sees but the effect of its impact upon him. As he himself defined that process, he sought to convey '... the synthesis of (either successive or spatially distinct) impressions ...'[67] Partly by the compound adjectives and juxtaposed neologisms he devised, he sought to impart the dynamic interaction of the scene's effect upon the mind, with literalist details blurred, or encoded into intensely individually conceived images. Stars, in *The Starlight Night*, become fire-folk sitting in bright boroughs, the doves, startled into flight, are transformed into floating flakes of light:

> ... the fire-folk sitting in the air!
> The bright boroughs, the circle-citadels there!
> Down in dim woods the diamond delves! the elves'-eyes!
> The grey lawns cold where gold, where quickgold lies!
>   Wind-beat whitebeam! airy abeles set on a flare!
>   Flake-doves sent floating forth at a farmyard scare! ...[68]

The resulting effect is remarkably close to Van Gogh's *The Starry Night* of 1889 (Fig. 28), where the scene, rejecting mimetic fidelity, conveys instead what Hopkins would have called the act of instress, the artist's perception of the stars as passionately-conceived whirls in the sky, transmuted not only by the excitement of the viewer but also by their echoing of the energized moon, as they and the landscape below become charged with associative ecstasy.

In Hopkins' sense of art as artefact rather than mimesis, in his fascination with the interplay of adjacent syllabic units, and in his advocacy of words retaining their primary hue, he provided for poetry, as the Neo-Impressionists and Post-Impressionists were at that same time providing for painting, an essentially new vision of the world, responsive, as is all great art, to the changing perspective or 'con-text' of his generation, the new conception of nature and of all objects within it as engaged in a ceaseless process of reciprocal interaction and interchange. It was a conception for which the poet and painter of the time needed to create new methods of artistic representation, inaugurating thereby the artistic and poetic modes of the twentieth century.

6

The Art of Henry James

The connecting of literature with contemporary movements in the visual arts demands at times a leap of the imagination, a perception of affinities between the media even where the writer himself may have been by nature apathetic towards painting and sculpture, and ignorant of current trends in those arts. Henry James, in contrast, not only invites such investigation, rendering justification for it redundant, but throughout his work insists, with unqualified verve, upon the intimate correlation between the craft of the author and the principles governing the kindred arts of painting, architecture, and sculpture. Although all three artistic media were referred to frequently in his writings, whether as fictional elements within his stories or as authorially evoked exemplifications of the literary techniques he was employing, it was especially to the art of painting that he resorted in his critical work, employing it as a paradigm for the creative processes relating to his own profession of letters. He claimed categorically that '. . . the analogy between the art of the painter and the art of the novelist is, so far as I am able to see, complete.'[1]

Because of its visible and hence more demonstrable form, painting offered him a number of helpful parallels. It provided an object lesson for illustrating the limitations implicit in representationalism itself, it revealed the potentialities art possessed for overcoming those restrictions, and, above all, it demonstrated the impressive achievements to which aesthetic sensitivity and artistic ingenuity could eventually lead. His retrospective exposition of the narrative techniques developed within his novels, the famed passage on the 'house of fiction', presents the author in terms of a painter judiciously selecting the window through which he can best frame his proposed scene, thereby ensuring that the central figure of the literary work be 'placed' effectively within its setting.[2]

James's awareness of the bond connecting the sister arts was, as he readily acknowledged in his various autobiographical reminiscences, rooted in his earliest experiences. There were his frequent visits to art galleries during his childhood, as well as the parental encouragement afforded him to try his own hand at painting. In Newport, he had been delighted to accompany his elder brother William, while the latter was contemplating painting as a professional career, to the studio of the distinguished American artist, William Morris Hunt, to whom his brother had been apprenticed. Those were, the novelist recalls nostalgically, '. . . hours of Art, art definitely named, looking me full in the face and accepting my stare in return – no longer a tacit implication or a shy subterfuge, but a flagrant unattenuated aim'; and when he (at that time also considering painting as a career) eventually deserted it for letters, he comforted himself with his awareness of the consanguinity of the two media, '. . . the dawning perception that the arts were after all essentially one and that even with canvas or brush whisked out of my grasp I still needn't feel disinherited'.

Throughout those memoirs, the contribution of the visual arts to the process of his intellectual and aesthetic development, both as practitioner and as connoisseur, is repeatedly recorded. No student of James can be unaware of the emotional impact made upon him by his first visit, at the age of thirteen, to the Musée du Louvre, in one hall of which the ceiling fresco by Delacroix proved a revelation to him, symbolizing for him both then and through his subsequent years the very finest that art could achieve:

> . . . in those beginnings I felt myself most happily cross that bridge over to Style constituted by the wondrous Galerie d'Apollon, drawn out for me as a long but assured initiation, and seeming to form with its supreme coved ceiling and inordinately shining parquet a prodigious tube or tunnel through which I inhaled little by little, that is again and again, a general sense of glory. The glory meant ever so many things at once, not only beauty and art and supreme design, but history and fame and power, the world in fine raised to the richest and noblest expression.

Such visits to the Louvre, he claimed, were '. . . educative, formative, fertilising, in a degree which no other "intellectual experience" our youth was to know could pretend, as a comprehensive, conducive thing, to rival'; and his sense of personal debt to the visual arts, together with his identification of them as the ideal analogue for the novelist's craft, were to accompany him throughout his career.[3]

That aspect of his writings has received full acknowledgement in criticism, resulting in a number of important full-length studies, quite apart from numerous briefer treatments. Edwin Bowden some years ago examined sensitively the ways in which the analogy with painting functioned within the novels, especially in regard to the visual 'perspective' it offered him. Viola H. Winner has focused upon his relationship to nineteenth-century aesthetic theories, including his indebtedness to Ruskin, and has, through close study of the references to specific paintings both in his art reviews and within the novels themselves, sought to establish James's own artistic preferences, most notably his fondness for the Mannerist painters, of whom Tintoretto was his declared favourite. Marianna Torgovnick, in a broader investigation, selected James as one of the three novelists on whom to focus in her examination of the function of pictorialism within the modern novel, while Adeline Tintner, who has devoted a lifetime to the 'museum world' of James's novels, has recently – some forty years after the stimulating article which first attracted attention to the significance of that facet of his work – produced a major study, exhaustively recording and evaluating almost every allusion within his writings to the art galleries, private collections, individual works, and country houses with which he was acquainted, and which served as contributory elements within his novels. She notes, for example, the symbolic function of ancient statuary in his story 'The Solution', in which figures of Roman senators represent those Republican notions of honour to which Wilmerding must remain faithful in the contemporary American ferment over democratic principles; and she identifies with acuity the visual pun as Daisy Miller, whose putative 'innocence' forms the central theme of that story, is, in a secluded nook in the Doria-Pamphili Palace in Rome, located beneath Velasquez' portrait of Pope Innocent X. The juxtaposition, as a male admirer notes within the tale, brings together a superb portrait and a strikingly pretty picture, yet for the reader it possesses at the same time a submerged thematic significance concealed within the pontiff's name.[4]

The insights which these critics and others have offered have undoubtedly deepened our understanding of the part played by James's recourse to painting as an analogue to the novel. But as these advocates of such interdisciplinary enquiry themselves admit, the results of the investigation are strangely unsatisfactory. The conclusions concerning his relationship to painting are either negative in implication – with James himself expressly disparaging the aesthetic styles or painters identified by those critics as the models for his art – or, at best, only mildly relevant to his writing because of discrepancies or vagueness in the supposed parallels. That he was a close friend and a personal admirer of Burne-Jones seems to have little bearing on the literary techniques that he developed for his novels, he himself recording how the Brotherhood had aroused in him only a passing interest, creating the briefest of impressions upon him during his youth: 'The very word Pre-Raphaelite wore for us that intensity of meaning, not less than of mystery, that thrills us in its perfection but for one season, the first hour of initiations . . .'[5] Walter Pater's *Studies in the History of the Renaissance,* which he read soon after its appearance in 1873, was a contemporary influence that James consciously resisted, referring to its author slightingly in later years as 'faint, pale, embarrassed, exquisite Pater', who, he maintained, had provided for his readers only a meagre phosphorescence instead of a flame.[6] Ruskin, whose authority was indeed powerful during James's formative years, did leave his mark upon him, especially in his insistence upon the moral function of art; and the revival of interest in early Florentine painters, initiated in large part by Ruskin, was no doubt responsible for James's personal enthusiasm for that school, his own art reviews often echoing certain of the master's aesthetic criteria, even though he carefully resisted what he termed the strange 'falsetto key' in which Ruskin wrote. But there was a chasm separating their focal concerns, a divergence of interest related to the most cherished of James's own principles, which invalidated Ruskin as a major force in his own professional career – 'Look into Ruskin and he's all about Nature – splendidly often, but loathing Art' when it was art itself which was of primary concern to the novelist.[7] On the other hand, the Aesthetic movement, which was indeed concerned with art, James treated with a ridicule and scorn evocative of the contemporary parodying of Wilde in Gilbert and Sullivan's operetta *Patience.* The young narrator in 'The Author of Beltraffio' describes with disdain the pale and angular 'medieval' lady he meets, garbed in a faded velvet robe, and gazing at him intently with mournful eyes. She was, he concludes on recovering from his initial astonishment:

. . . a singular fatuous artificial creature, and I was never more than half to penetrate her motives and mysteries. Of one thing I'm sure at least: that they were considerably less insuperable than her appearance announced. Miss Ambient was a restless romantic disappointed spinster, consumed with the love of Michael-Angelesque attitudes and mystical robes; but I'm now convinced she hadn't in her nature those depths of unutterable thought which, when you first knew her, seemed to look out from her eyes and to prompt her complicated gestures.[8]

His comments on Wilde himself, and on his younger contemporary Beardsley, were no less scathing. The former he described as '. . . the repulsive and fatuous Oscar Wilde' who, he insisted, was 'never in the smallest of degree' interesting to him,[9] while Beardsley, whom he admitted to be unmistakably intelligent and personally possessed of a melancholy grace, appealed considerably less to him as an artist. James acknowledged in him a disconcerting talent, circumspectly adding: '. . . my appreciation of which seems to me, however, as I look back, to have stopped quite short.' The drawings themselves James strongly disliked, describing them as 'extraordinarily base'. He did agree to become associated with the Yellow Book, but only under personal protest, driven to it by his financial needs and remarking to his brother that he hated '. . . too much the horrid aspect and company of the whole publication'.[10] To judge from his own comments, therefore, James would seem to have gained little inspiration from any of these contemporary artists or aesthetic schools.

In some despair at finding any convincing evidence of intermedia relations which would justify the extraordinary prominence of art themes and analogues in his work, focus has understandably been directed at the most important movement occurring on the contemporary European scene, the rise of Impressionism. Peter Stowell has in fact coined the term 'literary Impressionism' to suggest the way in which James absorbed the principles of that movement into his own writings, and that relationship has been pursued by many others. It has been remarked, for example, that, from *The Portrait of a Lady* onwards, his novels gradually move outside the art gallery or studio into the open, adopting the ideal of *plein air* associated with such painters as Pissarro, Monet, Sisley, and Renoir, while both F.O. Matthiessen and Charles Anderson identified the luncheon and boating scenes in *The Ambassadors* as being, in their delicate play with light, literary versions of paintings by Manet and Renoir. More recent critics, however, especially those most identified with intermedia research, have, on a closer reading of the text, admitted that the only real connection is that of subject-matter. There is no hint in those scenes of the refraction of light and the dissolution of reality which constituted the most striking element of Impressionist art.[11] A more substantial connection has been perceived in James's narrative technique. Percy Lubbock pointed many years ago to the innovative strategy, discernible primarily in *The Ambassadors* but functioning in many other novels, whereby the stories are often presented through the impressions (a word repeatedly employed in that connection by the novelist himself) made upon the mind of a fictional narrator within the tale; and he sugggested that this strategy paralleled, and may even have been derived from the similar practice adopted by those painters. Yet in this aspect too, the technique, one must record, never functions in James's writings as a means of transforming reality, that difference from the Impressionists being, perhaps, more substantial than any supposed similarities.[12]

Moreover, in this instance too the idea of an indebtedness becomes suspect in the light of James's marked and often vigorous antipathy towards that school of painters both on the continent and in England. His comment on Whistler's *Nocturnes* and *Impressions* in an 1877 art review, his refusal to discuss them 'because I frankly confess they do not amuse me', insisting that a picture, to be interesting, must have some relation to life, indicates his allegiance at that time to conventional realism in art. A year earlier, he had, more specifically, dismissed the Impressionists themselves on the grounds that none of them showed any signs of possessing a first-rate talent – thereby revealing, not for the first time, that his own talents as a critic of contemporary art were themselves somewhat less than first-rate – and singled out for disapproval their tendency to be 'absolute foes to arrangement, embellishment, selection'.[13] To regard, after that specific condemnation, his own careful compositional technique as consciously imitative of theirs must assume some significant, subsequent change of opinion. Although he did become more sympathetic to the Impressionists in later years, when his friendship with Sargent no doubt modified his opposition, the only laudatory comment recorded by him is from 1905, too late to have influenced the writing of his novels, all of which had been completed by that date.[14] During the period of his creativity, his comments are consistently negative towards them. In *The Reverberator*, the paintings of the 'rising Impressionist' artist Waterlow are treated disparagingly by the visitors to his studio, where the productions struck them '. . . for the most part in the category of those creations known to ladies as frights, and our friends retired with the lowest opinion of the young American master.' That is not an authorial comment, but it is left unqualified, the effect of amused disapproval being reinforced a little later. Gaston Probert, we are informed, defended certain of the purples and greens produced by his friend Waterlow as he would have defended his own honour, even though, the narrator wrily adds, those purples and greens 'were far beyond him'.[15]

As I have tried to indicate both here and, more fully, in the bibliographical notes to this chapter, this scepticism concerning James's indebtedness to contemporary artists and artistic theories is shared, often reluctantly, by the critics most eager to establish such parallels. They acknowledge a puzzling discrepancy between, on the one hand, James's repeated citation of painting and sculpture as the aesthetic paradigm and authority for the novel genre he was attempting to redesign and, on the other, the marked lack of interest he displayed, frequently even a disdain for those contemporaries engaged in the same task within the visual arts. The result has been a thrusting back of the search for models into earlier centuries, an enquiry how far he may have been affected by the antique sculpture of Rome appearing so often in his work, by the classical collections of the Louvre, or by the revered masters of the eighteenth century, all remote in time from the ferment of artistic production in his own day which might be thought more relevant to his own creative pursuits and with which he had himself been so intimately connected in his earlier years. *Roderick Hudson*, the young American sculptor whose tastes are carefully nurtured by the art-connoisseur Rowland, is introduced by his mentor not to the contemporary art of Europe but to Italy's ancient ruins. And here too, the result of that supposed influence is far removed from the kind of literary experimentation in James's own novels. Roderick's much-lauded genius eventuates in a masterpiece which, while clearly approved by the authorial voice of the novel, is disappointing to a reader familiar with the plastic arts of the time. It is as staid and conventional a work as could be conceived. At an exciting time in the arts, when Rodin was experimenting with such startlingly anti-academic sculpture as his *Bronze Age*, Roderick, in the bust of his mother which he did eventually complete, captures with all the conventional sentimentality of contemporary sculpture, the characteristics of her face, '. . . its sweetness, its mildness, its minuteness, its still maternal passion, with the most unerring art. The truth was all tenderness, the tenderness all truth.' This is standard Victorian statuary of the least interesting kind, free from the innovative elements in James' own art. In *The Tragic Muse* too, a novel more obviously concerned with the immediately contemporary world, where Nick Dormer must choose between the promise of a brilliant career in politics and dedication to the poorly-paying profession of artist, the splendid portrait retrospectively justifying his choice and amazing his connoisseur friend by its brilliance, so far from revealing artistic originality merely echoes in style, pose, and timbre – apparently to the contentment of the author if not of his reader – the eighteenth-century painting hinted at in the title, Reynolds' *Mrs Siddons as the Tragic Muse*:

> Her beautiful head was bent a little, broodingly, and her splendid face seemed to look down at life. She had a grand appearance of being raised aloft, with a wide regard, a survey from a height of intelligence, for the great field of the artist, all the figures and passions he may represent. Peter asked himself where his kinsman had learned to paint like that.[16]

It is a question we may well ask ourselves in connection with James' own tastes. He had certainly not gained that preference from William Morris Hunt and John La Farge with whom he had studied in his youth, nor was it from the Pre-Raphaelites, the Yellow Book artists, or the Impressionists of his day. And the same holds true for his use of imagery drawn from painting. Aurora Coyne is evocative of a sixteenth-century Titian or Veronese, Milly Theale is compared to a Bronzino, Mme de Vionnet's head recalls the image stamped on some 'old precious medal' from the period of the Renaissance; and the buildings and art works that form the background for his scenes – the Colosseum at Rome where Roderick attempts an act of bravado to impress Christina, 'The Dying Gladiator' in the Capitoline Museum before which, symbolically, Warburton must suffer his final rejection by Isabel, the Correggio *Madonna and Child* to which the seemingly career-minded Harriet Stackpole feels, on the threshold of her marriage, inexplicably drawn on her visits to the Uffizi – all these derive not from the challenging innovations in the art of his time, to which James might have been expected to turn as models for his own experiments with form, but from an antiquity divorced from his own period by many centuries.

In attempting to deal with this discrepancy, we shall need once again to resort to the distinction between the diachronic approach to intermedia studies adopted by most historians and the synchronic system advocated in this present book. The former method searches for verifiable or at least chronologically justifiable cause and effect, speculating on the influence exerted upon James by his teachers Hunt and La Farge, by the painting and sculpture to which he was exposed on visiting European galleries in his youth, by the art criticism current in his day (wherever there is evidence that he had read or commented upon it), and by his recorded contacts with practising painters. All this is perfectly legitimate. But in such interdisciplinary studies, James has been conceived primarily as a recipient, however adept at transforming such models to his own needs, as a writer absorbing ideas and lessons from others, adopting or modifying already formulated theories and methods for use in developing his own practice as a novelist. He is rarely, if ever, viewed in such studies as an independent initiator, performing within the literary sphere and without direct influence from outside that realm, the same creative function as the painters and sculptors of his day – searching himself for means to express within his work the altered philosophical and cultural patterns of his time, patterns to which he is responding directly, while being to a large extent either oblivious of, or even inimical to similar manifestations within the visual arts of his generation.[17] A principle adopted in this synchronic approach, it will be recalled, is that, in establishing parallels between the media, no personal contact need be proved between a writer and the specific contemporary canvas to which the text is being compared, nor even his or her awareness of the contemporary changes occurring within the kindred arts, on the assumption that the similarities, insofar as they exist, derive from the shared complex of inherited ideas and dominant impulses to which they are simultaneously, yet individually, responding. In this instance, James's repeated evocation of painting and sculpture in his novels has seemed to justify a contrary approach, encouraging and even authorizing a search for the precise works or aesthetic schools which he personally admired and to which his stylistic and compositional innovations might be indebted.

It may be, however, that the prominence of artists and art-related themes in his novels derives from an entirely different motivation, his turning away from social realism as the main theme of the novel, from the depiction of middle-class or provincial scenes of daily life such as had occupied his immediate predecessors, in favour of a new topic, a concern with art itself as the new principle for living. In one respect that meant the introduction to the novel of a new type of character, of intellectuals refined in their tastes and aesthetic discernment, whose visits to museums and whose collections of *bibelots* and rare antiques provide the setting for their sophisticated activities. On the other hand, that concern formed in itself only the external manifestation of a more profound interest, the response of a sensitive writer to a major change in the ideological configuration of the era which was reaching its apogee at the very time James was writing, and for which his fiction was to provide literary expression. In order to comprehend that emerging pattern, we shall need to penetrate behind the surface changes in contemporary art in order to perceive the deeper impulses which were to affect so radically both literature and the plastic media.

The final decades of the nineteenth century marked in many respects the culmination of a movement originating in the 1830s, the growing awareness that Nature could no longer function, as it had for so long in the past, as the major source of inspiration for writer and artist. Ruskin, it is true, had continued to advocate the meticulous recording of natural phenomena as a prerequisite for all great art, the Pre-Raphaelites exemplifying that mimetic accuracy in the detailed depiction of fauna and flora on their canvases, while the Realists both in England and on the continent, in the novel as well as in painting, had espoused fidelity to the natural scene as the cornerstone for their aesthetic practice. But the very conception of Nature had changed, such fidelity being in essence close to the geological, botanical, or sociological researches of the empirical sciences, an objective representationalism far removed from the Romantic tradition. What has disappeared from such scenes, or become so diluted as to be negligible, is the idea of Nature, whether in Christian, Deistic, or vaguely pantheistic terms, as the divine, mystical force, whose harmonies, beauty and universal benevolence were to imbue man with his noblest ideals, providing a true model for art whose rules both poet and painter must subserviently follow. The long-established principle inherited from classical times, reinforced by Renaissance Neoplatonism with its sense of human harmonies echoing those of the heavens, had been adopted and re-formulated for the eighteenth century by Alexander Pope in unequivocal terms in the command 'First follow Nature, and your judgement frame / By her just Standard, which is still the same', with the conclusion that it must serve at all times as '. . . the Source, and End, and Test of Art.'[18] For the Romantic poet, the principle was to be softened and personalized, its validity enhanced by the mystical quality with which Nature was now endowed and by the revived vision of the poet as the instrument through whom its moral messages were to be transmitted to mankind. But as that period drew to its close, such time-venerated belief in Nature as the primary model for morality, for poetry and for art could no longer be preserved.

The crisis of religious faith, with the concomitant doubts concerning the divine origin and order of creation, had wrought part of the effect; but such suspicions were being significantly reinforced by the changing conception of Nature itself in the light of scientific determinism. Impulses from vernal woods benignly instructing man in his moral responsibilities seemed singularly outmoded for a generation now made aware of Nature in terms of predatory creatures viciously battling for survival within a harsh, impersonal system. Even the Darwinists themselves, who had originally perceived an overall beauty in the universal progression of the evolutionary process, were being confronted with mounting evidence that the cruelty and callousness within the economy of Nature were not minor aberrations which must be accepted as part of the larger whole, but rather elements essential to the operation of the entire system. George J. Romanes, soon to be appointed Professor of Physiology at Edinburgh University and himself a leading Darwinist, admitted that the picture emerging from current empirical studies was far from comforting: '. . . we find that more than half of the species which have survived the ceaseless struggle are parasitic in their habits, lower and insentient forms of life feasting on higher and sentient forms; we find teeth and talons whetted for slaughter, hooks and suckers moulded for torment – everywhere a reign of terror, hunger, and sickness. . . .'[19]

Within the multifarious and often contradictory forms of Aestheticism in its nineteenth-century manifestations, from the moral decadence of Verlaine and Baudelaire, through the preciosity of Pater, the Japonisme of Whistler, the symbolism of Arthur Symons, and the movement of Art Nouveau, one powerful underlying theme co-ordinating them all is, it would seem, this growing distrust of Nature as the source of inspiration, the recognition that its function as the aegis of art had drawn to a close.[20] Poet, novelist and painter were forced back to the realization that, with Nature disqualified, art must now constitute its own justification, to be regarded henceforth as an autonomous practice, valid in its own right. It was, they pointed out with increasing confidence, ultimately superior to

Nature, transcending the latter's mutability and ephemerality, discarding its blemishes, and attaining thereby to idealized and permanent forms to which Nature itself could never aspire. The hero of Huysmans' seminal novel *A Rebours*, published in 1884, declared that Nature could no longer be of service to writer and artist. She merely wearied them by the 'disgusting uniformity' of her landscapes and skies. Artificiality, he maintained, was the true distinguishing mark of human genius, and Wilde could now pronounce for his generation: 'It is through Art, and through Art only, that we can realise our perfection; through Art, and through Art only, that we can shield ourselves from the sordid perils of actual existence.'[21]

How far-reaching this tendency was may be perceived in the linkage between apparently disparate movements of the time. The devotional Tractarianism of Keble and Pusey in the mid-century may seem the very antithesis of the superbly executed yet sexually perverse drawings of Beardsley towards its close, exulting in sadism and in the 'unnatural' impulses of man; but unifying them in one important respect was their shared proclivity for ritualized and stylized forms removed from the natural world, including a fascination, shared by Pater's Marius, for the liturgical symbols, the typological exegesis, and the formal sacraments of the Catholic church. It was a fascination which Newman, Beardsley and Wilde were all eventually to endorse in their own lives, by their eventual conversion to that faith.[22]

In a stimulating study of this period, Linda Dowling has argued, on the basis of modern linguistic theory, that the Decadent movement arose from a crisis in Victorian attitudes towards language, a crisis brought about by the innovations in comparative philology imported from the continent. She points out how, as forerunners of Saussure and Derrida, such German philologists as Bopp, Grimm, and, even more importantly, Max Müller, who lectured in England and was widely admired there, proposed that language should be seen as entirely divorced from the cultural context and human values of its time, and should be regarded as emerging instead from sound-associations. In contrast to the Romantic tradition, which had viewed language in its finest form as a means of expressing emotion, a 'language of the heart' to use Wordsworth's term, achieving its fullest effects in poetry, the Neogrammarians on the continent attributed the primary authority of language to plebeian oral forms, to the local dialect spoken by the common people and over which the educated man of letters exerted no control and could provide no direction. While, Müller argued, it may be in the power of an individual to change empires, to abolish laws, or to introduce new forms of government, in contrast '. . . no King or Dictator has ever been able to change the smallest law of language.'[23] He accordingly rejected the traditional assumption that the idioms of Greece, Rome, or modern European tongues, as preserved in literary records, should serve as the basis for the syntactical or grammatical principles of those languages. The corollary of that theory was a disqualification of literature as being the highest form of language and its relegation to the status of constituting a mere debasement. As Henry Sweet (the model for Shaw's Professor Henry Higgins) declared with the provocative misspelling which Shaw was partially to adopt for his own writing: 'Fonetics alone can breathe life into the ded mass of letters which constitute a writn language.'[24]

The next stage in argument is the one relevant to the period we are examining, for, as Dowling concludes, all that was left for the intellectual, in the face of that disqualification of poetry and sophisticated letters, was to rescue something from the wreck by attempting to bestow a 'belated and paradoxical vitality' on a literary form of writing which linguistic science had declared to be dead. Hence the nineteenth-century Aesthetes defiantly moved away from natural forms of speech in the direction of the fastidious and eclectically euphuistic style, as advocated by Pater.

The theory is both illuminating and persuasive, except for her tendency to divorce that linguistic crisis from its cultural context, from the larger configuration examined here. It is surely significant that, as has been mentioned in connection with Hopkins, the new conceptions of language developed by the nineteenth-century philologists were the outcome of an application to linguistics of the current theory of evolution, and hence were themselves an offshoot of it. The philologists now assumed for language an impersonal process of natural selectivity, ensuring the perpetuation only of those linguistic forms able to survive and profilerate among the masses, a process resistant to interference or control on the part of any individual and oblivious to such criteria as progressive refinement or sophistication. August Schleicher, one of the most important of this group of German philologists, entitled his major work *Darwinism Tested by the Science of Language.* Moreover, the response these theories elicited closely parallels the intellectual's shift in mood at that time from an initially optimistic regard for evolution, as marking a progression from the primitive to the highly civilized, and its eventual replacement by the chilling realization that Darwinism implied no such advancement, that natural selection most frequently resulted in the survival of the parasitical or brutish rather than the compassionate and humane. In 1862, reflecting the optimistic response, George Eliot eagerly welcomed Müller's published lectures, recommending them to others as a 'great and delightful' work, while Newman at the same time selected it as a prize-book for his students; but by 1885, when the less encouraging implications of evolutionism had been grasped, Oscar Wilde rejected Müller's work with scorn, especially for its disparaging treatment of mythology, the treasure-house of imaginative literature, as being no more than 'a disease of language'.[25] It marked a reversal of the nineteenth-century focus upon the vernacular, the conception of language as evolving from the everyday speech of the common people, revealing its replacement by a new appreciation of it as essentially an instrument for intellectual discourse, in that respect reflecting the growing distaste for the popularist, evolutionary reading of history. Those changes in comparative philology, therefore, should be seen not as the cause of the Decadent movement but as one facet or manifestation of a broad cultural change.

The more general distancing from natural forms and the preference for the consciously stylized and mannered reached its fullest expression during the final decades of the century, just as James was composing his major novels. In the plastic arts, it was to be represented most clearly by the movement of Art Nouveau, with its invariable insistence upon the precedence to be accorded to Art over Nature. Vegetal forms were frequently employed, often as the basic paradigms for this art-form, but no longer as models to be reverentially reproduced on the canvas with lifelike accuracy. They are instead only prototypes, to be transmuted by the craftsman into patterned or formalized shapes in order to demonstrate the superiority of the artificial over the natural, to highlight their distancing from the herbaceous and floral which are ever subject to imperfection and decay. The Favrile glass, from which Louis Tiffany moulded vases in the shape of flowers, was selected by him, after lengthy experimentation on his part, not for mimetic reasons but because of the unreal, metallic iridescence of its sheen and the unnatural colours the glass was able to absorb.[26] His lampshades, at the time thought shockingly eccentric, were hybrid forms of deliberately contrived design (Fig. 29), with a tree-like stem supporting a canopy of purple-green fruit and foliage, mosaically wrought in stained glass; or, in another instance, ornamented with stylized dragonfly emblems, arranged in orderly sequence against a vivid yellow background. The wallpaper produced by William Morris for his Arts and Crafts Movement similarly metamorphosed the natural scene, working the flowers and birds into patterns distinguished for their artistry rather than their naturalism. There too, the forms of nature were often employed as starting-points, but only as models out of which the artist was to construct aesthetically pleasing variants. Morris, for example, even though he remained somewhat closer to natural forms than other Art Nouveau artists, declared that the artist '. . . should not copy Nature, but recreate it', and although birds and plants remain recognizable in his wallpapers and textiles, it is the artistic patterning that produces the major impression.[27] Beardsley, echoing the Japonisme adopted by Whistler and Van Gogh, in designing a book-cover for an edition of *Morte d'Arthur* in 1893, orientalized the floral models into ceremonial figures so remote from nature that they are more reminiscent of the world of the kimono (Fig. 30).

The rise of Japonisme during this period has often been attributed to the opening up of trade with Japan in the mid-nineteenth century and the consequent influx of imported curios from that country. But, as always, that process needs to be examined in reverse. We need to enquire what pre-existent need in contemporary society made the arrival of those curios so fascinating to artists, at a time when the opening up of trade with so many other countries and colonies as part of England's imperial expansion produced no similar vogue. Its attraction was the authorization which Japanese culture provided for this burgeoning Victorian cult of the artefact. The expressionistic drawings by the Japanese artist Kiyotada, with areas of unmodulated colour sharply outlined in defiance of mimetic realism, the ceremonial porcelain vases with their sophisticated ornamentalism, and the ritualized drama of the Noh and Kabuki plays, where a bamboo rod, held horizontally, sufficed symbolically to represent a bridge, provided cultural credentials from the past for the stylized forms remote from the natural to which the new generation was attracted.[28] Hence the shift in this period from *japonaiserie*, a casual interest in the decorative aspects of that art-form paralleling the vogue of *chinoiserie* popular since the eighteenth century, to the serious desire to absorb its techniques into Western art. And a major aspect of that process was the urge to capture the 'concept' of an object rather than its physical form. Arthur Mackmurdo, one of the most influential designers of that period, included within the fretwork detailing of a mahogany cabinet from 1882 the image of a tree, which made no pretence at literal representation. It was a symbol, embodying the essence of biological growth. And his fabric and wallpaper designs, highly admired at the Liverpool Exhibition of 1886, desert the Romantic naturalism of Wordsworth or the fidelity to observed detail advocated by Ruskin, preferring to capture the 'idea' or notion of flowers swaying rhythmically in the wind.

Within Mackmurdo's designs, moreover, may be discerned a quality characteristic of the artistic productions of this period at large, expressing, it would seem, the submerged responsiveness of their creators to the new, less attractive theories of evolution. There is, in contrast to the Romantic tradition, a sense of vegetation thrusting upwards in fierce struggle for survival, competing for the limited light and air available, a conception often producing in such work a claustrophobic effect of sickly proliferation, as in Beardsley's *L'Abbé*, the central figure hemmed in by huge overblown flowers, thick bushes, and dark foliage. Christopher Dresser, who was among the first to treat organic forms in this way, had, in fact, been trained as a botanist before he transferred his interests to design. In 1870, he declared that it was his purpose in such drawings '. . . to embody chiefly the one idea of power, energy, force, or vigour . . . when the energy of growth is at its maximum.'[29]

While Dresser did acknowledge his affinity to current ideas of evolution, such symbolic elements may not always have been entirely conscious on the part of an artist, arising rather from instinctual associations, like our own altered feelings on gazing at the moon after having witnessed an astronaut stepping upon its surface or, in an earlier era, Milton's baroque depiction of the heavens in terms of numberless stars, each a solid entity like earth itself, '. . . that shone/ Stars distant, but nigh hand seem'd other Worlds', in the light of Galileo's revelation that the Milky Way, so long believed to be a celestial stream, was in fact composed of myriads of whirling planetary bodies.[30] So here, the nineteenth-century artist could no longer depict organic forms in nature without expressing at some level of consciousness the disquieting new theories concerning its ruthlessly competitive processes. Mackmurdo's patterns incorporating vegetal forms are, in fact, distinguished by a 'counter-change' system, as one art historian has named it, in which, as the rhythm gathers momentum in one direction, it suddenly switches course to move mysteriously in the other.[31] That element has merely been noted as a personal characteristic, but it should be seen rather as representing one of the most deeply disturbing elements in evolutionary theory, the realization that, in an unpredictable world so different from the fixed and preordained harmony of the universe as it had been traditionally conceived, sudden changes in environmental conditions could demand a dynamic redirection of species-development as a prerequisite for survival. The 'whiplash' motif so widespread in Art Nouveau designs – exemplified by Hermann Obrist's *Cyclamen*, which was described by a contemporary as representing '... the forceful outburst of the elements of nature'[32] – echoes this same concern, translating into iconic or emblematic form these swift developmental changes of direction in an art now stylistically remote from the calm, rural scenes that had so often served as models for poetry and painting in previous generations.

James clearly is not to be identified either in his personal life or in the themes adopted for his fiction with the moral decadence of the *fin de siècle* which he so abhorred, nor indeed with the exhibitionistic dandyism of its more notorious figures – those elements which have discouraged critics from suggesting any identity between them. But with regard to the deeper shared impulse motivating those artistic trends and their larger manifestations at the close of the century, there is much not only in common but of direct relevance to the literary innovations he introduced to the novel genre. The distinguishing element there is his new conception of the writer or artist, including the fictional projection of himself into the created work, in terms of this new emphasis, finding inspiration not in the picturesque hamlet, in the dark mists shrouding the city, in the lonely shepherd, or in the wildness of storm and tempest, but rather within the sculptor's studio, the art gallery, and the museum where, isolated from the vulgarity of the outside world and from the ephemeral setting of nature, he could apply to the eternal artefacts they contained the aesthetic discrimination of a cultivated mind. That realignment of interest demanded, both for the author and for the ideal reader at whom the new novel was aimed, a distancing from the emotional involvement in human affairs which had animated the fiction of Dickens, Eliot and Trollope, the sympathetic depiction of people in the natural cycle of daily activity, such as had formed the staple ingredient of the three-volume novel of the day. Such emotional identification became replaced by the more detached scrutiny of the critic, for whom life had now itself become a form of artefact, to be judged and evaluated rather than experienced. As Arthur Symons defined the ideal of that generation, '. . . the making of one's life into art is after all the first duty and privilege of every man'.[33]

The new interest, accordingly, is in the sophisticate, in the refined judgements of an artistic élite, relishing the intellectual gratification which such interpretive exercise provides. There had been movements in this direction in the later novels of George Eliot which James so admired, notably in *Middlemarch* and *Daniel Deronda*, both concerned with the ideals by which life should be lived; but they were expressed there largely in terms of religious or spiritual striving, in a Dorothea longing for a life of asceticism and dedication or a Deronda impelled to fulfil a prophetic vocation. But here an aesthetic fastidiousness has taken over, in which life itself has become something to be assessed and commented upon, rather than lived.

This stance of critical detachment is espoused not only by the author/narrator but by the fictional characters themselves, who frequently employ a similar objectivity towards their own existence, observing their own decisions, their friendships, and even their experience of love with the cool scrutiny of the *cognoscente*, or of the creative artist moulding his life into the aesthetic form most satisfying to him. Osmond reminds Isabel of the bond between them, the tendency they share which first drew him to her: 'Don't you remember my telling you that one ought to make one's life a work of art?' he remarks, adding, '. . . it was exactly what you seemed to me to be trying to do with your own.' As James asserted in defending himself against H.G. Wells' criticism of his novels, his own purpose was not to reproduce nature: 'It is art that makes life, makes interest, makes importance . . . and I know of no substitute whatever for the force and beauty of its process.'[34]

If James is not to be identified with the moral decadence of Verlaine and Baudelaire, there is nevertheless within his novels a perceptible shift in values. For all its relative moderation, it partook of their recognition that ethical principles were no longer to be regarded as part of a benevolent and divinely supervised natural order, and were therefore no longer mandatory. The very criteria for distinguishing the 'good' characters from the 'bad' have been unobtrusively replaced in his fiction. Those qualities of honesty, kindness, loyalty and generosity that had previously served to identify the nobler figures in the nineteenth-century novel were now gently shunted aside in favour of exquisite sensibility, impeccable manners and artistic refinement.[35] The Prince and Charlotte in *The Golden Bowl* enjoy, without alienating the reader's sympathy, an adulterous relationship which, in the mid-century novel, would have condemned them irrevocably – witness George Osborne in *Vanity Fair*, disqualified as hero solely for the despatch of a billet-doux after his marriage. And despite their exploitation of the Ververs' trust for the crassest of financial reasons, they retain our regard in the context of the novel through the perfect refinement and unfailing good taste which both possess, so that, with no more than a re-arrangement of location, they can at the close be re-instated in their marital positions.[36] The worst reproof the Prince suffers is a hint in his closing dialogue with Maggie that discretion must be preserved and the delicacy of their relationship maintained:

> 'You spoke just now of Charlotte's not having learned from you that I "know". Am I to take from you then that you accept and recognise my knowledge?'
>
> He did the inquiry all the honours – visibly weighed its importance and weighed his response. 'You think I might have been showing you that a little more handsomely?'
>
> 'It isn't a question of any beauty', said Maggie; 'it's only a question of the quantity of truth.'
>
> 'Oh, the quantity of truth!' the Prince richly, though ambiguously, murmured.

As Whistler had claimed in 1878, art was now to be autonomous, unfettered by conventional sentiments or ethical precepts:

> Art should be independent of clap-trap – should stand alone, and appeal to the artistic sense of eye or ear without confounding this with emotions entirely foreign to it, as devotion, pity, love, patriotism, and the like. All these have no kind of concern with it . . .[37]

In James's work too, moral values have become almost irrelevant in the search for 'beauty' and aesthetic impeccability in lifestyle. Within that setting, the flawed golden bowl functions not only as a symbol of the blemished relationship between the characters, but also as a testing-ground for the delicacy of perception which distinguishes them. It serves as the touchstone for their artistic sensibility, confirming for us in Maggie, as much as in the two lovers, the refined taste which attracts them on separate occasions to the same beautiful ornament, while qualifying them to discern the delicate crack hidden beneath the gilt, unidentifiable except to the true expert.

The presence of an art object, as a means of demarcating those characters who possess the taste necessary for acceptance into the select circle of interest to James, pervades all his writings in a manner suggesting that the works of painting and sculpture recurring so frequently in his novels appear there not, as has been generally believed, as aesthetic analogues for his literary innovations, as models for the specific 'perspective' or impressionistic 'brush-work' he was to introduce into his narrative practice. They are there to mark the new priority in his writing, the connoisseur's *appreciation* of those art works irrespective of the latters' period or specific style. The studios which his fictional characters visit, the expensive *bibelots* with which they grace their homes and, above all, the critical acumen requisite for such activity create the ambience necessary for a novel no longer reliant for its themes upon the tribulations of lovers, except insofar as those experiences reflect or reveal aesthetic qualities. In *The Spoils of Poynton*, it is Fleda Vetch's responsiveness to artistic elegance which first endears her to her patroness, her pleasure in the latter's exquisitely designed home; and, exemplifying James's projection of this artistic discrimination on to life itself, the point of the story at large is Fleda's own delicacy of judgement in dealing with the problematic situation into which she finds herself drawn. Adam Verver's avocation as a distinguished collector in *The Golden Bowl*, transporting with him throughout his journeys valuable *objets d'art* to render graceful his hotel rooms and rented *palazzi*, sets the tone for his own treatment of Charlotte, his welcoming of her as a rare acquisition rather than as a wife. The prospect of marriage to her he contemplates much as he would evaluate the purchase of an antique: '. . . he still but held his vision in place, steadying it fairly, with his hands, as he had often steadied for inspection a precarious old pot or kept a glazed picture in its right relation to the light . . .'[38] In that, he reflects the central theme of the novel, the price Maggie must pay for acquiring so very rare and refined a work of art as her Prince. If there is an ambivalence in James's treatment of such acquisitiveness – the suggestion that in this latter instance the price may have proved excessively high – the desire shared by these leading characters for the very finest rarities is in itself invariably treated as a noble and admirable quality.[39] Within that novel, even the metaphor invoked to characterize Maggie's mental processes is of a richly-ornamented fabrication, gracefully constructed to delight the responsive viewer:

> This situation had been occupying, for months and months the very centre of the garden of her life, but it had reared itself there like some strange tall tower of ivory, or perhaps rather some wonderful beautiful but outlandish pagoda, a structure plated with hard, bright porcelain, coloured and figured and adorned at the overhanging eaves with silver bells that tinkled ever so charmingly when stirred by chance airs.[40]

The employment of the art object as a touchstone for aesthetic sensibility operates as a motive force, therefore, in many of the novels. In *The Portrait of a Lady*, Gilbert Osmond instantly discerns in Madame Merle's rare piece of china the infinitesimally small crack that reduces its value, a scene serving not only as a symbol of their own dubious relationship but as evidence establishing for the reader the genuineness of his expertise. He may be proved lacking in moral qualities, despicable in other aspects of his character but it was, we must recall, his civilized deportment that originally attracted Isabel to him, his social grace and perfect manners forming part of his sophistication as an evaluator of art, those traits outshining in her eyes the more solid but less brilliant virtues of Lord Warburton. Moreover, that aspect of her choice is one she never changes nor regrets. She carries away from her early visit to him, we are informed by the narrator, the image of a quiet, clever, sensitive, distinguished man '. . . which her subsequent knowledge of him did nothing to efface . . .'

Although Osmond emerges by the end of the book as self-centred, calculating, and cruel, his aesthetic sensibility is never seen by Isabel as part of those failings. Her reason for regretting her marriage even before she discovers his duplicity with Madame Merle is, as we are explicitly told, not his selfishness. That trait, she generously acknowledges, forms part of the very refinement of taste she had always admired – for there is always an element of selfishness in acquiring personal ownership of art objects. What has proved bitterly disappointing to her is in fact integral to the respect she has for his taste – the discovery, so painful to her ego, that she herself has not merited Osmond's high estimation as a valued acquisition, her retrospective realization that she had been possessed for her wealth rather than for her character, and that the lively independence of judgement on which she prides herself is to him no more than a nuisance. As she recognizes at that moment of self-revelation, her respect for his discrimination remains unimpaired:

> A mind more ingenious, more pliant, more cultivated, more trained to admirable exercises, she had not encountered; and it was this exquisite instrument she had now to reckon with . . . He said to her one day that she had too many ideas and that she must get rid of them. He had told her that already, before their marriage; but then she had not noticed it: it had come back to her only afterwards.

Her continued respect for his sensibility is, James hints, in large part responsible for her returning to Rome at the close of the novel despite her personal disillusionment with their marriage, the fact that, even at his worst, he remains always the epitome of courtesy and good taste. In reply to Harriet's brash enquiry whether Osmond had 'made a scene' over her leaving to visit the dying Ralph, Isabel, correcting such obtuseness, answers with dignity that he had indeed objected, but it '. . . was a very quiet conversation'.[41]

The veneration for the aesthetically exquisite which James shared with contemporary Art Nouveau is equally manifest within the novels in its obverse form. For, if the only figures proving of any lasting interest to him are those belonging to this cultural élite, those unfortunate enough to lack such delicacy of judgement, whether through inferior upbringing or natural ineptitude, can never qualify, whatever their other merits, for more than an amused condescension. Miss Amanda Pynsent in *The Princess Casamassima*, selflessly devoting herself to the care of an adopted orphan, struggling uncomplainingly at her meagre milliner's trade in order to provide the child with his needs, would in a Dickens novel have been presented as an angel of mercy, however humble her status or educational qualifications. But for James she is, by her exclusion from the privileged class of the artistic intellectual – indeed, precisely because of that defect – intrinsically comic in the muddled processes of her thinking and the clumsy method of their execution:

> . . . if Amanda's thoughts were apt to be bewildering visions they sometimes led her to make up her mind, and on this particular

September evening she arrived at a momentous decision. What she made up her mind to was to take advice, and in pursuance of this view she rushed downstairs and, jerking Hyacinth away from his simple but unfinished repast, packed him across the street . . .[42]

The primacy accorded to delicacy, in preference even to ethical integrity, at times functions as the central theme of a novel. James, as has been noted, never approached in his own life, nor in his fictional writings, the defiance of traditional morality flaunted by leaders of the Decadent movement but he did reveal a realignment of values. Mrs Gereth's 'theft' of her son's possessions in *The Spoils of Poynton*, an inheritance indubitably bequeathed to him by his late father, can be condoned neither on legal nor ethical grounds, with Fleda Vetch admitting that the act itself was quite indefensible on those terms. Nonetheless, the older lady's purpose in removing that superb collection of *objets d'art* – consisting of priceless French furniture, oriental china, and invaluable ornaments impeccably arranged with charm and tact – and her desire to rescue them from falling into the hands of an uncouth Mona Brigstock, transforms what might have been an ugly tale of parental interference into a delicate exploration of the conflict between good taste and vulgarity, an enquiry whether any limits, including those of conventional morality, are to be held operative when defending the purity of art from the gross inroads of philistinism. Disgust at Mona's love of 'cheap gimcracks' is seen as justifying for both author and reader the act of pillage itself.[43]

This disdain for Mona, the exclusion of the crude and uncouth from the select circle of the exquisite, was a sentiment shared by the leading proponents of Art Nouveau. Walter Pater had defined style itself as being flight '. . . from a certain vulgarity in the actual world', while his disciple Oscar Wilde, flamboyantly despising the public as coarse and ignorant, revelled in the opprobrium poured upon him as testimony to the common people's lack of taste, dismissing journalists too as writing '. . . with the conscientiousness of the illiterate.'[44] Even William Morris who, in the tradition of Carlyle and Ruskin, claimed that he designed his works with the common people in mind, hoping to bring into ordinary homes articles of daily use which should be aesthetically pleasing, in fact shared this élitism, catering stylistically only for the wealthy patron, and instinctively aligning himself, despite the socialist fervour of his speeches, with the tastes and sensibilities of those artistic circles. The elaborately illustrated edition of Chaucer's work produced by him at the Kelmscott Press was certainly not intended for the road-labourer. As his colleague Frank Colebrook recalled, his insistence upon using paper manufactured from hand-made linen, as well as ink of the very finest quality costing ten shillings a pound, ensured that his prices could never be within the reach of any but the well-to-do.[45] It was not fortuitous, as part of this élitism, that the products of the Arts and Crafts Movement found their main outlet in such expensive stores as Liberty & Co. in London and Tiffany's in New York, and that the most admired Art Nouveau works consisted of exotic jewellery, such as the corsage ornament in the form of a human dragonfly, created in France especially for Sarah Bernhardt by René Lalique.

It is in the context of this cult of refinement, of distancing from the crude and common, that one recognizes how, throughout James's work, vulgarity has become the one unpardonable sin, to be shunned at all times by the initiated. Those persons of civilized intellect and temperament who provide the main interest of his fiction do so in large part by virtue of their fastidiousness, of their being '... properly impressed with the infinite vulgarity of things and of the virtue of keeping one's self unspotted by it.' True nobility, in the Jamesian dispensation, lies not in birth but in this critical aloofness, the ability to discriminate from a position of superiority. The 'aristocratic situation', James informs us through one of his characters, consists of having the supreme good fortune to be in a better position for appreciating people than they are for appreciating you.[46]

James's identification of intellectual discrimination with artistic sensibility explains an element in his novels for which he has often been criticized, the sympathy he extends to the desire of his characters for wealthy marriage even at the expense of love. It is a theme recurrent in his fictional work, deserting the earlier tradition in the novels of Trollope, Dickens or Thackeray where true love accompanied by poverty was to be preferred by their heroes and heroines over the attractions of marital wealth, less highly-principled characters being dismissed as mercenary. For in James's philosophy, to be surrounded by works of art and to possess the financial means to visit the palaces and museums of Europe constituted more than mere comfort or leisure entertainment. As in Art Nouveau at large, such aesthetic pursuits had become a prerequisite for living to which all else must be subordinated, imperative for the preservation of that artistic sensibility which a lack of funds inevitably coarsens and destroys. Hence the indulgence James feels towards the decision of Prince Amerigo and Charlotte to forgo marriage as being quite out of the question on their limited incomes, and his sympathy for Charlotte's choice of a much older man who could supply her with the tasteful ambience, the charming clothes and expensive jewels so essential to her being. If the initial decision of the lovers to part was to lead to near-tragedy, the fault lay, James suggests, in the proximity which their later complex marital situation imposed rather than in the original separation understandably dictated by their needs.

There was a further departure in James's novels from the established practice of earlier fiction, a change in technique to which he himself drew especial attention. George Eliot, he noted with due respect for her achievements, had presented the events in her novels in a manner which made them appear to arise organically out of the specific traits of her fictional characters, their success or failure being 'determined by their feelings and the nature of their minds'. Her reader is thus encouraged to watch the plot developing naturalistically, unfolding before his eyes. James, however, preferred those events to be mediated for the reader, observed through the 'mirror' of a commentator placed between the reader and the events themselves, such individuals selected because they were, as he termed them, 'intense perceivers' of the action.[47] What goes unremarked in his own analysis is perhaps the most significant element in that technique, namely the nature of the commentators whom he chooses for the task. They are not only, as he says, '. . . the most polished of possible mirrors' in reflecting the action. As we discover in the process of reading, they function as far more than passive recorders or transmitters. They analyse and evaluate the events, they ponder them at each stage of their sequential occurrence, and such 'perceivers' – Ralph Touchett in *The Portrait*, Strether in *The Ambassadors*, Fanny Assingham in *The Golden Bowl* – are individuals whose sensibilities are always of the most delicate. When they assess such events, they do so – as projections of James himself – with the critical fastidiousness of an art collector appraising some rare item. The result is, in effect, and again as in Art Nouveau design, a threefold distancing from nature, with the main fictional figures viewing their own lives as artefacts, the 'reflector' figures screening such activity through their aesthetically refined commentary, and James himself providing a third authorial appraisal equally discriminating in its refinement. In place of events intended to evoke the reader's empathic identification with the joys and sufferings of the characters, the criterion now assumed, not only for the leading fictional figures and choric commentator but for the reader too, is the intellectual and artistic pleasure of adding a further specimen of human behaviour to one's collection, a jewelled instance to be stored away for future leisurely contemplation. As the narrator in *The Sacred Fount* revealingly remarks on meeting Guy Brissenden: 'It took but a minute then to add him to my little gallery – the small collection, I mean, represented by his wife and by Gilbert Long . . .'[48] The effectiveness of the novel hence depends less upon emotional response than on the degree to which it satisfies this cerebral faculty of discriminatory evaluation, art existing for art's sake in the fullest sense of the term.

The triple sequence of critical evaluation adopted by James may at times create a certain ambiguity as to the source of a comment, whether, for example, the metaphor of the pagoda originates in Maggie Verver's mind or in the narrator's.[49] At other times, it suggests a play or correspondence between two stages of observation. Ralph Touchett, who comments chorically upon the inner action, is specifically described by James as paralleling in artistic acumen the sensibilities of Gilbert Osmond. The latter's refinement, we learn, had

> . . . made him impatient of vulgar troubles and had led him to live by himself, in a sorted, sifted, arranged world, thinking about art and beauty and history . . . Ralph had something of this same quality, this appearance of thinking that life was a matter of connoisseurship.

The evaluative criteria applied by Osmond to Isabel are, for all their resultant contrasts (emanating from the disparate characters of the assessors), not essentially different from those applied to her by Ralph, both drawing upon artistic sensibility. Ralph, disqualified by his illness from a more intimate relationship, can apply those principles to Isabel's experiences a trifle more freely, providing in the imagery he employs ample evidence of the theme suggested here, the use of art works as the standards for assessing life itself. She had been blessedly handed to him, he notes happily, as a Titian or Greek bas-relief, as some beautiful edifice for which the key had been thrust into his hand with permission to walk in and to admire. Yet she was more than an edifice, she was a fine free nature, intelligent and beautiful, raising the question one asks of so few women, what she would do with herself, how fulfil her intentions: 'Whenever she executes them', said Ralph, 'may I be there to see!'[50] The novel itself is, we may conclude, the study of Isabel as an art work in progress, the portrait of a lady not as a finished product – the specific portrait James may have had in mind is thus scarcely relevant – but a portrait sequentially judged during the process of its creation, a process so stimulating for the critic to watch. Indeed, one recalls how frequent in James's novels are accounts of visits to the studios of artists and sculptors while they are engaged in their work: Rowland with difficulty restraining himself from visiting Roderick Hudson too often lest he disturb the sculptor's concentration; Peter Sherringham impatient to witness Nick Dormer's progress with the portrait of Miriam; the visit of the ladies to view Waterlow's work; and the endless round of calls at the studios of artists and sculptors in Rome, instances so numerous in the fiction as to suggest that the theme held a special significance for James. They are to be seen, in fact, as inner vignettes, representing, from within the narrative, the larger purpose of the novels themselves as studies of life conceived no longer in terms of nature but in terms of art in process.

Historically, this aspect of James's novels marks a further stage in that burgeoning interest in art collection and artistic creativity of a previous generation, represented by such figures as Browning's Bishop ordering his tomb at St. Praxed's, his Fra Lippo Lippi and his Andrea del Sarto. In those poems, the primary purpose had been the achievement of dramatic immediacy, the selection of painters and art patrons as his fictional or semi-historical characters being secondary, as is evidenced by his introduction of other characters demented by jealousy or perverted justice. Now, however, the interest in artistry has intensified, becoming the controlling vision of the work itself, as author, choric figures, and fictional protagonists examine the foibles and aspirations of mankind in search of the 'beauty' or aesthetic pleasure such scenes could supply. Where Wordsworth's *Solitary Reaper* had provided a 'holy' scene of moral import to be treasured in the mind for further contemplation – 'Stop here or gently pass' – and Dickens' harrowing scenes were aimed at arousing social indignation, the new focus is upon the rare and beautiful. As Fanny Assingham warns her husband, while speculating on Maggie's likely response to the crisis of the Prince's infidelity:

'We must keep our hands off, we must go on tiptoe. We must simply watch and wait. And meanwhile', said Mrs Assingham, 'we must bear it as we can. That's where we are – and serves us right. We're in presence.'

And so, moving about the room as in communion with shadowy portents, she left it till he questioned again. 'In presence of what?'

'Well, of something possibly beautiful. Beautiful as it may come off.'[51]

The centrality of this aesthetic pursuit in his novels places in doubt the extraordinary comment made recently by a respected critic, Marianne Torgovnick, that the visits to studios and the concern with painters and sculptors are entirely peripheral, such scenes of artistic creativity being mere props or adjuncts in James's work. She remarks that since, in *The Tragic Muse*, we are never offered any detailed description of Nick Dormer's paintings, they are of no real significance to the novel and '. . . poor Nick might as well be knitting.'[52] But it is surely not the specific painting Nick is engaged upon nor the specific school of art with which he aligns himself that is significant for the novel. It is the principle he suggests of dedication to artistic form, a withdrawal from political activity into the world of the artefact, symbolizing the novel's major concern. All fiction involves a transformation of life into art, but the philosophy of 'Art-for-Art's-Sake' constituted an intensification or doubling of that principle. Roland Barthes, in *The Pleasure of the Text*, which develops in semiotic terms Gombrich's interpretation of art as illusion and Wittgenstein's concept of language as signs, has demanded that the modern writer and artist acknowledge the synthetic quality of their work, the fact that it is only a series of signifiers. But the originality of that approach has been recently questioned by George Levine, whose *The Realistic Imagination* has revealed the extent to which nineteenth-century writers, long before such post-modernist demands, had been acutely conscious of the representational aspects of their medium.[53] There is, however, a vital distinction; for if those earlier writers were aware of the problem, they continued, in conformity to the long-established maxim *ars est celare artem*, to attempt to conceal or camouflage the factitiousness. Art Nouveau, in contrast, turned the maxim on its head, seeking as a principal aim to highlight the work's remoteness from the natural, with James reflecting the new mode by his direction of reader response away from spontaneous emotional identification with his characters in favour of an intellectual savouring of each scene in terms of its artistic representation, evaluated through the eyes of a sophisticated observer employing the fastidiousness of a gourmet testing the bouquet of a rare-vintage wine.

The contrast with previous tradition afforded by that *fin-de-siècle* view finds its fullest expression, I believe, in Yeats' poem *Sailing to Byzantium*, where the speaker, longing to escape from the endless Darwinian struggle for survival within nature, the proliferating salmon-falls and swarming mackerel-crowded seas, yearns for the gold eternity of a Byzantine mosaic, remote from such mutability and ephemerality. Underlying the poem may be perceived an intertextual evocation of Keats' *Ode to a Nightingale*, with its essentially similar yearning for escape from the mortality of the human condition, 'Where palsy shakes a few, sad, last gray hairs,/ Where youth grows pale, and spectre-thin, and dies . . .' But while Keats, still seeing art as integral to nature and attempting to capture in his verse the harmonies and beauties of the natural world, had visualized poetry in terms of the living nightingale, its song renewed from generation to generation, Yeats, eschewing natural form as being part of that same wearisome reproductive cycle, rejects the image in favour of the bird as jewelled artefact:

> Once out of nature I shall never take
> My bodily form from any natural thing,
> But such a form as Grecian goldsmiths make
> Of hammered gold and gold enamelling
> To keep a drowsy Emperor awake;
> Or set upon a golden bough to sing
> To lords and ladies of Byzantium
> Of what is past, or passing, or to come.[54]

It is the same conception, it would seem, as had motivated his contemporary Carl Fabergé in producing, for the royalty and aristocracy of Europe, those exquisite birds, animals, and flowers deliberately wrought as artefacts, fashioned unnaturally of nephrite and diamonds, in rock crystal and sardonyx – including (Fig. 31) a bird carved from white opal, its eyes set with Siam rubies, perched upon a golden bough within a golden cage.[55] Most famous of those creations was his series of jewelled eggs, such as the 'Coronation Egg' presented by Nicholas II to the Czarina to commemorate their accession to the throne in 1896 (Fig. 32), and containing a replica in gold of the ceremonial coach used by them on that occasion. The egg, the progenitor of natural life, is here stylized to the highest degree. Meticulously crafted of enamelled, translucent lime-yellow, caged in green-gold trellis-work and studded with brilliant diamonds, it discards all pretence at verisimilitude. So Mark Ambient in *The Author of Beltraffio*, embodying both the author's dedication to art and the dangers such dedication may involve, echoes James's own compositional techniques as he visualizes the form of his forthcoming novel:

> 'This new affair must be a golden vessel, filled with the purest distillation of the actual; and oh how it worries me, the shaping of the vase, the hammering of the metal! I have to hammer it so fine, so smooth . . .'

adding a few moments later: 'The effort to arrive at a surface . . . if you could see the surface I dream of as compared with the one which I've to content myself. Life's really too short for art – one hasn't time to make one's shell ideally hard . . .'[56]

In a sense, Yeats' Byzantium, the world of golden mosaic isolated from a distasteful Nature, is the analogue to James' Europe, whose museums and galleries serve similarly as the admirable repositories of an aesthetic past. The polished manners of European aristocratic society, representing the ancient patronage and cultivation of those arts, constituted for him an intellectual refuge from the brash 'naturalism' of young America, thrusting towards conquest of its open spaces as part of its own vigorous struggle for survival and characterized by him, with a certain ironic humour, through the Henrietta Stackpoles and Caspar Goodwoods of his novels. F.O. Matthiessen many years ago suggested a parallel between the zest for life in Whitman and what he saw as a similar urge in James, expressed in such figures as Roderick Hudson, although he admitted that there was a certain 'attenuation' in the Jamesian version, a detachment in which (as the author himself described it) the only form of riot or revel he would experience would be 'of the visiting mind'.[57] That supposedly minor difference may indeed be fundamental, divorcing James from Whitman and perhaps even accounting for James's spiritual and physical expatriation. For while Whitman continued the Romantic tradition of passionate response to the world around him and Thoreau, like the Hudson River artists, perpetuated its revelling in the beauties of unspoilt nature, James

had moved away from that natural world to the seclusion of the art
gallery, and to the adoption of a new code in which cerebral discrimination, the dispassionate, considered assessment of the spectator, has displaced such emotional fervour and spontaneity. It is
worthy of note that James's authorial identification was, in fact,
not with the young explorer of life nor with the creative artist
as Matthiessen suggested, but with the connoisseur – not with
the sculptor Roderick but with his patron and advisor Rowland.
As James himself remarked in his 'Preface' to the novel:

> My subject, all blissfully, in the face of difficulties, had defined
> itself – and this in spite of the title of the book – as not directly,
> in the least, my young sculptor's adventure. This it had been but
> indirectly, being all the while in essence and in final effect another
> man's, his friend's and patron's, view and experience of him.[58]

Similarly, while the youthful Chad, experiencing the zest of life,
may be the object of the expedition in *The Ambassadors*, it is the
observer Strether with whom James empathizes, an observer too
detached and withdrawn from the vigour of life to accept the offer
of Miss Gostrey's love. James could depict such eagerness for living
in others, but his own preference, both in the sympathies he manifested for his fictional characters and in the conduct of his own life,
was withdrawal into the golden eternity of art, into the cultivated
world of Europe in which he found his imaginative Byzantium.[59]

In this context, therefore, the underlying contrast in his novels
between a somewhat uncouth young America and the cultivated
modes of an older Europe takes on a more symbolic function,
expressing in literary form the contemporary turning away of Art
Nouveau from an aggressive, self-generating Nature, no longer satisfying the poetic soul. As I argued in the introduction to this volume, the way the artist sees the world about him is intimately related
to the vision he has of the universe at large, his 'perspective' of the
relationship of daily existence to it, whether in terms of a divinely
ordered creation, of a metaphysical entity transcending reality, of
a rationally conceived mechanism or, as in this present instance, of
a nature driven by impersonal forces of eternal struggle, imaged
in Yeats as the swarming mackerel seas. From such a world, James,
like so many artists of his generation, retreated with disfavour, finding his comfort and his understanding of the human condition in the
aesthetic pleasure which, like the more sensitive American characters

in his novels, he sought in the elegant houses, studios and architectural splendours of Rome, Paris and London, fascinating in their very remoteness from that vigorously thriving country across the seas which had come to symbolize for him many of the distasteful elements in that thrust for survival. He was fully aware of the moral decay inherent in civilized Europe, in the faded glory of the De Bellegardes and in the dubious heritage of aristocratic families distinguished for past crimes, scandals, and abominable cruelties no less than for their erstwhile wealth and ancient patronage, so that the contrast is not always favourable to that older civilization. Yet in that respect too, in his implicit admission that moral decay does not nullify the artistic pursuit, he was reflecting the new standards formulated in the art circles of his day, with their elevation of aesthetic criteria above established moral values.

Literary style is, at its best, organically related to content, expressing in outward form the philosophical or aesthetic assumptions inherent in the work itself. The complaint, so frequently voiced, that James's novels are excessively stylized would seem in this setting to be a judgement based, paradoxically, on the very standards James consciously rejected. F.R. Leavis complained of James's obsession with mere technique, with exhausting delicacies, and with an incapacity for directness, Edmund Wilson condemned the gratuitous verbiage and roundabout locution, such pejorative observations frequently echoed, if less mordantly, by later critics up to and including our own day. The emphasis now, still generally negative, has shifted to structuralist, formalist and deconstructive analysis identifying, as in Mary Cross's recent study, his 'verbal machinations and disorienting effects' as resulting from a doomed quest for truth.[60] But James's stylistic aim had not been the naturalistic flow of George Eliot, the boisterous vitality of Dickens, or the provincial realism of Trollope. The verbal preciosity of his style, like the jewelled eyes of the Fabergé bird, represented, as we have seen, an aversion to the mundane, a desire to distance his work from the hackneyed and commonplace. Hence that feature so characteristic of his writings, the introduction within quotation marks of colloquial terms, as though he were holding aloft with amused antipathy some grubby phrase in natural, common usage, with which neither he nor the reader would normally soil their speech. Roderick Hudson, pondering whether he is still formally engaged to be married, asks himself: 'Was the old understanding "off", or was Mary, in spite of humiliation, keeping it on?'; Fleda Vetch acknowledges that it would seem intolerably vulgar to her 'to have "ousted" the daughter of the Brigstocks'; and Peter Sherringham felt that, since '. . . he had "taken up" the dark-browed girl and her reminiscential mother', he must face the consequences of his act.

Such fastidiousness frequently constitutes the bond, the source of implicit understanding between the more refined characters, allowing for a dialogue elevated above the banal by its unstated assumptions. There is an allusive quality which assumes on the part of the interlocutor – and, by extension, on the part of the reader too – a heightened perceptiveness and delicacy of judgement which makes mere words unnecessary, as each responds less to the content of a previous remark than to its nuances, picking up an unfinished phrase, weighing it, querying it, often completing it to the satisfaction of the speaker. Thus Strether finds in Miss Gostrey a confidante sensitive enough to share, without explicit statement, a reflective appraisal of the progress of his enquiry:

'I admit I was surprising even to myself.'
   'And then, of course', Maria went on, 'I had much to do with it.'
   'With my being surprising – ?'
   'That will do', she laughed, 'if you're too delicate to call it *my* being! Naturally', she added, 'you came over more or less for surprises.'
   'Naturally!' – he valued the reminder.
   'But they were to have been all for you' – she continued to piece it out – 'and none of them for her.'[61]

In the Jamesian sentence, adverbs obtrude in unnatural positions, interrupting the normal speech-flow. But designedly so. The effect of such usage is to encourage a pause for leisurely assessment of the depicted scene, a reconsideration of it in accordance with an undefined but assumed hierarchy of values which merges moral, social and intellectual criteria into an all-embracing aesthetic standard – 'Maggie, wonderfully, in the summer days . . .' he will comment authorially, or 'It was, beautifully, . . .' Such adverbial insertions have their counterpart in his technique of placing the attributions of quoted speech not, as in accepted usage, at the end of the sentence cited nor at a convenient comma which rounds off a logically completed phrase, but rather at a point of obvious intrusion, to create that same evaluative pause in which to ponder the significance of the judgement and, at the same time, to break up the natural flow, reminding us that the scene as presented is an artefact, transmitted through the critical assessment of the fictional narrator:

'It really', said Mrs Assingham, 'was, practically, the fine side of the wedge. Which struck me as also', she wound up, 'a lovely note for the candour of the Ververs.'

The effect is once again to focus attention away from the actual events of the story – the plot development upon which the mainstream nineteenth-century novel had so heavily relied and which James had identified as the characteristic mode of George Eliot – to the task of appraising those events in terms of exquisite sensibility. Natural speech is deserted in his works in favour of a form of dialogue designed to sound stilted, a dialogue so sophisticated that it represents a distillation of thought processes rather than a realistic verbal exchange. Such dialogue provides, indeed, for his admirers one of the major gratifications offered by the novels, the recurrent pleasure in witnessing, as it were, two intellectuals savouring the nuances in each other's critical pronouncements, enjoying, even more than the subject-matter itself, the aesthetic satisfaction such finely-tuned perceptiveness affords.

Final authenticity, then, as in the contemporary plastic arts, no longer resides in the faithful mirroring of reality or of 'nature' with art seen as imitatively subservient to the latter. It is now an accolade bestowed upon the artefact itself, whose preciosity or contrived stylization denotes a deliberate distancing from mimetic fidelity. The famous cartoon by George du Maurier, depicting a young bride holding aloft their newly-acquired piece of porcelain and earnestly exclaiming, 'Oh, Algernon, let us live up to it!' captured in humorous form a very serious principle of the time, and a recurrent motif in James's fiction. Throughout his writings there is a sense that the worthiest challenge for humanity is, indeed, to live up to the lofty standards of art. Milly Theale in *The Wings of the Dove*, moved by Bronzino's noble portrait of a lady, murmurs through her tears, 'I shall never be better than this'; and Strether in *The Ambassadors*, impressed by the beauty of the countryside, distills the experience by transforming the natural scene into a painting, visualizing it in terms of a Lambinet canvas: 'The oblong gilt frame disposed its enclosing lines; the poplars and willows, the reeds and river . . . fell into a composition, full of felicity, within them.'[62] Truth rests finally with the ideal work of art, with the perfect painting, novel or drama, of which (with echoes of Plato) life itself has now become only a poor shadow or reflection. *The Tragic Muse*, exploring as its central theme this altered aesthetic ranking, has Peter Sherringham apprehending in a moment of revelation how unimportant was the mundane existence of the brilliant actress Miriam Rooth in the real world, how irrelevant her daily life in comparison to the lasting supremacy of her art:

> Her character was simply to hold you by the particular spell; any other – the good nature of home, the relation to her mother, her friends, her lovers, her debts, the practice of virtues or industries or vices – was not worth speaking of. These things were the fictions and shadows; the representation was the deep substance.[63]

As he had declared earlier: 'I am fond of representation – the representation of life. I like it better, I think, than the real thing.' And Miriam Rooth herself, the counterpart to Nick Dormer the painter, offers James an opportunity of musing on the relationship between art and life, the validity to be accorded to each, and the demands they place upon the creative artist.

To maintain, as has been argued,[64] that James knew too little about the technicalities of the plastic arts to present effectively the struggles of a Roderick Hudson or Nick Dormer is to misunderstand his purpose, which was not to offer instruction to the contemporary painter or sculptor, but to present through those fictive figures a projection of his own dilemma as an author, eventually choosing in his own life – like Paul in 'The Lesson of the Master' – in effect to withdraw from the hurly-burly of living, to renounce love, marriage, home and children in favour of dedication to the eternal artifice, remaining, like Ralph Touchett, upon the sidelines of existence, in order to observe, comment, and evaluate with admirable finesse the activities of his fellow beings.[65]

My purpose in this chapter has not been to identify James with the specific form of 'Art-for-Art's-Sake' as represented by Wilde or Beardsley, of whom, as we have seen, he so strongly disapproved;[66] but rather to consider his novels as an independent expression, within literature, of the same fundamental impulses as had motivated Art Nouveau and stimulated the work of Tiffany, Lalique, and Fabergé, most notably the growing distrust, during the later decades of the century, of Nature as the inspiration and model for Art. It was in the fulfilment of that broader late-nineteenth-century impulse, the altered view of the relationship between Art and Nature, it may be argued, that James found it necessary to create new objectives for the novel, to restructure its forms, and to refashion its stylistic patterns. In the context of his desire to depict a cultural élite attempting to achieve in its lifestyle the rarefied quality of pure art, the museums and galleries, the paintings, the sculpture, and the architectural works recurring throughout his novels both as images and as plot elements serve not as paradigms for his own literary innovations, nor as specific models for his own stylistic forms, as critics have so long assumed. Rather, they serve as the *mise-en-scène* for the new type of fictional character engaging his interest. Those art works served instead as touchstones for the aesthetic perceptiveness of his leading figures, and as indications of the sensitivity they are to apply to their own careers, friendships and marital relations. The thematic and narrative forms he created for the novel may not be identical at all points with the theory and practice of Art Nouveau; but in that fundamental redirection of fiction from emotional empathy to the cerebral and the discriminatory, and from natural discourse to the preciosity of stylized formalism, he was fulfilling a cultural motivation shared by the artists of his time.

The changes we have been following marked a major reorientation in the arts, even within the comparatively brief period of Victoria's reign. The fervour of a Carlyle, his heroes inflaming their contemporaries with the blaze of a Turner canvas, the amusing animation of objects in Dickens' fiction reflecting the Victorian proclivity for impressing furnishings, architecture, and bric-à-brac with the personalities of their owners, and Hopkins' fascination, like the Post-Impressionist painters, with the mutual interaction of adjacency have been replaced in James's novels by a new concern with 'Art-for-Art's-Sake' and the sophistication of the connoisseur. Those changes epitomize the requirement from all the media, from literature as well as painting, architecture and sculpture, that they respond to the altered conditions and perspectives of the time, to challenges and conceptions varying not only from era to era but even from decade to decade, and, by such shared concerns, revealing illuminating affinities between those diverse forms of aesthetic expression.

Notes and References

INTRODUCTION

1. Roland Barthes, *S/Z* (Paris, 1970), p. 16. On intertextuality, see especially Julia Kristeva, *Semiotiké: récherches pour une sémanalyse* (Paris, 1969), p. 146, and on the oedipal conflict between writers and their predecessors, Harold Bloom, *The Anxiety of Influence: a theory of poetry* (New York, 1973).

2. Stephen Greenblatt, *Shakespearean Negotiations: the circulation of social energy in Renaissance England* (Berkeley, 1988), p. 86. Readers alert to the most recent trends in critical theory, in the areas both of literary research and of art history, will have perceived the emergence in the past decade of a swing back to the necessity once again of 'situating' works and events within the cultural motifs of their time. Donald Preziosi's *Rethinking Art History* (New Haven, 1989), for example, especially pp. 48–50, resists the view of art fostered by Baxandall, Fried and others, who had seen it as 'representation' in the narrower sense, as a second reality existing alongside the day-to-day. That view, Preziosi argues, has led to the near exclusion of the importance of art as a powerful social instrument for the creation and maintenance of the world we live in, and he claims that the time has come to reinstate the latter view, to replace art within the cultural and social setting of its time. For the earlier view, see Michael Baxandall, *Painting and Experience in Fifteenth-century Italy* (Oxford, 1972) and Michael Fried, *Absorption and Theatricality: painting and beholder in the age of Diderot* (Berkeley, 1980).

3. Cf. for example, the perception of Victorian Neo-Gothic architecture as a partially unconscious attempt to evoke the authoritative rule of past eras at a time of social unrest and threatened Jacobinism, in Alice Chandler, *A Dream of Order: the medieval ideal in nineteenth-century English literature* (Lincoln, Na., 1970); and on commodity culture, Jonathan Freedman, *Professions of Taste* (Stanford, 1990).

4. Arnold Hauser's stimulating study, *The Social History of Art* 4 vols (New York, 1951) adopted a primarily one-directional approach, assuming in Marxist terms that almost all developments in the arts are attributable to capitalist processes, rather than to the continuous interaction of artist or writer with a much wider range of fluctuations in contemporary society, including the philosophical, religious and scientific.

5. The Madonna painting depicted in Leighton's canvas and described in the title as a Cimabue was, in fact, identified in later years as a Duccio. William Gaunt's biography *Victorian Olympus* (London, 1952) describes the admiration aroused by the young Leighton.

6. The literary implications are examined in Earl Miner, 'That Literature is a Kind of Knowledge', *Critical Inquiry*, 2 (1976), 501; and W.J.T. Mitchell, 'Spatial Form in Literature: towards a general theory', *Critical*

Inquiry, 6 (1980), 539 (which quotes Wayne Booth's comment without recording the source). There is an account of the history of spatial concepts and their psychological implications in Max Jammer, *Concepts of Space* (New York, 1960), pp. 3–4, and of spatial metaphor in Rudolf Arnheim's essay 'Space as an Image of Time', in K. Kroeber and W. Walding (ed.), *Images of Romanticism* (New Haven, 1978), pp. 1–12.

7. As Alice herself remarks of this poem: 'Somehow it seems to fill my head with ideas – only I don't exactly know what they are.' The section devoted to him below, in the chapter on Dickens, provides details of Carroll's careful supervision of the drawings, as well as a fuller discussion of the way his work manifests his religious concerns.

8. As part of the distrust of interart studies related to historical periods, there has emerged in recent years a focus upon *ekphrasis*, the attempt by writers, especially poets, to describe or respond verbally to paintings or other artefacts, that response being seen in post-modernist criticism as revealing an intrinsic conflict between word and image. Such instances are outside the parameters of this present study, which concentrates instead upon the filaments connecting writer and artist as they function organically within their own media, not in those rarer instances of a hybrid art form. The two leading works in that critical field have been Murray Krieger's *Ekphrasis: the illusion of the natural sign* (Baltimore, 1991) and W.J.T. Mitchell's 'Ekphrasis and the Other' *South Atlantic Quarterly*, 91 (1992), 695, for which his *Iconology: image text, ideology* (Chicago, 1986) had laid the groundwork. For a recent and informative collection of essays on this theme, see Carol T. Christ and John O. Jordan (ed.), *Victorian Literature and Victorian Visual Imagination* (Berkeley, 1995).

1 CARLYLE'S 'FIRE-BAPTISM'

1. The oscillations in Carlyle's reputation are documented in Jules P. Seigel (ed.), *Thomas Carlyle: the Critical Heritage* (London, 1971); in G.B. Tennyson, 'Carlyle Today', published in K.J. Fielding and Rodger L. Tarr (eds), *Carlyle Past and Present: a collection of new essays* (New York, 1976); in Michael Goldberg, 'A Universal "howl of execration": Carlyle's Latter-day Pamphlets and their critical reception' in John Clubbe (ed.), *Carlyle and his Contemporaries* (Durham, NC, 1976), and in Fred Kaplan, *Thomas Carlyle: a biography* (Cambridge, 1983).

2. George Eliot's unsigned review in the *Leader*, 27 October, 1855. The biblical background to Carlyle's secular preaching is discussed in George P. Landow, 'Elegant Jeremiahs: the genre of the Victorian sage' in John Clubbe and Jerome Meckier (eds), *Victorian Perspectives: six essays* (London, 1989), pp. 21f.

3. In a letter to John Sterling who had criticized the un-Englishness of his writing, Carlyle replied by enquiring whether it was a time for purity of style when everything was in a state of flux, '. . . our Johnsonian English breaking up from its foundations, – revolution there as visible as anywhere else.' His response implies his conscious

dissociation from the Johnsonian tradition. The exchange of letters is reprinted in C.F. Harrold's edition of *Sartor Resartus* (New York, 1937), pp. 305–25. For a postmodern examination of the 'indecorousness' of Carlyle's style, see Geoffrey Hartman, *Criticism in the Wilderness: a study of literature today* (New Haven, 1980), pp. 133f., as well as David Riede, 'The Church of Literature and Carlyle' in Jerome J. McGann (ed.), *Victorian Connections* (Charlottesville, 1989), pp. 88f.

4.   Elizabeth Barrett (Browning), in *A New Spirit of the Age* (New York, 1844), pp. 333f. The review was probably altered, with her permission, by her editor Richard H. Horne, but is regarded by scholars as substantially her own composition.

5.   Thackeray's review of *The French Revolution* in *The Times*, 3 August, 1837.

6.   *Sartor Resartus* in *Complete Works: the 'University' edition* (New York, 1885), 1:168, all subsequent quotations being from this edition.

7.   Terry Eagleton, *Literary Theory: an introduction* (Minneapolis, 1983), especially pp. 601f., and Richard Rorty, *The Consequences of Pragmatism* (Minneapolis, 1982), p. 92.

8.   *French Revolution*, 3:137–8.

9.   Carlyle did write some poetry, but only in an amateur way. It is available in Rodger L. Tarr and Fleming McClelland (eds), *The Collected Poems of Thomas and Jane Carlyle* (Greenwood, 1986).

10.   Letter to J.H. Rigg dated 5 April, 1857 in *Charles Kingsley: his letters and memories of his life* edited by his wife (London, 1877) 2:22–3.

11.   Quoted in Fielding and Tarr, p. 18, from f. 4v of the manuscript. The Forster Collection in the Library of the Victoria and Albert Museum contains some early drafts for Carlyle's projected biography of Oliver Cromwell, a work which he never completed.

12.   Cf. David V. Erdman, *Blake: prophet against empire* (New York, 1954), a pioneer study in revealing the poet's relationship to contemporary politics, aesthetics, and social change, and my own *Prophet and Poet: the Bible and the Growth of Romanticism* (London, 1965), pp. 159–71, which connected Blake's 'prophetic' poems, both in their form and their passionate content, with Robert Lowth's eighteenth-century discovery, widely influential at the time, that the basis of biblical poetry was not quantitative or accentual metre, but a loose parallelism of phrases, a fervent repetition of sentiments.

13.   Karl Kroeber, 'Romantic Historicism: the temporal sublime', in Karl Kroeber and William Walling (eds), *Images of Romanticism: verbal and visual affinities* (New Haven, 1978) and developed in his *British Romantic Art* (Berkeley, 1986), pp. 143–52. The Tolstoy quotation is from the Everyman edition of *War and Peace* (New York, 1948), 3:319. For a comparison of this painting to Coleridge's *Ancient Mariner* in terms of the romantic sublime, see James B. Twitchell, *Romantic Horizons: aspects of the sublime in English poetry and painting, 1770–1850* (Columbia Mo., 1983), pp. 85f. There is a useful listing of vortex and whirlwind images culled from Carlyle's *French Revolution* in Chris Brooks, *Signs for the Times: symbolic realism in the mid-Victorian world* (London, 1984), pp. 16–17.

14. Peter Conrad, *The Victorian Treasure-House* (London, 1973), p. 43. Dickens was, of course, a great admirer of Carlyle, and is said to have carried a copy of the *French Revolution* everywhere with him on its first appearance – cf. J.A. Froude, *Thomas Carlyle: a history of his life in London, 1834–1882* (London, 1910), 1:93. The early influence is discussed in Michael Slater, 'Carlyle and Jerrold into Dickens: a study of The Chimes' in Ada Nisbet and Blake Nevius (eds), *Dickens Centennial Essays* (Berkeley, 1971), pp. 184f., and more generally in William Oddie, *Dickens and Carlyle: the question of influence* (London, 1972) and Michael Goldberg, *Carlyle and Dickens* (Athens, Ga., 1972). Dickens' most conscious imitation of Carlyle was, however, to be delayed until his *Tale of Two Cities* in 1859. The quotation is from *Barnaby Rudge*, Chapter 68. John Carey, *Here Comes Dickens: the imagination of the novelist* (New York, 1973), pp. 14–15, notes the prevalence of fire imagery in the novels.

15. Shelley, 'The Cloud', lines 9–12 in *Complete Poetical Works* (edited by Thomas Hutchinson) (Oxford, 1917).

16. J. Hillis Miller, '"Hierographical Truth" in *Sartor Resartus*: Carlyle and the language of parable', in John Clubbe and Jerome Meckier (eds), *Victorian Perspectives*, p. 1.

17. The prominence of 'light-fire' imagery in his work has long been noted, as in John Holloway, *The Victorian Sage: studies in argument* (New York, 1965), pp. 28–9, and G.B. Tennyson, *Sartor Called Resartus: the genesis, structure, and style of Thomas Carlyle's first major work* (Princeton, 1965), pp. 198–201. Gerry H. Brookes, *The Rhetorical Form of Carlyle's 'Sartor Resartus'* (Berkeley, 1972) is concerned with the thematic structure of the work and only tangentially with the literary style and imagery. The final quotation on the cities is from *Sartor Resartus*, 1:130.

18. Quotations from John Walker, *J.M.W. Turner* (New York, 1976), pp. 55–6.

19. *Collected Correspondence of J.M.W. Turner* (edited by John Gage) (Oxford, 1980), p. 99.

20. Cf. Claude Lévi-Strauss, *Myth and Literature* (London, 1975); Roland Barthes, *Mythologies* (trans. A. Lavers) (Frogmore, 1973); and Frank Kermode, *The Sense of an Ending* (New York, 1967). The application of these and other mythological approaches to nineteenth-century studies is exemplified in the collection of essays *The Sun is God: painting, literature and mythology in the nineteenth century* (edited by J.B. Bullen) (Oxford, 1989). For Victorian interest in solar mythology, which reached its peak in time for Ruskin but too late to influence Turner, see especially two essays in that collection, Dinah Birch, '"The Sun is God": Ruskin's Solar Mythology' and Gillian Beer, '"The Death of the Sun": Victorian Solar Physics and Solar Myth.' There was, within science, a general interest at this time in the sun as a source of light, Sir David Brewster, Joseph Plateau, and Gustav Fechner all severely damaging their eye-sight (Plateau became permanently blind) as a result of gazing directly at it for lengthy periods in order to investigate its effect upon the eye. For details, see Jonathan Crary,

Techniques of the Observer: on vision and modernity in the nineteenth century (Cambridge Ma., 1990), pp. 141f.

21. An overview of these early studies in anthropology is provided in B. Feldman and R.D. Richardson, *The Rise of Modern Mythology, 1680–1860* (Bloomington, 1972). The passage from Jones's essay 'On the Gods of Greece, Italy, and India' appears in A.M. Jones (ed.), *Works* (London, 1807), 3:385–6.

22. John Gage, 'J.M.W. Turner and Solar Myth' in *The Sun is God*, pp. 39f., examines the painter's debt to Knight, Jones, and others, but makes no distinction there between the earlier and later phases of his work.

23. A.G.H. Bachrach offers a detailed examination of Turner's relationship to the Dutch painters in the *Dutch Quarterly Review of Anglo-American Letters* (1976), 6:88f. On Lord Bridgewater's loan to the British Institution, see Martin Butlin and Evelyn Joll (eds), *The Paintings of J.M.W. Turner* (New Haven, 1984), text volume, p. 13.

24. Martin and Joll (eds), p. 173. John Gage's explanation has been challenged by Andrew Wilton, *Turner and the Sublime* (New Haven, 1980), p. 143, who identifies as Regulus one of the small figures to the right, while Cecilia Powell has argued in her *Turner in the South* (New Haven, 1987), pp. 145–51, for the small figure with his arms raised at the left. But Gage's reading is more convincing (and still generally accepted), as there is no logical justification for the artist's placing of the main character in a peripheral, even disputable location.

25. *Literary Gazette*, 4 February, 1837.

26. Andrew Wilton, *J.M.W. Turner: his life and art* (New York, 1979), p. 216f., supports the view that Petworth marks the turning-point, noting how critics in 1829 responded to the new works as marking a 'violent departure' from his former style. Philipp Fehl, in his important essay 'Turner's Classicism and the Problem of Periodization in the History of Art', *Critical Inquiry*, 3 (1976), 93, argues that the artist's continued admiration for Claude militates against any interpetation of his work as adumbrating Impressionism. I am not, of course, concerned here with his relationship to that later school, but the marked stylistic change during the Petworth period, while it did not end his admiration for the classicism Claude represented, would seem to reveal an essentially new commitment within his own work. Historical aspects of this period of his career appear in Martin Butlin, Mollie Luther and Ian Warrell, *Turner at Petworth* (London, 1989).

27. 'Lines Written Among the Euganean Hills', 206–13 in *Complete Poetical Works* (edited by Thomas Hutchinson) (Oxford, 1917), p. 552. The comparison of Turner to Shelley is discussed in Hugh Honour's perceptive interart study, *Romanticism* (New York, 1979), pp. 100–2.

28. *French Revolution*, 4:270–1.

29. *French Revolution*, 4:385 and 3:52.

30. The basic study is still C.F. Harrold, *Carlyle and German Thought, 1819–1834* (New Haven, 1934). But see also Terry Eagleton, *The Ideology of the Aesthetic* (Oxford, 1991), especially pp. 123f. for the shift in emphasis within German philosophy of this time.

31. John Gage, *Color in Turner: poetry and truth* (New York, 1969) examines the revolution in colour theory occurring during Turner's lifetime and the latter's reactions, both in theory and practice, to the various innovative ideas. Frederick Burwick has provided a detailed analysis of Turner's colour in *The Damnation of Newton: Goethe's color theory and Romantic perception* (Berlin, 1986); and see also Gerald Finley, 'Pigment into Light: Turner, and Goethe's Theory of Colours', *European Romantic Review*, 2 (1991), 39. In 1843, Turner exhibited two paintings based upon Goethe's theory, *Shade and Darkness: the Evening of the Deluge* and *Light and Colour: the Morning after the Deluge*. On aspects of the painter's development as an artist, see also John Gage's valuable study, *J.M.W. Turner: 'a wonderful range of mind'* (New Haven, 1987).

32. John Holloway, *The Victorian Sage*, especially in the opening chapter.

33. *Past and Present*, 12:184.

34. *Heroes and Hero-worship*, 1:329 and 381.

35. *Heroes and Hero-worship*, 1:309 and 296.

36. Cf. John P. McGowan, *Representation and Revelation: Victorian realism from Carlyle to Yeats* (Columbia Mo., 1986), p. 63.

37. From Brooks, *Signs for the Times*.

38. *Sartor Resartus*, 1:168–9.

39. Seemingly hesitant to pronounce his own judgement, Carlyle inserts, in one of his rare references to the visual arts, a protective parenthesis: 'Raphael, the Painters tell us, is the best of all Portrait-painters . . .', *Heroes and Hero-worship*, 1:322.

40. Ronald Paulson, 'Turner's Graffiti: the sun and its glosses', in *Images of Romanticism*, ed. cit., pp. 167–88. Quotations from Milton's invocation to Book 3 of *Paradise Lost* in *Complete Poems* (edited by Merritt Y. Hughes) (New York, 1957), p. 257, and Pope, *An Essay on Criticism*, 2:315–17, in the Twickenham edition, ed. John Butt (New Haven, 1970), p. 153. John Dixon Hunt suggests in 'Wondrous Deep and Dark: Turner and the sublime', *Georgia Review*, 30 (1976), 139, that the indefiniteness of Turner's paintings and his preference for uncompleted sketches, which '. . . pleased me beyond the best finishing', marked his acceptance of Burke's theory identifying the element of suggestiveness in the sublime.

41. Hazlitt's review appeared in *The Champion*, 12 May, 1816.

42. The genuineness of this painting is discussed in Butlin and Joll, p. 97. Alexander J. Finberg notes in his *Life of J.M.W. Turner* (Oxford, 1961) p. 476, that it was based upon a sketch made at the time of the eruption by Hugh P. Keane, Turner himself not having been present at the scene.

43. On the importance of this painting in Turner's development, see Carl Woodring, 'Road Building: Turner's *Hannibal*', *Studies in Romanticism*, 30 (1991), 19.

44. *Sartor Resartus*, 1:149.

45. Forster collection, f. 106.

46. *Sartor Resartus*, 1:200.

47. R.A. Foakes, *The Romantic Assertion* (New Haven, 1958).

48. M.H. Abrams, *The Mirror and the Lamp: romantic theory and the critical tradition* (New York, 1958), pp. 30f. Schelling's comment appeared in his 1807 essay 'On the Relationship of the Creative Arts to Nature'.
49. *Sartor Resartus*, 1:128. J. Hillis Miller's recent book, *Illuminations* (Cambridge, Mass., 1992), pp. 135f., has noted the possibility that the sun may represent Turner's own artistic creativity, but, as part of the deconstructionist's untiring search for *aporia*, assumes that his sunsets represent the artist's acknowledgment of his declining power. The splendour of those sunsets, however, seem to me far from pessimistic in their implications.
50. John P. McGowan, *Representation and Revelation*, especially the perceptive opening chapter.
51. *Sartor Resartus*, pp. 167–8. For the relationship of Fichte's philosophy to this aspect of Carlyle's work, see Jerry A. Dibble, *The Pythia's Drunken Song: Thomas Carlyle's 'Sartor Resartus' and the style problem in German idealist philosophy* (The Hague, 1978). For the lengthy bibliography relating to the eighteenth-century sublime and a discussion of its place in art and literature, the reader is referred to the chapter on that theme in my *Changing Perspectives*.
52. Anne K. Mellor, *English Romantic Irony* (Cambridge, Mass., 1980), pp. 5–25.
53. Jack Lindsay, *J.M.W. Turner, His Life and Work: a critical biography* (London, 1966), especially pp. 89f., and Gage, *Color in Turner*, p. 145. The mythological references appended to Turner's later works are typified by the quotation he chose for the canvas *Aeneas Relating his Story to Dido* of 1850:

> Fallacious Hope beneath the moon's pale crescent shone,
> Dido listened to Troy being lost and won.
>
> (*MS. Fallacies of Hope*)

The quotations often became the target of satirical comment, such as the caustic remark by the critic of the *Illustrated London News* on 1 June, 1850: '. . . the said fallacy being any hope of understanding what the picture means.'
54. Recorded in R.C. Trench (ed.), *Letters and Memorials* (London, 1897), 1:84. On the general situation at that time, cf. Walter E. Houghton, *The Victorian Frame of Mind, 1830–1870* (New Haven, 1972), pp. 54–61; E.P. Thompson, *The Making of the English Working Class* (New York, 1966); and, for the statistics of this movement into the cities, Eric E. Lampard, 'The Urbanizing World' in H.J. Dyos and Michael Wolff (eds), *The Victorian City: images and realities* (London, 1976) 1:3–58.
55. Cf. Bryan Jay Wolf, *Romantic Re-vision: culture and consciousness in nineteenth-century American painting* (Chicago, 1982), pp. 81f.; and R.W.B. Lewis, *The American Adam: innocence, tragedy, and tradition in the nineteenth century* (Chicago, 1955).
56. George P. Landow, *Images of Crisis: literary iconology 1750 to the present* (Boston, 1982).

57. J. Hillis Miller, *The Disappearance of God: five nineteenth-century writers* (New York, 1965), especially pp. 6–8.

58. *Sartor Resartus*, 1:167.

59. Ruskin, *Complete Works* (edited by E.T. Cook and Alexander Wedderburn) (London, 1903–12) 3:254. The passage was omitted from the 1846 edition onwards. The connection of this painting with Ruskin's description of Turner was first suggested by Jack Lindsay in his *J.M.W. Turner*, p. 213. On Ruskin's interpretation of the painting in pessimistic terms, probably reflecting his own mood at the time, see Elizabeth K. Helsinger's lucid discussion, *Ruskin and the Art of the Beholder* (Cambridge, Ma., 1982), pp. 248–9. That pessimistic reading has generally been accepted by subsequent critics, because of the scene of Cain's murder of Abel, and the presence of the serpent and death; but, as I have indicated in my discussion of the painting, they were conventional concomitants of apocalyptic visions, when the messianic era would drive out death and sin.

60. Rippingille's account appeared some years later in the *Art Journal* (1860), p. 100.

61. C.R. Leslie, *Autobiographical Recollections* (London, 1860), 1:202.

62. Lawrence Gowing, *Turner: Imagination and Reality* (New York, 1966), p. 45, an impressive study of Turner's art, arguing for the artist's use of pigment as an acknowledged ingredient of painting rather than as a camouflaged instrument for achieving mimetic effect.

63. Sir George Beaumont condemned the water in this picture as being '. . . like the veins on a Marble slab.' The comment is recorded in the manuscript of Joseph Farington's *Diary* in the British Museum, the entry being for 3 May, 1803. Richard L. Stein, *The Ritual of Interpretation: the fine arts as literature in Ruskin, Rossetti, and Pater* (Cambridge, Ma., 1975), pp. 17f., discusses the 'religion of art' that Ruskin attempted to create for his fellow Victorians, sometimes misusing Turner in the process. Ruskin's own delight in detail which he transferred attributively to Turner is also examined in Robert Hewison, *John Ruskin: the argument of the eye* (Princeton, 1976). On the reception of this painting by Turner's contemporaries, see J. Ziff, 'Turner's Slave Ship; What a Red Rag is to a Bull', *Turner Studies*, 3 (1984), 28.

64. *Heroes and Hero-worship*, 1:298. Cf. Patricia M. Ball, *The Central Self: a study in Romantic and Victorian imagination* (London, 1968), which discusses Carlyle's call for 'sincerity' of vision in the poet.

65. *Sartor Resartus*, 1:201.

66. Lady Simon's recounting of the incident to George Richmond is recorded in A.M.W. Stirling, *The Richmond Papers* (London, 1926), pp. 55–6. Turner's choice of this theme coincided with the high-point of railway expansion in England, 6,000 miles of track being completed by 1850. There is a full account in Herbert L. Sussman, *Victorians and the Machine: the literary response to technology* (Cambridge, Mass., 1968). How long it took before people became accustomed to the blurring of landscape at the comparatively high speeds then being achieved is evidenced in E.M. Forster's amusing account in *Howards End* (Chapter 23), as Meg, reluctantly persuaded to travel in the Wilcoxes'

motor car, attempts to enjoy the scenery: 'It heaved and merged like porridge. Presently it congealed. They had arrived.'

67. *Sartor Resartus*, 1:185.
68. J.A. Froude, *Thomas Carlyle, Life in London*, 1:65.

2 THE FALLEN WOMAN

1. Louis Montrose, 'The Place of a Brother in *As You Like It*: social process and comic form', *Shakespeare Quarterly*, 32 (1981), 28; and Marjorie Levinson, *Wordsworth's Great Period Poems* (Cambridge, 1986), pp. 14–57; and for the preferred name of the movement, Stephen Greenblatt, 'Towards a Poetic of Culture', in H. Aram Veeser (ed.), *The New Historicism* (New York, 1989), pp. 1–13.
2. Tzvetan Todorov, *'Le Vraisemblable'* in *Communications*, 11 (1968), pp. 1–4.
3. The convergence has long been noted. Its emergence in the minor literature of the time, including the penny weekly magazines, is examined in Sally Mitchell, *The Fallen Angel: chastity, class and women's reading, 1835–1880* (Bowling Green, Ohio, 1981).
4. For the Restoration drama, one may note Nell Gwynn's unembarrassed recital of the epilogue to Dryden's *Tyrannic Love*, admitting her role in real life: 'Here Nelly lies, who though she lived a slattern/ Yet died a princess acting in St. Catheryn.'
5. Thackeray, *The Newcomes* (New York, 1899), p. 311. Dumas's play was first performed on the English stage at the Vaudeville Theatre in 1852. Its subsequent popularity is discussed in James L. Smith (ed.), *Victorian Melodramas* (London, 1976), pp. 177–8. Cf. also the portrayal of Queen Guinevere in Tennyson's *Idylls of the Kings*, no longer the touchingly noble lover of Malory's version but now grovelling in torment at the king's feet and condemning herself for her shame and self-pollution (*Guinevere*, 602f.). Later instances in the century include, of course, Thomas Hardy's Fanny in *Far from the Madding Crowd* (1874) and the central figure in *Tess of the D'Urbervilles* (1891). They mark a continuation of this tradition, but with a shifting of focus to the cruelty of blind fate, epitomized by Fanny's error in identifying the church and the disappearance of Tess's letter under the carpet.

    It may be noted that Dickens' *Dombey and Son*, written in 1846, just before the emergence of this theme in the fifties, represents Alice Marwood as having been inducted into a life of prostitution by her evil mother (mark their surname) rather than corrupted by unfortunate events.
6. Rossetti's poem 'Jenny' falls outside the parameters of the genre examined here, as it deals with an unrepentant prostitute. Millais' *The Woodman's Daughter* of 1851 was based upon a poem by Coventry Patmore which ends with the seduced girl drowning herself in a pool. For a close examination of Rossetti's painting, see Linda Nochlin, 'Lost and Found: once more the fallen woman', *Art Bulletin*, 60 (1978), 139.
7. It should be noted that, while Ford Madox Brown's painting has

generally been interpreted as described here, there is no firm evidence that the artist was painting an unmarried mother. For that reason, although my own feeling leans strongly towards the traditional reading, I have not based any significant part of my argument upon this painting.

8.   Dickens' purpose in establishing Urania Cottage, together with the principles he had in mind for its general management, are summarized in his letter to Miss Burdett Coutts dated 26 May, 1846, in *Letters*, ed. Kathleen Tillotson (Oxford, 1977), 4:552–6. For accounts of similar attempts, such as the House of Mercy opened by the Community of the Holy Cross in 1857, cf. H.E. Manning, *Penitents and Saints . . . at Magdalen Hospital* (London, 1844); and Robert Liddell, *Account of the House of Refuge in Commercial Road, Pimlico* (London, 1854). For another instance, see Diane D'Amico ' "Equal Before God": Christina Rossetti and the Fallen Women of Highgate Penitentiary' in A.H. Harrison and B. Taylor (eds), *Gender and Discourse in Victorian Literature and Art* (DeKalb, 1992), 67f. The quotations in this passage are from Thomas Hood's 'The Bridge of Sighs' in *Poems* (Oxford, 1923), p. 167 and *David Copperfield*, p. 581, in the New Oxford Illustrated Edition, the series used for all subsequent quotations from Dickens.

9.   The incident is recorded in Diana Holman Hunt, *My Grandfather, His Wives and Loves* (London, 1969), p. 217.

10.   Dr William Acton, the Victorian physician who held wide-ranging interviews with such women, reached a conclusion very different from the view usually presented in art and literature of the time. He discovered that the majority worked in the profession in a casual part-time capacity, often marrying and settling down respectably later on, to become '. . . the wedded wives of men in every grade of society, from the peerage to the stable.' His important work, *Prostitution, considered in its Moral, Social, and Sanitary Aspects, in London and other Large Cities . . .* was first published in 1857. Some of the implications are discussed in Steven Marcus, *The Other Victorians: a study of sexuality and pornography in mid-nineteenth-century England* (New York, 1966), pp. 2–33, and in Christopher Wood, *Victorian Panorama: paintings of Victorian life* (London 1976), pp. 135–42. Lawrence Lipking's interesting study *Abandoned Women and Poetic Tradition* (Chicago, 1988) uses the term 'abandoned' in the sense of 'forsaken', not 'dissolute', and is hence more relevant to the topic examined at the end of this present chapter. On the life of Catherine Walters and similar courtesans of the time, see the account by William Hardman in S.M. Ellis (ed.), *A Mid-Victorian Pepys* (London, 1928), pp. 210–16 and Cyril Pearl, *The Girl with the Swansdown Seat* (London, 1955), pp. 126–40.

11.   James M. Brown, *Dickens: novelist in the market-place* (London, 1982), pp. 6f. The quotation is from *The Times*, 25 February, 1858.

12.   Amanda Anderson, *Tainted Souls and Painted Faces: the rhetoric of fallenness in Victorian culture* (Ithaca, 1993). See also Richard D. McGhee, *Marriage, Duty, and Desire in Victorian Poetry and Drama* (Lawrence, Ka., 1970), Tom Winnifrith, *Fallen Women in the Nineteenth-Century Novel* (New York, 1994) which provides a survey of such fictional figures,

and, for the sociological aspects, Jeffrey Weeks, *Sex, Politics and Society: the regulation of sexuality since 1800* (London, 1981). Charles Bernheimer's study, *Figures of Ill Repute: representing prostitution in nineteenth-century France* (Cambridge, Mass., 1989), is concerned neither with the 'fallen' woman nor with portrayals of penitence, but with the hardened professionals in France, the brazen courtesans and inhabitants of brothels who served as models for Balzac, Lautrec and others. On those professional women, there is an interesting chapter connected with Manet's *Olympia*, in T.J. Clark, *The Painting of Modern Life: Paris in the art of Manet and his followers* (New York, 1985), pp. 79f. There are also, of course, non-scholarly studies, such as Martin Seymour-Smith, *Fallen Women* (London, 1969), exploiting the prurient aspects of the subject.

13.   Statistics on prostitution are from W.R. Greg's contemporary article in the Westminster Review, 53 (1850), pp. 448–506. A detailed examination of the available statistics by E.M. Sigsworth and T.J. Wyke in their essay, 'A Study of Victorian Prostitution and Venereal Disease' in Martha Vicinus (ed.), *Suffer and Be Still: women in the Victorian age* (Bloomington, 1973), pp. 77–85, concludes that the information recorded is too vague and impressionistic to form any serious basis for comparison with other periods, the literature of the time merely confirming that the Victorians *thought* that prostitution was on the increase (p. 80). For the assumption that the convergence on this theme in literature reflected an increase in sexual licence during the period, cf. Walter E. Houghton, *The Victorian Frame of Mind* (New Haven, 1972), p. 365. There are studies of the problem from both sociological and feminist viewpoints, in Helene E. Roberts, 'Marriage, Redundancy or Sin: the painter's view of women in the first twenty-five years of Victoria's reign' in the collection *Suffer and Be Still*, pp. 63–76, as well as in Nina Auerbach, 'The Rise of the Fallen Woman', *Nineteenth Century Fiction*, 35 (1980), 29, incorporated into her *Woman and the Demon: the life of a Victorian myth* (Cambridge, Ma., 1982), pp. 150f.

Other valuable discussions of the theme are Judith R. Walkowitz, *Prostitution and Victorian Society: women, class, and the state* (Cambridge, 1980); George Watt, *The Fallen Woman in the Nineteenth Century English Novel* (London, 1984); Jane Flanders, 'The Fallen Woman in Fiction' in Diane L. Fowlkes and Charlotte S. McClure (eds), *Feminist Visions* (Alabama, 1984), p. 97; Beth Kalikoff, 'The Falling Woman in Three Victorian Novels', in *Studies in the Novel*, 19 (1987), 357; and Lynda Nead, *Myths of Sexuality: representations of women in Victorian Britain* (Oxford, 1988). Michel Foucault, *The History of Sexuality* (London, 1979) has studied the subject of nineteenth-century discourses on sex in terms of a power struggle with political implications.

The portrayal of the female in painting is surveyed in Susan P. Casteras, *Images of Victorian Womanhood in English Art* (Rutherford, 1987), and her depiction in literature, with occasional side-glances at painting, in Rod Edmond, *Affairs of the Hearth: Victorian poetry and domestic narrative* (London, 1988).

14. Hippolyte Taine, *Notes on England* (trans. W.F. Rae) (London, 1872), p. 36. The Defoe quotation appears without source in Lawrence Stone, *Family, Sex and Marriage in England 1500–1800* (New York, 1979), p. 392, which itself offers an illuminating insight into the sexual mores of earlier generations. The growth of London's population within the context of the worldwide process of urbanization is recorded in H.J. Dyos and Michael Wolff (eds), *The Victorian City: images and realities* (London, 1976), 1:105f. Françoise Barret-Ducrocq, *Love in the Time of Victoria: sexuality, class, and gender in nineteenth-century London* (translated from the French by John Howe) (London, 1991), draws mainly on the archives of the Thomas Coram Foundling Hospital, archives which had been opened briefly to the public. Somewhat naïvely, the author accepts unquestioningly the unwed mothers' accounts of their forcible seduction, not recognizing that such claims of freedom from complicity improved the chances of the child's adoption.

15. As he neared the end of his journal, Boswell developed an affection for it which prevented him from ordering the diary burned on his death. By then, therefore, he may have cherished some idea that it would be preserved and read in later generations. But initially he had intended it only for himself, as he had been advised by Dr. Johnson that the keeping of a personal diary '... would be a very good exercise, and would yield me infinite satisfaction when the ideas were faded from my remembrance.' See the entry for 16 July, 1763 in his *London Journal* (edited by Frederick A. Pottle) (New York, 1956), p. 269.

16. The importance of the *Ecclesiologist* in influencing church architecture of the period was first traced in Chapter 8 of Kenneth Clark's classic study *The Gothic Revival: an essay in the history of taste* (New York, 1962), originally published in 1928.

17. Ruskin, *Complete Works* eds. E.T. Cook and Alexander Wedderburn (London, 1903–12), 4:264–65. Ruskin's emphasis upon symbolic reading is discussed in Elizabeth K. Helsinger, *Ruskin and the Art of the Beholder* (Cambridge, Mass., 1982), pp. 201–31. Holman Hunt recorded the experience in his *Pre-Raphaelitism and the Pre-Raphaelite Brotherhood* (London, 1905), 1:90. There is a helpful examination of this aspect of their work in George P. Landow, *William Holman Hunt and Typological Symbolism* (New Haven, 1979).

18. D.G. Rossetti, *Poetical Works* (ed. William M. Rossetti) (New York, 1886), p. 326. For further examination of these iconological aspects, cf. G.B. Tennyson, 'The Sacramental Imagination' in *Nature and the Victorian Imagination* (edited by U.C. Knoepflmacher and G.B. Tennyson) (Berkeley, 1977) and Chris Brooks, *Signs for the Times: symbolic realism in the mid-Victorian world* (London, 1984), Chapter 13, which examines this aspect of the Gothic revival.

19. Hunt explained his intention in a letter to J.E. Pythian dated 21 January, 1897, preserved in the Manchester City Art Gallery. But the allegorical intent was perceived immediately without such guidance by W.M. Rossetti in a review in *The Spectator*, reprinted in his *Fine Art, Chiefly Contemporary* (London, 1867). For conjectures on further

symbolism in this painting, see John Duncan Macmillan, 'Holman Hunt's *Hireling Shepherd*: some reflections on a Victorian pastoral', *Art Bulletin*, 54 (1972), 190 and Leslie Parris, *Landscape in Britain, c.1750–1850* (London, 1973), p. 128.

20. From the opening description in the novel. Her response to painting in general is discussed in a later chapter. As is noted in Hugh Witemeyer, *George Eliot and the Visual Arts* (New Haven, 1979), she was an enthusiastic admirer of Ruskin, whose third and fourth volumes of *Modern Painters* she reviewed and who exerted a major influence on her work. It has long been known that she maintained a personal relationship with certain Pre-Raphaelite painters, introduced to them by Edward Burne-Jones who joined her intimate circle of friends in 1867.

21. George P. Landow, *Victorian Types, Victorian Shadows: biblical typology in Victorian literature, art and thought* (London 1980), in addition to his work on Holman Hunt mentioned above. That aspect was also explored in a slightly earlier study by Herbert L. Sussman, *Fact into Figure: typology in Carlyle, Ruskin and the Pre-Raphaelite Brotherhood* (Columbus, 1979).

22. Cf. Stephen Orgel, *The Illusion of Power: political theatre in the English Renaissance* (Berkeley, 1975) and Roy Strong, *Splendour at Court: Renaissance spectacle and the theatre of power* (Boston, 1973). Both studies preceded the formal emergence of New Historicism under the aegis of Stephen Greenblatt, but are recognized as having prepared the way for its advent. From the host of Marxist-oriented works appearing in the last two decades, one may instance Fredric Jameson, *The Political Unconscious: narrative as a socially symbolic act* (Ithaca, 1981) and, from the realm of art history, John Barrell, *The Dark Side of the Landscape* (Cambridge, 1980), the latter reinterpreting eighteenth-century painting in terms of the class struggle between the rural poor and their employers.

23. See, for example, Catherine Hall, 'The Early Formation of Victorian Domestic Ideology' in Sandra Burman (ed.), *Fit Work for Women* (London, 1979), pp. 15–32. Eric Trudgill, *Madonnas and Magdalens* (New York, 1976) is primarily interested in Victorian ideas of prurience, but does discuss briefly the concept of the home (pp. 38f.). Jeff Nunokawa, *The Afterlife of Property: domestic security in the Victorian novel* (Princeton, 1994) suggests that marriage in the Victorian novel conceives of the wife in terms of 'a form of estate that replaced insecure marketplace property' (p. 98).

24. From a lecture delivered by Broadhurst in 1877, quoted in Jeffrey Weeks, *Sex, Politics, and Society*, p. 68.

25. Cf. Helena Michie, *The Flesh Made Word: female figures and women's bodies* (Oxford, 1987), and Hilary Schor, 'The Plot of the Beautiful Ignoramus: *Ruth* and the tradition of the fallen woman', in Regina Barreca (ed.), *Sex and Death in Victorian Literature* (London, 1990), 158–77. Susan Gubar had written earlier on the female as a text in 'The Blank Page and the Issues of Female Creativity' in Elizabeth Abel (ed.), *Writing and Sexual Difference* (Chicago, 1982), pp. 73–93.

26. Ruskin's lecture 'Of Queens' Gardens' delivered in Manchester in 1864 and incorporated into his *Sesame and Lilies* in *Works*, 18:122. For details of John Cadbury of Birmingham and for a perceptive feminist study of this period, see Leonore Davidoff and Catherine Hall, *Family Fortunes: men and women of the English middle class, 1780–1850* (London, 1987), especially pp. 57 and 151f.

27. R.I. and S. Wilberforce, *The Life of William Wilberforce* (London, 1838), 3:487.

28. A. Dwight Culler, *The Poetry of Tennyson* (New Haven, 1977), p. 131, notes that the religion of love which Tennyson helped propagate in his generation may have been formed in part through the influence of his friend Arthur Hallam, who had studied those sources closely during his residence in Italy.

29. A comment by Aubrey de Vere dated 14 October, 1850 recorded in Wilfrid Ward, *Aubrey de Vere* (London, 1904), pp. 158–9. For further praise of Emily Tennyson, see Christopher Ricks, *Tennyson* (New York, 1972), pp. 208–10, notably Edward Lear's light-hearted yet obviously sincere comment: 'I should think computing moderately that 15 angels, several hundred ordinary women, many philosophers, a heap of truly wise and kind mothers, 3 or 4 minor prophets, and a lot of doctors and school-mistresses, might all be boiled down, and yet their combined essence fall short of what Emily Tennyson really is.' Among the suffragettes, of course, the male idealization of women was regarded as a mere sop or substitute for social equality.

30. Samuel Smiles, *Self-Help: with illustrations of character and conduct* (London, 1859), p. 294.

31. Cf. Mikhail Bakhtin, *The Dialogic Imagination* (edited by Michael Holquist) (Austin, 1981).

32. For a study of the growing awareness of the plight of the poor within the writings and and engravings of the time, see Sheila M. Smith, ' "Savages and Martyrs": images of the urban poor in Victorian literature and art' in Ira Bruce Nadel and F.S. Schwarzbach (eds), *Victorian Artists and the City: a collection of critical essays* (New York, 1979), pp. 14f.

33. I do not argue that every instance of such literary characterization was symbolic in the sense depicted here, but that the sudden outcrop of interest in the 1850s owed its main impetus to that deeper theme. The figure of Carry Battle, for example, in Trollope's later novel, *The Vicar of Bullhampton* (1868), a sympathetic portrayal of a fallen woman from the labouring class, was introduced by him for different reasons. In response to an anti-feminist article in the *Saturday Review* (14 March, 1868), attacking the woman of independence for losing the 'pretty bashful modesties' of the past in favour of 'the fashions of prostitutes', Trollope introduced Carry into the novel in order to accentuate by contrast the moral uprightness of the self-reliant heroine. And as was mentioned in an earlier note, Hardy, although continuing this interest in the fallen woman in novels he wrote later in the century, altered both its focus and its implications.

34. The conception of the Victorian woman as the repository of ideals,

postponed within a corrupt world, is crystallized towards the end of that period in Conrad's *Heart of Darkness*, written in 1899, where Kurtz's noble and faithful fiancée, never named, is referred to throughout by the profoundly ambivalent appellation, his 'Intended'.

35.   *Hard Times*, pp. 35 and 217. The transfer of the Angel from the middle-class home to that of the working-class, now seen as the truer preserver of moral values, is reinforced in the novel by the secondary figure of Rachael, repeatedly described in those terms, as in Stephen's reiterated cry: 'Thou art an Angel. Bless thee, bless thee!' (p. 88). Mrs Gaskell's concern in *Ruth* with the harsh conditions under which seamstresses worked reflects the protest at this time in Thomas Hood's popular poem *The Song of the Shirt* and in Richard Redgrave's painting of 1846 depicting a seamstress wearily watching the dawn rise after having worked throughout the night.

36.   Steven Marcus, *Dickens: from Pickwick to Dombey* (London, 1965) first sensitized critics to the parallelistic structure of Dickens' novels in general, to be followed by H.M. Daleski, *Dickens and the Art of Analogy* (London, 1970), and, on the paradigm of parent–child relationship, Alexander Welsh, *From Copyright to Copperfield: the identity of Dickens* (Cambridge Mass., 1987).

37.   Peggotty remarks on Emily's wandering in foreign countries: 'I know'd in my mind, as he'd have told her wonders of 'em, and how she was to be a lady theer, and how he got her to listen to him fust, along o'sech like.' *David Copperfield*, p. 498. How far this was an English phenomenon, closely related to the new industrialism, may be seen in the different cultural context of Hawthorne's *The Scarlet Letter*, whose setting is the stern Puritan morality of the 1640s, far removed from the immediate problems of urban congestion and commercial exploitation. The passage concerning Em'ly as a child angel appears on p. 32.

38.   *David Copperfield*, p. 251; and *Adam Bede*, 1:193 and 172, in the Cabinet Edition of *The Works of George Eliot* (Boston, 1901). Michael Steig, *Dickens and Phiz* (Bloomington, 1978), p. 30, has deduced from the disproportionate frequency of Emily's and Martha's appearance in the illustrations to the novel that Dickens was more interested in his fallen women than in either Agnes or Dora. Whatever Dickens' personal preferences, that evidence does at least suggest that the scenes of fallen women in the novel were more dramatically interesting, and hence more conducive to illustration.

39.   Thackeray, careful to avoid offending contemporary moral standards and to remain within the parameters of what was permissible in literature, avoids any unequivocal statement of Becky Sharp's adultery; but his own conviction is obvious from the placing within her jewellery case of an unexplained bank-note for one thousand pounds received from Lord Steyne, and by his authorial comment, cautiously phrased as a rhetorical question: 'Was she guilty or not? She said not; but who could tell what was truth which came from those lips; or if that corrupt heart was in this case pure?' *Complete Works* (New York, 1903), 3:115.

40. *Carlyle Past and Present* in *Complete Works*, the 'University' edition (New York, 1885), 12:143. On Ruskin's concern with Mammon, cf. Jeffrey L. Spear, *Dreams of an English Eden: Ruskin and his tradition in social criticism* (New York, 1984), p. 8.

41. Erwin Panofsky, *Meaning in the Visual Arts* (New York, 1955), p. 31, and, for the medieval cathedral, his *Gothic Architecture and Scholasticism* (New York, 1957). For subsequent examinations of that theme, see Georges Poulet, *Metamorphoses of the Circle* (translated by C. Dawson and E. Coleman) (Baltimore, 1966) and W.J.T. Mitchell, 'Metamorphoses of the Vortex' in R. Wendorf (ed.), *Artistic Images: the sister arts from Hogarth to Tennyson* (Minneapolis, 1983), p. 125. The equipoise of the heroic couplet and arabesque is discussed, in that context, in my *Changing Perspectives*, Chapter 3.

42. There is, of course, no authority in the text of the Gospels for identifying the 'sinner' who anoints the feet of Jesus in *Luke*, 7:36–50 with Mary Magdalene, but the identification became so widespread in subsequent Christian exegesis as to be regarded as axiomatic.

43. Rossetti's poem 'Why wilt thou cast the roses from thy hair . . .' was written to accompany this drawing. See Virginia Surtees, *The Paintings and Drawings of Dante Gabriel Rossetti: a catalogue raisoné* (Oxford, 1971), 1:62.

44. For Fielding, Hogarth's contemporary, the village slut Molly Seagrim, ineffectively hiding the philosopher Square behind a curtain while negotiating with Tom, is treated, as in the second scene in Hogarth's sequence, as a subject for light humour or mock epic, devoid of serious moral reverberations. Tom Jones' lecture to Nightingale later in the novel – a chapter headed 'Which we hope will be very attentively perused by young people of both sexes' – grants that sleeping with women who know what they are about is forgivable and warns only against philandering with innocent girls, who may be misled by such casual dalliance into genuine affection and false hopes of marriage.

45. Helene E. Roberts, 'Marriage, Redundancy or Sin', p. 72.

46. *Hard Times*, p. 274. There is a brief survey of the fallen women of Dickens's novels in Michael Slater, *Dickens and Women* (London, 1983), pp. 339–48. For an analysis of the Egg triptych, see Martin Meisel, *Realizations: narrative, pictorial, theatrical arts in nineteenth-century England* (Princeton, 1983), pp. 25–7, which examines the attempt there to create a cross-referential continuity, symbolized by the unifying appearance of the moon in the two latter scenes.

47. Fred Kaplan, *Sacred Tears: sentimentality in Victorian literature* (Princeton, 1987).

48. Robert Rosenblum, for example, a critic remarkably sensitive to symbolic elements in art, nonetheless describes the painting in exclusively social terms as an expression of the conflict 'between sexual innocence and experience'. See his *Nineteenth Century Art* (New York, 1984), p. 259, written jointly with H.W. Janson (who contributed only the sections on sculpture).

49. Michael Baxandall, *Painting and Experience in Fifteenth-Century Italy* (Oxford, 1972), pp. 36–40.

50. Hunt recorded his conception of the two paintings as being complementary in his *Pre-Raphaelitism and the Pre-Raphaelite Brotherhood*, 2:429–30, from which his account of the symbolism is quoted, while Ruskin's analysis appeared in his letter to *The Times* dated 5 May, 1854, reprinted in *Works*, 12:329–30. The shared interest in the companion piece is discussed in William Gaunt, *The Pre-Raphaelite Dream* (New York, 1966), pp. 70–3. Nina Auerbach, *Romantic Imprisonment: women and other glorified outcasts* (New York, 1985), pp. 150f., offers a feminist reading of Lewis Carroll's *Alice*, symbolically connecting Alice's 'fall' with the Victorian fear of becoming the fallen woman and noting that the author's favourite painting was Rossetti's *Found*.

51. The centrality of this concept, the idea of the soul's conversion to higher ideals, is noted in Jerome H. Buckley, *The Victorian Temper: a study in literary culture* (Cambridge Mass., 1951), pp. 89f. It formed the main theme of William James' brilliant study, *Varieties of Religious Experience*.

52. Cf. Wood, *Victorian Panorama*, p. 137.

53. Tennyson, *Mariana*, lines 1–4, in *Poems* (edited by Christopher Ricks) (London, 1969), pp. 187–8. The place of the moated grange in the symbolic use of buildings throughout his poetry is discussed in Valerie Pitt, *Tennyson Laureate* (London, 1969), especially pp. 39–42.

54. The ideal, of which these instances presented the negative aspect, was depicted in Tennyson's poem 'The Beggar Maid' (1842) based on the ballad appearing in Percy's *Reliques of Ancient English Poetry*. His poem in its turn inspired Edward Burne-Jones's painting *King Cophetua and the Beggar Maid*, in which the monarch sits humbly at the feet of the beautiful but impecunious maiden, doffing his jewelled crown, the symbol of his wealth and power, in deference to love.

3 COMMODITY CULTURE IN DICKENS AND BROWNING

1. Dickens' preface to *The Pickwick Papers*, p. xi. All quotations are from the New Oxford Illustrated Dickens of 1948–58. In this connection, see J.R. Harvey, *Victorian Novelists and their Illustrators* (New York, 1971), p. 12. There is a discussion of Dickens' somewhat amateurish art criticism in Richard Lettis, 'Dickens and Art', *Dickens Studies Annual*, 14 (1985), 93, and a detailed account of his knowledge of painting, architecture and sculpture in his *The Dickens Aesthetic* (New York, 1989). See also two articles by Leonee Ormond, 'Dickens and Painting: the Old Masters' and 'Dickens and Painting: Contemporary Art' in *The Dickensian*, 79 (1983), and 80 (1984), 3. There is a more general discussion of the subject in David Skilton, 'The Relation between Illustration and Text in the Victorian Novel: a new perspective', in K.J. Höltgen, P.M. Daly and W. Lottes (eds), *Word and Visual Imagination* (Erlangen, 1988), 303.

2. Dickens' comment on the relationship between illustration and text was recorded by Charles Dickens the Younger in an introduction he contributed for a later edition of *The Pickwick Papers*, while the

praise of Cruikshank appeared in *Household Words*, 8:184. It seems likely that Dickens' insistence upon the priority to be accorded to the writer contributed in some degree to Seymour's suicide. See, for example, Edgar Johnson, *Charles Dickens: his tragedy and triumph* (New York, 1977), pp. 99f. Michael Steig, *Dickens and Phiz* (Bloomington, 1978), p. 26, notes that Phiz did sometimes elaborate, inserting, for example, a kitten attacking the remains of a meat-pie in his depiction of *Job Trotter Encounters Sam*, but he remained faithful to the details in the text he was illustrating.

3. Peter Conrad, *The Victorian Treasure-House* (London, 1973), p. 68.
4. *Little Dorrit*, p. 542.
5. Blanchard Jerrold, *London: a pilgrimage with illustrations by Gustave Doré* (London, 1872), pp. 69–70. Alexander Welsh, *The City of Dickens* (Oxford, 1971) provides a valuable social study of the metropolis as Dickens presented it; and the theme was developed in F.S. Schwarzbach, *Dickens and the City* (London, 1979). Ira Bruce Nadel, 'Gustave Doré: English Art and London Life', devoted mainly to his illustrations for Jerrold's book, makes no mention of this deliberate exploitation of Dickens' popularity. See her essay in *Victorian Artists and the City* which she edited with Schwarzbach.
6. Fielding's preface to *Joseph Andrews,* and the fictional letter dated July 10 in Smollett's *Humphrey Clinker* (Oxford, 1925), 1:266.
7. *David Copperfield*, p. 352. For information on the influence of Daumier on Hablot Browne, I am indebted to J.R. Harvey, *Victorian Novelists*, pp. 132–3. The mutual admiration expressed by Hogarth and Fielding has been frequently documented as in Roger E. Moore, *Hogarth's Literary Relationships* (Minneapolis, 1948) and, more recently, in Ronald Paulson, *Hogarth: his life, art, and times* (New Haven, 1971), 1:468–71.
8. Dorothy Van Ghent, 'The Dickens World: A View from Todgers's', *Sewanee Review*, 58 (1950), 419–38, later incorporated into *The English Novel: form and function* (New York, 1953), pp. 125–38. The passage on the four-poster bed quoted from *Great Expectations*, p. 347. R.D. McMaster, 'Man into Beast in Dickensian Caricature', *University of Toronto Quarterly*, 31 (1962), 354, extended Van Ghent's theory by providing instances of the interchange between man and the animal world within the imagery of the novels. On the intensive investigation of animism in the novels resulting from Van Ghent's study, cf. James R. Kincaid, *Dickens and the Rhetoric of Laughter* (Oxford, 1971), pp. 10–11 and, on the general prevalence of animism in the novels, John Carey, *The Violent Effigy: a study of Dickens' imagination* (London, 1973), pp. 101–3.
9. J. Hillis Miller, in *Charles Dickens and George Cruikshank: papers read at a Clark Library seminar* (Los Angeles, 1971), refers to Roman Jakobson's theory as he presented it in his essay 'Linguistics and Poetics' in T.A. Sebeok (ed.), *Style in Language* (Cambridge, Mass., 1966), p. 375. The quotation is from *Martin Chuzzlewit*, p. 625. Further discussion of synecdoche in Dickens' writings, can be found in Garrett Stewart, *Dickens and the Trials of Imagination* (Cambridge, Mass., 1974), especially pp. xixf. There is an analysis of the speech idiosyncrasies of the

fictional characters in Robert Golding, *Idiolectics in Dickens* (London, 1985).

10.   As Prince Albert wrily remarked in a letter to Frederick William IV of Prussia: 'The mathematicians worked out that the Crystal Palace must collapse after the first strong wind; the engineers claimed that the galleries would break up and crush the visitors; the economists predicted that prices would rise drastically as a result of the vast influx of people . . . while the theologians argued that this second Tower of Babel would also incur the vengeance of an insulted God.'

11.   *The Crystal Palace Exhibition: the Art Journal illustrated catalogue* (London, 1851), p. I in the Appendix, and p. xxi in the Introduction. This catalogue, excellently illustrated, was, at the time, the unofficial guide to the exhibition, and it contains the interesting contemporary essay on 'The Exhibition as a Lesson in Taste' by R.N. Wornum. There is a useful survey of the items displayed at Crystal Palace in Nikolaus Pevsner, *High Victorian Design: a study of the Exhibition of 1851* (London, 1951).

12.   Recorded in C.H. Gibbs-Smith, *The Great Exhibition of 1851* (London, 1964), which culls excerpts from contemporary responses to the various items in the exhibition without, unfortunately, providing bibliographical sources. Further contemporary responses to the exhibition are recorded in Christopher Hobhouse, *1851 and the Crystal Palace* (New York, 1937). One of the antagonistic responses was Charles Babbage, *The Exposition of 1851*, reprinted as Volume 10 in *Works* (edited by Martin Campbell-Kelly) (New York, 1989). It was recognized at the time as the response of a disgruntled inventor, whose model engine had been refused exhibition by the committee.

13.   For helpful surveys of the major changes in production methods introduced by furniture manufacturers at this time, see R.W. Symonds and B.B. Whineray, *Victorian Furniture* (London, 1962), especially pp. 20–5, and Clive D. Edwards, *Victorian Furniture: technology and design* (Manchester, 1993).

14.   John Steegman, *Victorian Taste: a study of the arts and architecture from 1830 to 1870* (Cambridge, Ma., 1979), originally published in 1950 as *Consorts of Taste*, has noted that around 1830 there was a shift from '. . . the signposts of authority to the fancies of the individual' (p. 4).

15.   *Pickwick Papers*, p. 560.

16.   Thomas Richards, *The Commodity Culture of Victorian England: advertising and spectacle, 1851–1914* (Stanford, 1990), p. 8. From this account, as from E.S. Turner's lively work, *The Shocking History of Advertising* (New York, 1953), it becomes apparent that there was a notable shift in the nature of advertising in the final decades of the century. At the time of the Great Exhibition and throughout the period that Dickens was writing, it was designed to sell items tailored to individual taste, while at the turn of the century it was aimed at arousing consumer interest in mass-produced items, such as factory-made soap or patent medicines.

17.   Clive Edwards' recent study, quoted above, argues for a more conservative view of the impact of new technology on Victorian furniture,

pointing out that traditional methods continued to be used side-by-side with the new. But that claim is to a large extent countered by the evidence quoted in his own study, his acknowledgment of the 'tremendous growth in the choice of materials available' (p. 90), of the way machinery began to replace handwork in the ornamentation of furniture (p. 52), and of the major influence of the bentwood and improved lamination processes upon the shape of furniture itself (p. 96).

18. The catalogue illustrations of couches is reproduced in *A Pictorial Dictionary of British Nineteenth Century Furniture Design*, published by the Antique Collections Club of England in 1977, pp. 294 and 332.

19. The Victorian conception of the cosy armchair as initiating dreams and fantasy is evidenced by Robert Buss's portrayal of Dickens himself, asleep in the armchair in his study, surrounded by a cloudy throng of characters drawn from his books. Similarly, Cruikshank depicted himself, in the frontispiece to his *Table Book* of 1845, plunged in reverie in his armchair, the smoke from his pipe (the engraving was designed before he foreswore tobacco) being transformed, as it curled upward, into the characters that peopled his own drawings; while Hablot K. Browne's frontispiece to *Martin Chuzzlewit* (1843–5) presented Tom Pinch in a similar position, dreaming up the characters of the novel.

20. *Pickwick Papers*, pp. 183–4.

21. Quoted in Asa Briggs, *Victorian Things* (London, 1988), p. 61.

22. *The Old Curiosity Shop*, p. 5.

23. *Our Mutual Friend*, pp. 10 and 131.

24. *David Copperfield*, pp. 216 and 641.

25. J. Hillis Miller's 'Afterword' to the Signet edition (New York, 1964).

26. *Our Mutual Friend*, pp. 45–6 and 56.

27. Stubbs was also interested, later in his career, in scenes of violence in nature, such as his *Lion Attacking a Horse* of 1770, an interest stimulated by a visit to North Africa.

28. See on this subject, Basil Taylor, *Animal Painting in England: from Barlow to Landseer* (Harmondsworth, 1955); Kenneth Clark, *Animals and Men: their relationship in Western art from prehistory to the present day* (London, 1977); and Jessica Rawson (ed.), *Animals in Art* (London, 1977).

29. The reprimand concerning irreverence is from a letter to an unknown recipient, in *Letters*, edited by Morton N. Cohen (New York, 1979), 2:1116, the rebuke to William Boyd Carpenter, Bishop of Ripon appears in 2:677, and the remark concerning his dislike of religious discussion in a letter to Edith Rix, 2:618.

30. On the genesis of the poem, see Morton N. Cohen, 'Hark the Snark', published in Edward Guiliano (ed.), *Lewis Carroll Observed: a collection of unpublished photographs, drawings, poetry and new essays* (New York, 1976), p. 95.

31. Cf. Carl Menger, *Principles of Economics* (1871) and Leon Walras, *Elements of Pure Economics* (1874). I am grateful to Regenia Gagnier for kindly allowing me to read the manuscript of her forthcoming article, *On the Insatiability of Human Wants: Economic and Aesthetic Man*, which offers considerable support to the theory adduced here.

32. Robert Kerr, *The Gentleman's House* (London, 1864), quoted in Roger Dixon and Stefan Muthesius, *Victorian Architecture* (London, 1985), p. 33. On the revisionist approach to Victorian art and architecture, cf. John Betjeman, *First and Last Loves* (London, 1952).

33. For further details, see Mark Girouard's excellent study, *The Victorian Country House* (New Haven, 1979).

34. Georg Germann, *Gothic Revival in Europe and Britain: sources, influences, and ideas* (Cambridge, Ma., 1973), pp. 112–16. Although cast-iron churches were authorised in the colonies, where prefabricated parts sent from England could be assembled without the need for trained craftsmen, no such churches were in fact erected in England itself, despite the Society's approval in principle. The introduction of polychromy into Victorian architecture is examined in Stefan Muthesius, *The High Victorian Movement in Architecture, 1850–1870* (London, 1972), pp. 59f.

35. Cf. W.R. Lethaby, *Philip Webb and his Work* (London, 1935), p. 73. There is a well-known limerick by Rossetti satirizing what he regarded as Burges's immaturity. It is preserved in *Rossetti Papers* (edited by W.M. Rossetti) (London, 1903), p. 494. For a detailed study of the architect, see J. Mordaunt Crook, *William Burges and the High Victorian Dream* (Chicago, 1981). I should like to take this opportunity of thanking the Cardiff City Council for their kindness in granting me a private and fascinating tour both of Cardiff Castle and of Castell Coch.

36. Walpole, who set up a committee of three to supervise the amateur Gothicizing of Strawberry Hill, found it necessary to issue to the public free tickets in advance in order to reduce congestion among visitors. Although Beckford did move into Fonthill in 1807, it had been designed only as a reconstruction of the ancient ruins there, a summer or weekend home, and proved unsuited to permanent residence even before the tower collapsed.

37. *Sketches by Boz*, p. 40.

38. *Little Dorrit*, p. 654.

39. Van Ghent, pp. 130–1.

40. *Great Expectations*, pp. 280 and 197. The interest in gadgetry was at its height at this time, as the Great Exhibition testified. Among numerous other examples, there was a suitcase which, in the event of an emergency, converted into a life-saving raft, a lady's parasol which doubled as a driving whip, and a sofa or ottoman which could be used simultaneously for storing coal.

41. *Little Dorrit*, p. 246.

42. Charles Dickens' *Book of Memoranda*, transcribed and annotated by Fred Kaplan (New York, 1981), p. 14.

43. Cf. Harry Stone, *Dickens and the Invisible World: fairy tales, fantasy, and novel making* (Bloomington, 1979). John Romano, *Dickens and Reality* (New York, 1978) argued against the author's championing of fancy, but the evidence is strongly against him. There is Dickens' attack on Cruikshank in an article in *Household Words*, 184, which charged him with distorting the pristine purity of fairy tales, as well as Dickens' own defence of fancy in the lecture he delivered in 1857 (*Speeches of*

Charles Dickens, edited by K.J. Fielding (Oxford, 1960), p. 230), from which the quotation is taken.

44. Van Ghent, p. 130.
45. *Martin Chuzzlewit*, p. 810. On Dickens' metaphorical usages, cf. Nancy K. Hill, *A Reformer's Art: Dickens' picturesque and grotesque imagery* (Athens, Ohio, 1981).
46. *Dombey and Son*, p. 472.
47. *Bleak House*, p. 404.
48. *Sketches by Boz*, p. 239.
49. For details, see Lewis F. Haines, 'Mill and Pauline: the Review that Retarded Browning's Fame' in *Modern Language Notes*, 69 (1944), 410; and William C. DeVane, *A Browning Handbook* (New York, 1955), pp. 45–6.
50. The dramatic monologue was not, of course, entirely new to English literature, John Donne, whom Browning greatly admired, having developed the pattern some two centuries earlier. But it had functioned very differently in Donne's hands, producing, as I examined in *The Soul of Wit: a study of John Donne* (Oxford, 1974), an intensely mannerist yearning in both his secular and his religious verse, a form of one-sided dialogue in which the speaker strives to bridge the metaphysical gulf separating him from his silent partner, God. That dimension is absent from the nineteenth-century versions.
51. The principle is explored in Harold Bloom's *The Anxiety of Influence: a theory of poetry* (New York, 1973), his *A Map of Misreading* (New York, 1975) and his *Agon: towards a theory of revisionism* (New York, 1982). In these he strives to counter what he terms the nihilism of deconstructionism by an assertion of the active force of poet or writer, applying in his interpretive reading a conscious 'misprision' of Freud's Oedipal theory, with the powerful author-predecessor viewed as a father-figure whom the later author must resist and overpower.
52. Ruskin, *Modern Painters*, 3:4:1 published in 1856. For the rise of the terms 'subjective' and 'objective' in this period and their adoption by English critics, see M.H. Abrams, *The Mirror and the Lamp: Romantic theory and the critical tradition* (New York, 1958), pp. 235f. Browning's *Essay on Shelley* is interestingly discussed in the opening chapter of Philip Drew, *The Poetry of Browning: a critical introduction* (London, 1970) and, from a somewhat different angle, in Thomas J. Collins, *Robert Browning's Moral-Aesthetic Theory, 1833–1855* (Lincoln, Na., 1967), pp. 113f.
53. Robert Langbaum, *The Poetry of Experience: the dramatic monologue in modern literary tradition* (New York, 1963), especially pp. 75–108. Langbaum offers there the stimulating theory that the subjectivity of the Romantic poets, their filtering of experience through the self, may have been adopted by them only as a prerequisite for revalidating the material world and for coping with the disequilibrium between experience and idea resulting from the cold pragmatism of the Enlightenment. He is especially persuasive in his discussion of the Victorian dramatic monologue as rooting personal sensitivity in a firmly conceived physical setting. The relationship of the dramatic

monologue to the growing interest in psychological analysis is discussed in Ekbert Faas, *Retreat into the Mind: Victorian poetry and the rise of psychiatry* (Princeton, 1988), pp. 64f. See also Park Honan, *Browning's Characters: a study in poetic technique* (New Haven, 1961), pp. 104f.

54. Jacob Burckhardt's influential study, *The Civilization of the Renaissance in Italy* of 1860, both expressed and stimulated this tendency by its focus upon rugged individualism as the dominant feature of that age. The later reactions to that approach have been traced in W.K. Ferguson, *The Renaissance in Historical Thought: five centuries of interpretation* (Cambridge, Mass., 1948). On details of this rising interest, see John Hale, *England and the Italian Renaissance: the growth of interest in its history and art* (London, 1954), and, more recently, Hilary Fraser, *The Victorians and Renaissance Italy* (Oxford, 1992).

55. *Letters*, edited by F.G. Kenyon (London, 1897), 1:448. This incident probably gave rise to his poem, *Old Pictures in Florence*. In 1848, the Arundel Society was formed in England to encourage the preservation of early paintings, chiefly Italian frescoes, and to diffuse a knowledge of them among the public. The Society remained active for some fifty years.

56. David Robertson, *Sir Charles Eastlake and the Victorian Art World* (Princeton, 1978) traces the history of the acquisitions to the National Gallery during his period of office and the public response to his efforts, the quotation from Trollope appearing on p. 286. Prince Albert, who worked closely with Eastlake, was himself a respected art connoisseur, being in large part responsible for directing Eastlake towards Early Renaissance painters at a time when the Trustees were in favour of High Renaissance art. He himself purchased for the royal collection works by Gentile da Fabriano, Fra Angelico, and Gozzoli, as is recorded in J.H. Plumb and Huw Wheldon, *Royal Heritage: the treasures of the British Crown* (London, 1977), pp. 255f.

57. Lines 25–33. All quotations are from *Poetical Works*, edited by Ian Jack (Oxford, 1980).

58. Cf. Wolfgang Iser, *The Art of Reading* (London, 1978), and Roland Barthes, *The Pleasure of the Text* (London, 1976). The greater applicability of post-modern critical theory to twentieth-century texts is noted, for example, in Terry Eagleton, *Literary Theory* (Minneapolis, 1983), p. 136f. M.M. Bakhtin, in his essay 'From the Prehistory of Novelistic Discourse' in *The Dialogic Imagination: four essays by M.M. Bakhtin* (edited by Michael Holquist) (Austin, 1988), p. 82, remarks that the rich tradition of parody in the Renaissance created dialogistic elements paving the way for the genre of the novel.

59. Roland Barthes argues the point in *The Pleasure of the Text*.

60. Richard Wollheim, *Art and its Objects* (Cambridge, 1987), especially pp. 205–26, distinguishing, in connection with pictorial representation, between 'seeing-as' and 'seeing-in'. There is a brief discussion of this poem in terms of *ekphrasis* in James A.W. Heffernan, *Museum of Words: the poetics of ekphrasis from Homer to Ashbery* (Chicago, 1993), pp. 139f.

61. One may note here a contrast with the earlier use of the dramatic monologue by John Donne, where the *persona*, especially in the devotional poems, is so obviously a projection of the poet himself that it is difficult, if not impossible, to distinguish them. The variety and range of Browning's *personae*, on the other hand, seem deliberately created to discourage such identification.

62. Quotations are from *A Spanish Cloister*, 1–4, *A Woman's Last Word*, 1–4, *Holy-Cross Day*, 13–17, and *The Lost Mistress*, 17–20.

63. The expanded version of *Saul*, published in *Men and Women*, printed the poem in long lines rather than with alternating insets, but the metrical form remained otherwise unchanged.

4 GEORGE ELIOT AND THE HORIZONS OF EXPECTATION

1. On the distinction between mimesis and representationalism, cf. Roman Jakobson and Morris Halle, *Fundamentals of Language* (The Hague, 1956), pp. 81f.; and Ludwig Wittgenstein, *The Blue and Brown Books* (New York, 1965), pp. 104–9f. And for its relevance to George Eliot, John P. McGowan, *Representation and Revelation: Victorian realism from Carlyle to Yeats* (Columbia, 1986), pp. 132f. George Levine, *The Realistic Imagination: English fiction from Frankenstein to Lady Chatterley* (Chicago, 1981), pp. 16–17, arguing convincingly that the post-modern distinction is not new, demonstrates that Eliot was fully conscious of it.

2. *Westminster Review*, 66 (July, 1856), 55. For the identification of the 'great novelist' to whom she refers in this essay, see Gordon S. Haight, *George Eliot: a biography* (Oxford, 1978), p. 202.

3. 'The Sad Fortunes of the Reverend Amos Barton' in *Scenes of Clerical Life*, 1:64. As there is no definitive edition of George Eliot's novels, the Clarendon edition still being in process, I have used the Cabinet edition of her *Works* (Boston, 1901) for all quotations.

4. Mario Praz, *The Hero in Eclipse in Victorian Fiction* (trans. Angus Davidson) (Oxford, 1969), pp. 319f. On the change in target population, cf. Q.D. Leavis's classic study, *Fiction and the Reading Public* (London, 1932), pp. 143–60. The bourgeois source of the nineteenth-century novel is discussed interestingly in Arnold Hauser, *The Social History of Art* (trans. Stanley Godman) (New York, 1951), 4:132f., while Richard D. Altick, *The English Common Reader* (Chicago, 1957), has noted how difficult it still was for the hard-working lower classes to find time, energy, and even appropriate lighting conditions for the reading of books despite the growing interest.

5. Hugh Witemeyer, *George Eliot and the Visual Arts* (New Haven, 1979), especially pp. 106f., and Joseph Wiesenfarth, '*Middlemarch*: the language of art', *PMLA*, 97 (1982), 363.

6. *Adam Bede*, 1:246.

7. Karl Popper, *Theorie und Realitat* (edited by H. Albert) (Tübingen, 1964), pp. 87–102.

8. Hans Robert Jauss, *Toward an Aesthetic of Reception* (trans. Timothy Bahti) (Minneapolis, 1982).

9.   Courbet, from a letter in the *Courrier du dimanche* dated 25 December, 1861. There is a valuable account of this art movement in Linda Nochlin, *Realism* (New York, 1976), and a helpful collection of sources and documents in her earlier *Realism and Tradition in Art, 1848–1900* (Englewood Cliffs, NJ, 1966).

10. Quotation from *Adam Bede*, in Gillian Beer, *George Eliot* (Brighton, 1986), p. 61.

11. In her review of the third volume of Ruskin's *Modern Painters* in the *Westminster Review*, 65 (1856). Lewes's essay on 'The Lady Novelists' in the *Westminster Review*, July, 1852 had argued for a profounder awareness in literature of the feelings and sufferings of common humanity, and those views were expanded in his essay on 'Realism in Art' published in the same journal in October, 1858. The connection between the two in relation to this aspect of Eliot's work is discussed in George Levine, 'George Eliot's Hypothesis of Reality', *Nineteenth-Century Fiction*, 35 (1980), 1. See also, G.A.W. Davis, 'Ruskin's *Modern Painters* and George Eliot's Concept of Realism', *ELN*, 18 (1981), 194; and, for the philosophical background, Valerie A. Dodd, *George Eliot: an intellectual life* (London, 1990), especially pp. 261f.

12. From an unsigned review by Lewes, entitled 'Realism in Art: recent German fiction' in the *Westminster Review* of 1858, quoted in John P. McGowan, *Representation and Revelation*, p. 132. See also John Murdoch, 'English Realism: George Eliot and the Pre-Raphaelites', *Journal of the Warburg and Courtauld Institutes*, 37 (1974), 313.

13. *Letters* (ed. Gordon S. Haight) (New Haven, 1954–55), 2:291, 2: 344–5, and 347–9; and on Dutch art, 2:292. U.C. Knoepflmacher, *George Eliot's Early Novels: the limits of realism* (Berkeley, 1968) explored the conflict expressed in her novels between her faith in some higher ethical ideal (subsequent to the loss of her religious belief) and her commitment to the actuality of this world. He notes correctly that Eliot's pursuit of realism applies to the earlier part of her career and that in her later work she began to desert that principle in favour of idealism. See also Ian Adam, 'The Structure of Realisms in *Adam Bede*', *Nineteenth-Century Fiction*, 30 (1975), 127, and, for the relationship to painting, Joseph Wiesenfarth, '*Middlemarch*: the Language of Art', *Publications of the Modern Language Association*, 97 (1982), 363.

14. The response to Courbet's work is discussed in G. Mack, *Gustave Courbet* (New York, 1951), pp. 143–6.

15. Roland Barthes, *S/Z* (Paris, 1970), p. 16.

16. *Scenes of Clerical Life*, 1:33 and 58.

17. For George Eliot's connection with the French realistic novel, cf. note 30 below, and the comments related to it within the text.

18. Daniel Cottom, *Social Figures: George Eliot, social history, and literary representation* (Minn., 1987) provides an essentially Marxist reading of these changes.

19. Nochlin, *Realism and Tradition*, pp. 50–3. See also Charles Rosen and Henri Zerner, *Romanticism and Realism: the mythology of nineteenth-century art* (New York, 1984).

20. *Adam Bede*, 1:270.

21. Marjorie H. Nicolson, *Newton Demands the Muse* (Princeton, 1946) discussed the way Newton's discovery of the spectrum affected the concept of light in English literature of the late seventeenth and early eighteenth centuries.

22. The beginnings of the modern Zionist movement in terms of a nationalist revival have been generally related by historians to the 1896 appearance of Theodore Herzl's *Der Judenstaat*, published some twenty years after *Daniel Deronda*.

23. *Adam Bede*, 1:9.

24. *Adam Bede*, 1:3–4. For an allegorical reading of *The Wheat Sifters*, interpreted as a projection on to the agricultural scene of the painter's own craft, see Michael Fried, *Courbet's Realism* (Chicago, 1990), pp. 152–5.

25. Although Alphonse Legros was French by birth and upbringing, he settled in England in 1863 and became part of the English artistic scene. Paintings devoted to the suffering of the poor are examined in Julian Treuherz (ed.), *Hard Times: social realism in Victorian art* (London, 1987), produced for a collection exhibited in 1988 at the Manchester Art Galleries, the Rijksmuseum, and the Yale Center for British Art.

26. Quoted, without source, in Linda Nochlin, *Realism*, pp. 90 and 113. The growing interest in the lower classes as subject for the novel is documented in P.J. Keating, *The Working Classes in Victorian Fiction* (New York, 1971).

27. *Scenes of Clerical Life*, 1:2. That aspect is examined in Henry Auster, *Regionalism in the Early Novels of George Eliot* (Cambridge, Mass., 1970).

28. Details of the reaction to architectural 'restoration' can be found in E.P. Thompson, *William Morris: romantic to revolutionary* (New York, 1976), pp. 228–41. The changes, structural and theological, effected at this time within the smaller country churches are examined in Olive Cook and Graham Hutton, *English Parish Churches* (London, 1976), pp. 211f.

29. The attack appeared in *Household Words*, May, 1856.

30. Quoted in William J. Hyde, 'George Eliot and the Climate of Realism', *Publications of the Modern Language Association*, 72 (1957), 147. Her relationship to the European novel is discussed, primarily in Marxist terms, in Georg Lukàcs, *Studies in European Realism* (New York, 1964). Barbara Smalley, *George Eliot and Flaubert: pioneers of the modern novel* (Athens, Ohio, 1974) comments on the paucity of studies connecting Eliot with the French novelists, but confines her own study of those authors to their psychological concern with the inner life of their characters rather than to the attempt at realistic depiction.

31. Erich Auerbach, *Mimesis: the representation of reality in western literature* (trans. William Trask) (New York, 1957), pp. 407 and 417–18.

5 HOPKINS AS POETIC INNOVATOR

1. Cf. Roland Barthes, *Writing Degree Zero* (New York, 1979), especially pp. 63f.

2. *The Wreck of the Deutschland*, stanza 4. Quotations from Hopkins' poems throughout this chapter are from the Oxford Authors text, edited by Catherine Phillips (Oxford, 1990), a corrected version of the 1986 edition.

3. The break-away from Impressionism in the 1880s did not constitute in the eyes of the artists themselves a clear or public dissociation from that mode, nor did they form a homogeneous group with unified ideas. They saw themselves rather as advancing the ideas and practices of the Impressionists, fundamental as the change was in fact to be. The one cohesive element in Neo- and Post-Impressionism which divided them from the older group and constituted their inauguration of Modernism was, it would seem, this new conception of art as no longer mimetic but hieratic.

4. Although the recognition of Cézanne as the first Modernist painter and of Hopkins as the first Modernist poet needs no substantiation, cf. for confirmation such standard texts as Linda Nochlin, *Impressionism and Post-Impressionism: sources and documents* (Englewood Cliffs, 1966), p. 83, and David Perkins, *A History of Modern Poetry: modernism and after* (Cambridge Ma., 1987), p. 129.

5. Wordsworth's *Preface to the Lyrical Ballads,* championing the use there of 'language really used by men', rejects '. . . the false criticism which has been applied to Poetry in which the language closely resembles that of life and nature.'

6. Cf. Cézanne's liaison with Hortense Fiquet, whom he only married after sixteen years in order to legitimize their son retrospectively. Gauguin's affairs with native women in Tahiti and Toulouse-Lautrec's scenes of Parisian brothels did much to further this popular view. See John Rewald, *Paul Cézanne: a biography* (New York, 1968), pp. 111–12.

7. Henry James' dismissal of the Impressionists is reprinted in *The Painter's Eye: notes and essays on the pictorial arts by Henry James* (edited by John L. Sweeney) (Cambridge, Mass., 1956), pp. 114–15. There is a well-known attempt to connect Hopkins with James stylistically in Georgio Melchiori, *The Tightrope Walkers: studies of Mannerism in modern English literature* (London, 1956), but Melchiori's book is typical of the initial responses to Sypher's *Four Stages of Renaissance Style,* identifying as 'manneristic' anything that happens to be idiosyncratic or highly personalized. See also Graham Storey, 'Hopkins as a Mannerist', *Studies in the Literary Imagination,* 21 (1988), 77.

8. Letter to Baillie, 10 July, 1863 in *Further Letters of Gerard Manley Hopkins* (edited by C.C. Abbott) (Oxford, 1956), p. 201. For his lessening interest in the Pre-Raphaelites, see Robert B. Martin, *Gerard Manley Hopkins: a very private life* (London, 1991), pp. 72–3.

9. Pissarro's wife contemplated suicide in despair at their poverty. In February 1890, Theo managed to sell a painting by Van Gogh, *The Red Vineyard,* at approximately the time that Toulouse-Lautrec, in a famous incident, challenged De Groux to a duel for having, in public, called Van Gogh an ignoramus and a charlatan. Details are recorded in John Rewald's two volumes on this period, his *History*

of Impressionism (New York, 1980, orig. 1946), p. 431; and his *Post-Impressionism: from Van Gogh to Gauguin* (New York, 1956), p. 374.

10. Roger Fry's review of the 1906 exhibition, held by the International Society at the New Gallery and containing paintings by Cézanne. There are useful collections of reviews and comments representing the English response to the French school in Kate Flint (ed.), *Impressionism in England: the critical reception* (London, 1984) and J.B. Bullen (ed.), *Post-Impressionists in England* (London, 1988). S.K. Tillyard, *The Impact of Modernism 1900–1920* (London, 1988), connects the English response to Post-Impressionism with aesthetic criteria which had already been established by the Arts and Crafts Movement. There are further studies of British painters following French developments during the early twentieth century (a subject not directly related to this present chapter) in Simon Watney, *English Post-Impressionism* (London, 1980) and Laura Wortley, *British Impressionism: a garden of bright images* (London, 1988).

11. Gerard Hopkins, the poet's nephew, recalls the reaction of his generation in his 'Foreword' to W.H. Gardner, *Gerard Manley Hopkins: a study of poetic idiosyncrasy in relation to poetic tradition* (New Haven, 1948), 1:xiv.

12. Félix Fénéon, 'Le Néo-Impressionisme', *L'Art moderne*, (May 1, 1887), p. 138.

13. *Diverses Choses* (1896–7), an unpublished manuscript by Gauguin, quoted in Herschel B. Chipp, *Theories of Modern Art* (Berkeley, 1968), p. 66, and Strindberg's letter to Gauguin, 1 February, 1895.

14. The comments on this canvas appear in two successive letters from Van Gogh to his brother, in *The Complete Letters of Vincent Van Gogh* (Greenwich, 1958), 3:86 and 89.

15. Robert Bridges' letter has not been preserved, but Hopkins quotes the phrase 'presumptious jugglery' in his reply, whimsically rejecting it not because of its application to his poem but on the grounds that the adjective is unacceptable English usage. See *The Letters of Gerard Manley Hopkins to Robert Bridges* (edited by C.C. Abbott) (Oxford, 1955), p. 46.

16. *The Wreck of the Deutschland*, lines 210–13.

17. Clement Barraud, S.J., 'Recollections of Father Gerard Hopkins', *The Month*, July, 1891.

18. *Letters to Bridges*, pp. 66, 50, and 265–6 (my emphasis), respectively.

19. *Letters to Bridges*, p. 46.

20. *Letters to Bridges*, p. 265. The convoluted syntax of the poetry is discussed in Todd K. Bender, *Gerard Manley Hopkins: the classical background and critical reception* (Baltimore, 1966), pp. 97f., and in Bernard Bergonzi, *Gerard Manley Hopkins* (New York, 1977), pp. 71f.

21. *The Journals and Papers of Gerard Manley Hopkins* (edited by Humphry House and Graham Storey) (Oxford, 1959), pp. 270–1.

22. *Letters to Bridges*, p. 66.

23. Gauguin, *Diverses Choses*, ed. cit., and *A Sketchbook*, trans. Raymond Cogniat (New York, n.d.), p. 62.

24. Michel-Eugène Chevreul, *La loi du contraste . . .* (Paris, 1839) 2:1:78.

25. Robert Wilhelm Bunsen had worked together with G.R. Kirchoff around 1859 on new methods of spectrum analysis, while Ogden N. Rood's *Modern Chromatics* (New York, 1879) was read by Seurat in French translation.

26. Delacroix seems to have been alone in the interest he took in Chevreul's discoveries, but his proposed meeting with Chevreul never took place. Delacroix's experimentation with colour was later seized upon by certain Post-Impressionists to justify their own experiments, as in Signac's *D'Eugène Delacroix au néo-impressionisme* (Paris, 1899). See Phoebe Pool, *Impressionism* (London, 1967), pp. 26–7. The importance of spectral analysis in the work of Seurat and others was admirably defined at the time in Félix Fénéon's study, *Les Impressionistes en 1886*, which appeared in response to the exhibition of that year and helped publicize their ideas.

27. O.B. Hardison, Jr., *Christian Rite and Christian Drama in the Middle Ages: essays in the origins and early history of modern drama* (Baltimore, 1965), especially the opening chapters. His insights into the evolutionary assumptions of nineteenth-century criticism were developed in Stanley J. Kahrl, *Traditions of Medieval English Drama* (Pittsburgh, 1975). The broader impact of evolutionism upon Victorian thought is examined in Jerome H. Buckley, *The Triumph of Time: a study of the Victorian concepts of time, history, progress and decadence* (Cambridge, Mass., 1966), and the effects upon the novel most recently in Gillian Beer, *Darwin's Plots: evolutionary narrative in Darwin, George Eliot and nineteenth-century fiction* (London, 1983), and George Levine, *Darwin and the Novelists: patterns of science in Victorian fiction* (Cambridge, Mass., 1988).

28. Bishop Thomas Burnet's widely-read *Sacred Theory of the Earth*, published in 1681 and based upon contemporary scientific findings, argued that the divinely-sent Flood had, as a second stage in the process of Creation, wiped away the beauty of a still Paradisial world, replacing it with raging oceans, bleak mountains, and desert wastes in punishment for human sin and corruption.

29. The classic account of 'plenitudinism' is, of course, A.O. Lovejoy, *The Great Chain of Being: a study of the history of an idea* (New York, 1960, originally 1936). The eighteenth-century manifestations were examined in further detail in M.C. Battestin, *The Providence of Wit: aspects of form in Augustan literature and the arts* (Oxford, 1974), which relates to that theory the formal literary genres of that time.

30. Charles Lyell, *Principles of Geology* (Philadelphia, 1837), 1:166, and Charles Darwin *Origin of Species* (London, 1872) chapter xv.

31. In a letter by Ruskin dated 24 May, 1851, in *Works* (London, 1903–12), 26:115. The importance of reciprocity in Darwin's theory is discussed in P. Kropotkin, *Mutual Aid: a factor of evolution* (New York, 1916), originally published in 1902.

32. Discussed in my *Milton and the Baroque* (London, 1980), pp. 22f.

33. Julius Laforgue, in an article originally published in 1883 and reprinted in *Mélanges posthumes* (Paris, 1903), related Impressionism to evolutionary theory but in a very different way from that suggested here.

He argued that the innovation of these painters represented a more advanced stage in the evolution of the human eye, now more sensitive to subtle nuances of colour. Seurat, during the period of his studies with Mathias Duval, applied Darwinist theory to examining the physiognomy of humans and animals. See Albert Boime, 'The Teaching of Fine Arts and the Avant-Garde in France during the Second Half of the Nineteenth Century', *Arts Magazine*, 60 (1985), p. 50.

34. Richard Shiff, *Cézanne and the End of Impressionism* (Chicago, 1984), p. 66.

35. Emile Bernard, 'Paul Cézanne', *L'Occident*, (July, 1904), 23.

36. William Innes Homer, *Seurat and the Science of Painting* (Cambridge, Mass., 1964), p. 69. Homer was the first to recognize that Signac's retrospective account of Neo-Impressionism, long regarded as authoritative, was in fact misleading in many respects, overstressing the debt to Delacroix and underplaying the scientific aspects of their work in order to lend dignity to a movement still under attack. I am grateful to Homer's book for many insights into the technicalities of pointillist painting. See also Floyd Ratliff's account of *Paul Signac and Color in Neo-Impressionism*, originally published in French in 1921, recently made available in an English translation by Willa Silverman (New York, 1992).

37. Paul Signac, 'Les Besoins individuels et la peinture', *Encyclopédie française* xvi, 16.

38. Fénéon, 'Signac' in *Les Hommes d'aujourd'hui*, viii (1890).

39. 'As for stippling *[le pointillé]* and making haloes and other things, I think they are real discoveries, but we must already see to it that this technique does not become a universal dogma any more than any other.' Letter to Theo, 26 August, 1888.

40. 'Lecture on Rhythm and Other Structural Parts of Rhetoric-Verse' in *Journals and Papers*, p. 269.

41. For Hopkins' knowledge of Müller's work, see James Milroy, *The Language of Gerard Manley Hopkins* (London, 1977), pp. 33f., and Cary H. Plotkin, *The Tenth Muse: Victorian philology and the genesis of the poetic language of Gerard Manley Hopkins* (Carbondale, 1989), pp. 65f. T. Zaniello, *Hopkins in the Age of Darwin* (Iowa City, 1988) offers a general survey of the interest in evolutionary theory at the time Hopkins was a student at Oxford. See also Peter Morton, *The Vital Science: biology and the literary imagination, 1860–1900* (London, 1984).

42. An entry in his diary, 9 September, 1864, in *Journals and Papers*, p. 15.

43. Fénéon, 'Exposition des Artistes-Indépendants', *L'Art Moderne* (27 October, 1889), p. 339.

44. *Journals and Papers*, p. 5.

45. *Letters to Bridges*, pp. 83 and 218. There is a helpful discussion of Hopkins' vocabulary and syntax structures in W.A.M. Peters, S.J., *Gerard Manley Hopkins: a critical essay towards an understanding of his poetry* (Oxford, 1948), especially pp. 62f. For his relationship to contemporary philological research, see Linda Dowling, *Language and Decadence in the Victorian Fin de Siècle* (Princeton, 1986).

46. On the practice of sketching, cf. Constable's sketch for his *Haywain*

in the Victoria and Albert Museum, which has long been admired for its vitality, but which the artist felt obligated to transform into a finished canvas before submitting it to the Royal Academy. On the continental scene, the transition has, in a fascinating study by Albert Boime, been traced to a gradual shift within the French Academy which, in the early nineteenth century, began to concentrate on the generative phase of art. He points out in his study, *The Academy and French Painting in the Nineteenth Century* (London, 1971), especially pp. 166–84, that it encouraged respect for that phase by introducing at the Ecole des Beaux-Arts, which it then controlled, a competition for compositional sketches.

47. *The Sea and the Skylark*, lines 4–7.
48. *Letters to Bridges*, p. 217. Hopkins as a student had been singled out by Jowett with the comment that he had 'never met a more promising pupil', and the poet continued his interest in classical studies. 'I have been reading the Choephori carefully', he wrote in 1887, 'and believe I have restored the text and sense almost completely in the corrupted choral odes', adding that he was thinking of submitting an article on it for the *Classical Review*. A year later, he was considering the possibility of writing an article on Greek negatives. See *Letters to Bridges*, pp. 255 and 270.
49. Michael Sprinker, *A Counterpoint of Dissonance: the aesthetics and poetry of Gerard Manley Hopkins* (Baltimore, 1980), which offers an excellent analysis of the etymological and sound elements in Hopkins' poetry, mentions Valéry's comment (p. 39) as recorded in the latter's notebook.
50. Cf. Marjorie H. Nicolson, *Science and Imagination* (Ithaca, 1956) and her *Newton Demands the Muse: Newton's Opticks and the eighteenth-century poets* (Princeton, 1946).
51. *Wreck of the Deutschland*, lines 265–9.
52. Geoffrey H. Hartman, *The Unmediated Vision: an interpretation of Wordsworth, Hopkins, Rilke, and Valéry* (New Haven, 1954), p. 49.
53. *That Nature is a Heraclitean Fire and of the comfort of the Resurrection*, 1–4.
54. Fénéon, *Les Impressionistes en 1886* (Paris, 1886).
55. *Spelt from Sibyl's Leaves*, lines 1–7.
56. Ezra Pound, *Pisan Cantos* cxv, in the New Directions edition of *The Cantos* (New York, 1983), p. 794. T.E. Hulme, a primary influence upon Pound, maintained that thought, preceding formulation into language, consists of the simultaneous presentation to the mind of two different images, and had argued accordingly that images in verse are not mere decoration '. . . but the very essence of an intuitive language.' See his 'Romanticism and Classicism' in *Speculations* (New York, 1924), pp. 134–5, a collection of his essays published posthumously.
57. *Hurrahing in Harvest*, lines 1–8. His discussion of what he called the 'Parnassian' habit of using elevated discourse as a substitute for true poetic creativity, a tendency he relates primarily to Wordsworth, appears in *Further Letters*, pp. 217f.

58. This eclecticism, whereby the choice of scriptural themes in each era reflects contemporary cultural shifts, was examined in my *Biblical Drama in England: from the Middle Ages to the Present Day* (London, 1968). For a more recent application of that approach, cf. Gary Taylor, *Re-Inventing Shakespeare: a cultural history from the Restoration to the Present* (New York, 1989), which studies the reinterpretations of and responses to Shakespeare's works in accordance with the changing proclivities of successive generations.

59. George Herbert, *The Windows*, lines 1–4.

60. *The Windhover*, lines 1–5. For close studies of this poem, see Herbert Marshall McLuhan, 'The Analogical Mirrors', *Kenyon Review*, (1944), reprinted in Geoffrey H. Hartman (ed.), *Hopkins: a collection of critical essays* (Englewood Cliffs, 1966), pp. 80–8, and Virginia R. Ellis, *Gerard Manley Hopkins and the Language of Mystery* (Columbia, Mo., 1991), pp. 194f.

61. The opening lines of *Pied Beauty*. Cf. Van Gogh's remark: 'The trees were superb; there was drama in each figure I was going to say, but I mean in each tree', *Letters*, 2:127.

62. *Sermons and Devotional Writings of Gerard Manley Hopkins* (edited by Christopher Devlin) (London, 1959), p. 195.

63. Van Gogh, *Letters*, 2:104. Monet wrote to Bazille in December, 1868: 'What I will do here has at least the merit that it will not resemble [the work of] anyone else . . . because it will be simply the expression of what I shall have personally deeply felt.'

64. *The Candle Indoors*, lines 1–8.

65. Van Gogh, inspired by Thomas à Kempis' *Imitation of Christ*, records in a letter to his brother in July 1878 how, in his attempt to work among the poor as an evangelist preacher of the Gospel, his novitiate had not been renewed by the authorities. A few years later, Van Gogh declared that 'the God of clergymen' was dead for him, and that he now believed only in a divine presence. There is an indication of the transference of his devotion to the sphere of aesthetics in his comment that the change of faith had not produced in him a mood of melancholy, as painting was now becoming his absorbing occupation. He also commented later in life: 'That does not keep me from being in terrible need of – shall I say the word? – of religion. Then I go out at night to paint the stars.' See *Complete Letters*, 1:288 and 3:56. There is a valuable discussion of the mystical and religious elements within Van Gogh's paintings in Robert Rosenblum, *Modern Painting and the Northern Romantic Tradition: Friedrich to Rothko* (New York, 1975), pp. 71–100.

66. Recorded in M. Denis, *Théories, 1890–1910, du Symbolisme et de Gauguin vers un nouvel ordre classique* (Paris, 1912), p. 163.

67. *Journals and Papers*, p. 126.

68. *The Starlight Night*, lines 2–7. On the use of images and compound adjectives in this poem, cf. Paul L. Mariani, *A Commentary on the Complete Poems of Gerard Manley Hopkins* (Ithaca, 1970), p. 335. M. Schapiro, *Vincent Van Gogh* (New York, 1950), pp. 33 and 100, while acknowledging the painter's rejection of scriptural allusion, believes that the

canvas, *The Starry Night*, and the pen-and-ink version here reproduced may have been inspired by the apocalyptic theme in the *Book
of Revelations*.

6   THE ART OF HENRY JAMES

1.   Henry James, *Partial Portraits* (London, 1888), p. 378.
2.   Preface to *The Portrait of a Lady*, written for the New York edition of
       1908 (3:x–xi). All subsequent quotations are from the same edition.
       James's image of the house of fiction is interestingly examined in
       Ellen E. Frank, *Literary Architecture: essays towards a tradition* (Berkeley,
       1979), pp. 172f. On the author's reservations concerning the Dutch
       artists, cf. his review of the 1871 acquisitions by the Metropolitan
       Museum, describing the Dutch works among them as being pleasant
       but lacking the intellectualism and stimulation of the imaginative
       faculty which were to be found in the finest paintings.
3.   *Notes of a Son and Brother* (New York, 1914), pp. 81 and 97, and *A Small
       Boy and Others* (New York, 1913), p. 364. Another edition of the latter
       volume was published in New York in the same year, but with dif-
       ferent pagination, the reference there being p. 361.
4.   Edwin T. Bowden, *The Themes of Henry James: a system of observa-
       tion through the visual arts* (New Haven, 1956); Viola H. Winner, *Henry
       James and the Visual Arts* (Charlottesville, 1970); Marianna Torgovnick,
       The Visual Arts, Pictorialism, and the Novel: James, Lawrence, and Woolf
       (Princeton, 1985); and Adeline R. Tintner, *The Museum World of Henry
       James* (Ann Arbor, 1986), a book-length study developed from her
       article, 'The Spoils of Henry James', *Publications of the Modern Lan-
       guage Association*, 61 (1946), 239. Laurence B. Holland, *The Expense of
       Vision: essays on the craft of Henry James* (Princeton, 1964) effectively
       applies to the novels Gombrich's conception of representationalism
       in art.
5.   *A Small Boy*, p. 328 (318 in the variant pagination).
6.   In a letter to Edmund Gosse in 1894, in *Letters* (edited by Leon Edel)
       (Cambridge, Mass., 1974–84), 3:492, where he adds a grudging
       admission that Pater '. . . is not of the little day – but of the longer
       time.' James' resistance to Pater is discussed in Adeline R. Tintner's
       subsequent study, *The Book World of Henry James: appropriating the
       classics* (Ann Arbor, 1987), especially pp. 146f.
7.   Quoted in E.V. Lucas, *Edwin Austin Abbey, Royal Academician: the record
       of his life and work* (New York, 1921) 1:416. The letter to Abbey, dated
       1906, is not included in Edel's collection. In a letter to his mother in
       1869 (*Letters*, 1:103), James recorded that his meeting with Ruskin
       confirmed the impression obtained from the latter's writings that
       Ruskin, '. . . has been scared back by the grim face of reality into the
       world of unreason and illusion, and that he wanders there without
       a compass and a guide . . .'
8.   *The Author of Beltraffio*, 16:24.

9. *Letters*, 9:372.
10. James's comments on Beardsley appear in the New York preface to *The Lesson of the Master*, 15:vi and in *Letters*, 4:691–2, while his comment on the Yellow Book is in *Letters*, 3:482. Camille Paglia, *Sexual Personae: art and decadence from Nefertiti to Emily Dickinson* (New Haven, 1990), p. 619, perceives only the negative qualities in James, castigating him for the Decadent aestheticism of his imagery whereby, she maintains, he joins '... Late Romantic sexual perversity to English high comedy of Carrollian absurdity ...' Some years ago, Giorgio Melchiori, *The Tightrope Walkers: studies of Mannerism in modern English literature* (London, 1956), pp. 13f., suggested similarities between Henry James and Gerard Manley Hopkins in terms of their complex syntactical structures and artificial language. Melchiori's assumption that Mannerism is a recurrent phenomenon, the modern era representing a later phase of the seventeenth-century version, was argued more fully in Arnold Hauser, *Mannerism: the crisis of the Renaissance and the origin of modern art* (trans. E. Mosbacher) 2 vols (New York, 1965). Persuasive as it may first seem, since both the seventeenth-century version and the modern employ convoluted and contrived forms, the theory is ultimately no more than a recognition of the so-called 'grandfather effect', whereby a generation rebelling against the ideas of its elders resembles in some respects, by process of oscillation, the ideas against which those elders had once rebelled.
11. F.O. Matthiessen, 'James and the Plastic Arts', *Kenyon Review*, 5 (1943), 535; Charles R. Anderson, *Person, Place, and Thing in Henry James's Novels* (Durham, NC, 1977), pp. 238f.; and Winner, pp. 88–9. The parallel is questioned by Tintner, pp. 108–9 and by Torgovnick, pp. 178–9, but has recently been mildly re-approved in Millicent Bell, *Meaning in Henry James* (Cambridge, Mass., 1991), pp. 4–7.
12. Cf. H. Peter Stowell, *Literary Impressionism: James and Chekhov* (Athens, Ga., 1980), especially pp. 48–9, and Percy Lubbock, *The Craft of Fiction* (New York, 1921), pp. 161f. Viola Winner, sceptical towards the influence of the Impressionists on James, suggests (p. 89) that such indebtedness applies only to his sense of the momentary and transitory nature of phenomena. But, as Morse Peckham argued long ago, that concern with ephemerality or changeability is no less characteristic of the Romantic imagination, and James would therefore have required no further guidance on that point from the Impressionists. Cf. Morse Peckham, 'A Theory of Romanticism' (1951) reprinted in his *The Triumph of Romanticism: collected essays* (Columbia, 1970) and, for an elaboration of that idea, Thomas McFarland, *Romanticism and the Forms of Ruin: Wordsworth, Coleridge, and modalities of fragmentation* (Princeton, 1981), especially pp. 276f.
13. *The Painter's Eye: notes and essays on the pictorial arts by Henry James* (selected and edited by John L. Sweeney) (Cambridge, Mass., 1956) reprints the comments on Whistler on p. 143, and on the Impressionists in general on pp. 114–15. Sargent, although a declared admirer of the Impressionists, was in practice only partially within that movement. Although his rougher brushwork revealed certain affinities,

the portraits, brilliant as they are, remain comparatively conventional in their treatment of their subjects. This conservatism is rightly noted in Barbara Novak, *American Painting of the Nineteenth Century: realism, idealism and the American experience* (New York, 1979), p. 243.

14.   In his essay, 'New England: an Autumn Impression' (1905), reprinted in *The American Scene*, he writes of '. . . wondrous examples of Manet, of Dégas, of Claude Monet, of Whistler, of other rare recent hands . . .' By then, however, he had completed all his novels, including *The Golden Bowl* (1904).

15.   *The Reverberator*, 13:35 and 40–1, *Roderick Hudson*, 1:362, and *The Tragic Muse*, 8:113.

16.   Robert L. Gale, *The Caught Image: figurative language in the fiction of Henry James* (Chapel Hill, 1964), p. 120, notes that the artists most frequently referred to in the imagery of the novels are Titian and Holbein, followed by Veronese, Gainsborough, Van Dyck, Michelangelo, Raphael and Velasquez. But that listing does not seem to reflect James's own preferences, as Tintoretto, the artist he most admired, emerges very low in this statistical listing.

17.   Jonathan Freedman's *Professions of Taste: Henry James, British Aestheticism, and commodity culture* (Stanford, 1990), which appeared after this chapter was completed, has at last acknowledged James' close relationship to the aesthetic movement, expressing a surprise similar to my own at the way that relationship has been ignored or suppressed in the otherwise exhaustive critical studies of James' sources during the past twenty years. Freedman analyses with admirable sophistication the philosophical subtleties of the movement, the socio-political implications of its response to an emergent commodity culture, and James' uneasy adoption and rejection of certain of its principles. But our approaches are very different, his study concentrating upon the political, philosophical and socio-economic aspects of Aestheticism as they affected James' writing, where my own interest is in the art works themselves, the specific paintings and artefacts produced by Art Nouveau and their relationship to James' stylistic and thematic innovations.

18.   Alexander Pope, 'An Essay on Criticism', 68f., in *Poems* (edited by John Butts) (New Haven, 1963), p. 146.

19.   George J. Romanes, *A Candid Examination of Theism* (Boston, 1878), p. 171, which he published under the pseudonym 'Physicus'. Thomas Huxley, who retained his optimism somewhat longer, wrote in his essay 'Science and Morals' (1886) of '. . . the order which pervades the seeming disorder of the world; the great drama of evolution, with its full share of pity and terror, but also with abundant goodness and beauty . . .' There is a perceptive discussion of the impact of Darwinism in that period in Peter Morton, *The Vital Science: biology and the literary imagination, 1860–1900* (London, 1984).

20.   Historians such as Aslin have warned against confusing Art Nouveau with the Aesthetic movement that preceded it, and I am aware of the important distinctions to be made between them. But both movements are, I would argue, clearly related in their shift away from the ideal-

ization of Nature to the idealization of the artefact. It is in that sense that I am comparing them here. See Elizabeth Aslin, *The Aesthetic Movement: prelude to Art Nouveau* (New York, 1969).

21. Oscar Wilde, 'The Critic as Artist' in *Complete Works* (New York, 1923) 5:185. He remarks there (5:236) that the nineteenth century was a turning point in history '. . . simply on account of the work of two men, Darwin and Renan, the one the critic of the Book of Nature, the other the critic of the books of God.' Adeline Tintner, in her important essay of 1946 cited above, cursorily mentions the possible relationship of James's early fiction to the Art-for-Art's-sake movement but examines the point no further, claiming moreover that *The Portrait of a Lady* marks the end of any such indebtedness. James's love–hate sentiment towards Pater's aesthetic philosophy is discussed in her article 'Pater in *The Portrait of a Lady* and *The Golden Bowl*, including some unpublished Henry James Letters', *Henry James Review*, 3 (1982), 80. Interart relationships in this period are examined in Lothar Hönnighausen, *The Symbolist Tradition in English Literature: a study of Pre-Raphaelitism and Fin de Siècle* (trans. Gisela Hönnighausen) (Cambridge, 1988).

22. G.B. Tennyson's essay on 'The Sacramental Imagination', in U.C. Knoepflmacher and G.B. Tennyson (eds), *Nature and the Victorian Imagination* (Berkeley, 1977), pp. 370f., notes the abandonment of unqualified faith in pantheism, and links that shift with the revived interest in Catholicism and the rituals of Christianity, exemplified by Coleridge's remark in *Anima Poetae*: 'Every season Nature converts me from some unloving heresy, and will make a Catholic of me at last.' See Carl Woodring, *Nature into Art: cultural transformations in nineteenth-century Britain* (Cambridge, Mass., 1989), p. 248, and Karl Beckson (ed.), *Aesthetes and Decadents of the Eighteen-Nineties* (London, 1981). There is a hint of all this in the attraction that the public ecclesiastical ceremonies and processions in Rome held for James during his earliest visit there, before the establishment of the Vatican city restricted such public rituals to its confines. His strong interest in those ceremonies is mentioned in *Letters*, 1:160.

23. Linda Dowling, *Language and Decadence in the Victorian Fin de Siècle* (Princeton, 1986). The quotation from Max Müller is from his 'Comparative Philology', *Edinburgh Review*, 94 (1851), 310. Suzanne Nalbantian, *Seeds of Decadence in the Late Nineteenth-century Novel: a crisis in values* (London, 1983), devotes one chapter to examining James in that context (pp. 37f.), but disappointingly assumes that the term Decadence is to be equated with structures or 'poetics' of postponement in his novels, that is, instances of a character's inability to seize opportunities. That is too narrow a focus to serve as an effective criterion. John R. Reed, *Decadent Style* (Athens, Ohio, 1985) provides a general survey of the movement in the various media, while the continental art forms are perceptively examined in Debora L. Silverman, *Art Nouveau in Fin-de-Siècle France: politics, psychology, and style* (Berkeley, 1989).

24. Henry Sweet, 'On the Practical Study of Language' (1884) in *Linguistics*

in Great Britain (edited by Wolfgang Kühlwein) (Tübingen, 1971),
p. 125. Bernard Shaw restricted his altered spelling to the insistence
that such abbreviations as 'don't' and 'didn't' should be printed in
his works without an apostrophe, on the grounds that flexibility of
common usage should prevail over the attempt of traditional philologists to petrify language in its inherited forms.

25.   George Eliot, *Letters* (edited by G.S. Haight) (New Haven, 1954–78),
       4:8 and Oscar Wilde, 'The Truth of Masks', appended to his 'Critic
       as Artist'. Frederic W. Farrar's 'Philology and Darwinism', *Nature*, 1
       (1870), p. 529, ventured to show how '. . . Mr Darwin's hypothesis
       may be confirmed and verified by the entirely independent researches
       of the comparative philologist.'

26.   Tiffany experimented with this medium from 1875, patenting his
       Favrile glass in 1880. He employed the technique of exposing it when
       hot to various metallic fumes and oxides in order to produce the
       iridescent effect for which it became famed.

27.   Quoted without source in Lara-Vinca Masini, *Art Nouveau*, trans-
       lated from the Italian by Linda Fairbairn (Secaucus, 1976), p. 38.

28.   Cf. Earl Miner, *The Japanese Tradition in British and American Literature*
       (Princeton, 1966); Aslin, *The Aesthetic Movement*, pp. 79f.; and Siegfried
       Wichmann, *Japonisme: the Japanese influence on Western art in the nine-
       teenth and twentieth centuries* (New York, 1980). The Japanese element
       in Van Gogh's work is not, perhaps, as obvious as in Whistler's, with
       the exception of a few canvases such as his *Bridge at Arles*; but he
       himself was conscious of its centrality, remarking in a letter to his
       brother dated 1886: 'In a way, all my work is founded on Japanese
       art.' See his *Complete Letters* (New York, 1958), no. 520.

29.   Christopher Dresser, from his caption to this illustration in *The
       Technical Educator* (London, 1870).

30.   See my *Milton and the Baroque* (London, 1980), pp. 90f.

31.   Cf. Mario Amaya, *Art Nouveau* (London, 1966), p. 37.

32.   The famous embroidered wall-hanging, *Cyclamen* by Hermann Obrist,
       received the sobriquet 'The Whiplash' after it was described in an
       article in the German magazine *Pan*: 'Its frantic movement reminds
       us of the sudden violent curves occasioned by the crack of a whip;
       now appearing as as a forceful outburst of the elements of nature, a
       stroke of lightning: now as the defiant signature of a great man, a
       conqueror.'

33.   Arthur Symons, *Studies in Prose and Verse* (London, n.d. [1904]),
       p. 291. Symons's statement: 'I affirm that it is not natural to be what
       is called "natural" any longer', and his search, like his friend Yeats,
       for a mask with which to hide his identity are discussed in Barbara
       Charlesworth (later Gelpi), *Dark Passages: the decadent consciousness in
       Victorian literature* (Madison, 1965), pp. 96f.

34.   *The Portrait of a Lady*, 4:15. His comment to H.G. Wells is recorded
       in *Letters*, 2:490.

35.   As Donald D. Stone rightly notes in his *Novelists in a Changing World:
       Meredith, James, and the transformation of English fiction in the 1880s* (Cam-
       bridge, Ma., 1972), pp. 224–45, the moral danger of James's artist-

heroes is 'that they move on a plane where conscience is replaced by artistic propriety'.

36. The moral ambiguity of James' novels has been examined in Sallie Sears, *The Negative Imagination: form and perspective in the novels of Henry James* (Ithaca, 1968). The switch in narrative 'reflectors' in this novel, the first half cultivating the Prince's perspective while the second half favours Maggie's, discourages, Sears points out, any unified moral viewpoint, balancing one against the other. With regard to the events in the story, it has been argued, in John Clair, *The Ironic Dimension in the Fiction of Henry James* (Pittsburgh, 1965), pp. 79f., that Prince Amerigo and Charlotte merely pretend to commit adultery in order to awaken Maggie from her dangerous complacency; but that interpretation has not received general acceptance.

37. From a letter written in 1878 and published in his *The Gentle Art of Making Enemies* (London, 1890), pp. 127–8.

38. *The Golden Bowl*, 23:210.

39. On the concern with wealth in James's novels, see Jan W. Dietrichson, *The Image of Money in the American Novel of the Gilded Age* (New York, 1969), especially chapters 1 and 2; and Donald L. Mull, *Henry James's 'Sublime Economy': money as a symbolic center in the fiction* (Middletown, 1973).

40. *The Golden Bowl*, 2:3.

41. *Portrait of a Lady*, 4:194 and 4:397. Isabel's continued respect for Osmond's civilized deportment is not the sole justification for her return to Rome, which involves the final scene with Goodwood as well as her own sense of moral commitment to the consequences of her choice. But the passage quoted here does suggest on the credit side the importance in Isabel's mind of Osmond's unfailing refinement. For a general assessment of the reasons for her return, see Dorothea Krook, *The Ordeal of Consciousness in Henry James* (Cambridge, 1967), pp. 357–62.

42. *The Princess Casamassima*, 5:22–3.

43. *The Spoils of Poynton*, 10:31. James's sympathy with Mrs Gereth, quite apart from the evidence provided by the text, is indicated by her having been modelled on his friend Isabella Gardner, who was at that time plundering Europe for the art works that were to form the basis of the museum now bearing her name.

44. Gerald Reitlinger, *The Economics of Taste: the rise and fall of the picture market, 1760–1960* (New York, 1961) locates the golden age of such artistic remuneration in the Victorian period. The sense of discomfort at the award of such honours is discussed in Paula Gillett, *Worlds of Art: painters in Victorian society* (New Brunswick, 1990), especially p. 17. The quotations here are from Walter Pater, *Appreciations* (London, 1889), p. 18, and from Wilde's 'Critic as Artist', *Complete Works*, 5:211–12. Pater's aesthetic standards have been interestingly discussed in Wolfgang Iser, *Walter Pater: the aesthetic moment* (translated by D.H. Wilson) (Cambridge, 1987), pp. 46f. and in Paul Barolsky, *Walter Pater's 'Renaissance'* (London, 1987).

45. Frank Colebrook in a lecture entitled *William Morris, Master Printer*

delivered in November 1896 and recently republished (Council Bluffs, Iowa, 1989). The conflict between Morris's socialist principles and the élitist aspect of his art is discussed in E.P. Thompson, *William Morris: romantic to revolutionary* (New York, 1976), pp. 655–67.

46. *Portrait of a Lady*, 4:197 and 3:271.

47. The author's preface to the New York edition of *The Princess Casamassima*. For somewhat generalized studies of these figures, cf. Ora Segal, *The Lucid Reflector: the observer in Henry James' fiction* (New Haven, 1969); and Sister M. Corona Sharp, *The Confidante in Henry James: evolution and moral value of a fictive character* (Notre Dame, 1963).

48. *The Sacred Fount*, which was not included in the New York edition. The passage appears at the end of Chapter 2.

49. Cf. Peter K. Garrett, *Scene and Symbol from George Eliot to James Joyce: studies in a changing fictional mode* (New Haven, 1969), pp. 141–4; and Ruth B. Yeazell, *Language and Knowledge in the Later Novels of Henry James* (Chicago, 1976), pp. 13f.

50. *Portrait of a Lady*, 3:377 and 3:87.

51. *The Golden Bowl*, 23:383–84. The theme of art collecting is as pervasive in the imagery of this novel as it is in his other writings, the Prince being informed: 'You're at any rate part of his collection . . . one of the things that can only be got over here. You're a rarity, an object of beauty, an object of price' 23:12. Daniel Brudney, 'Knowledge and Silence: The Golden Bowl and Moral Philosophy', *Critical Inquiry*, 16 (1990), 397, makes out an interesting case for the moral ambiguity of the novel, seeing each protagonist as trying to behave well but prevented from doing so by his or her treatment of others as mere surfaces on which to aestheticize.

52. Torgovnick, pp. 76–80 and 84. James's use of the artist as observer and as central character is perceptively discussed in Maurice Beebe, *Ivory Towers and Sacred Founts: the artist as hero in fiction from Goethe to Joyce* (New York, 1964), pp. 197f.

53. Roland Barthes discusses the need for 'healthy' signifiers in *The Pleasure of the Text* (London, 1976), following the semiotic approach of Roman Jakobson and Morris Halle, *Fundamentals of Language* (The Hague, 1956), p. 81 and Ludwig Wittgenstein, *The Blue and Brown Books* (New York, 1965), pp. 104–9, as well as E.H. Gombrich's *Art and Illusion: a study in the psychology of pictorial representation* (Princeton, 1960). The fact that Friedrich Nietszche, in his *The Will to Power*, paragraphs 515 and 521–2, had anticipated many of their ideas on the factitiousness of art strengthens the view that it is not a modern problem. See George Levine, *The Realistic Imagination: English fiction from Frankenstein to Lady Chatterley* (Chicago, 1981), especially pp. 16–17.

54. That search for the symbolic essence rather than the reality was exemplified in the widespread interest in this period in one of the most evanescent forms of art, the dance, seemingly divorced from the physical world of nature while yet dependent upon it for its existence. Artists and sculptors vied with each other in attempting to recapture the sensational effects created by the famous dancer Löie

Fuller, swirling her long coloured scarves about her – an interest which prompted Yeats' musings on Platonic beauty and its transcendence of reality in 'Among Schoolchildren', with its concluding lines: 'O body swayed to music, O brightening glance,/ How can we know the dancer from the dance?' The centrality of the dance image in Yeats's work is discussed in Frank Kermode, *Romantic Image* (London, 1966), pp. 62–106. For sculpture inspired by Löie Fuller, cf. Agathon Léonard's remarkable bronze figure of 1900 entitled *Le jeu de l'Echarpe*.

55.   Details of the precious stones and jewels incorporated in these ornamental creatures, plants and eggs are listed in the appendix to A. Kenneth Snowman, *The Art of Carl Fabergé* (London, 1968), pp. 144–66.

56.   *The Author of Beltraffio*, 16:42–3. Leon Edel, *The Life of Henry James* (Harmondsworth, 1977), pp. 190–1, records James's acknowledgment that J.A. Symonds was the model for Ambient, but that does not, of course, exclude the possibility of authorial self-projection as Ambient discusses the task of the novelist.

57.   F.O. Matthiessen, *Henry James: the major phase* (New York, 1944), pp. 27 and 31. A more conventional account of James's preference for the European continent is offered in Christof Wegelin, *The Image of Europe in Henry James* (Dallas, 1958). Byzantium functioned also as a model of decadence and corruption for the Symbolist writers and artists of the late nineteenth century. That aspect is explored in Philippe Julian, *Dreamers of Decadence: symbolist painters of the 1890s* (London, 1974), but to the exclusion there of the more positive inspiration Byzantium offered, representing, as for Yeats, the sacredness and eternity of art. Elizabeth B. Loizeaux, *Yeats and the Visual Arts* (New Brunswick, 1986) examines his relationship to painting primarily in terms of Pre-Raphaelite influences, despite the lengthy gap in time.

58.   Preface to *Roderick Hudson*, 2:1049.

59.   Frederick C. Crews, *The Tragedy of Manners: moral drama in the later novels of Henry James* (New Haven, 1957), p. 56, argued that Strether heroically declined Miss Gostrey's offer through a desire for greater life fulfilment. But Richard Poirier, in *The Comic Sense of Henry James: a study of the early novels* (London, 1960), pp. 252–4, has challenged that view, perceiving in Strether's act a reflection of James's own tendency to withdraw from active participation in life. The conclusion of the novel reveals, he maintains, as so often in James's fiction, a 'curious discontinuity between the significances that are finally evoked and the dramatic life that has been precedently created.'

60.   F.R. Leavis, *The Great Tradition: a study of the English novel* (New York, 1954), especially pp. 202–3; Edmund Wilson, 'The Ambiguity of Henry James', first published in *Hound and Horn*, 7 (1934), 385; and Mary Cross, *Henry James: the contingencies of style* (New York, 1993), p. 3. Cf. Seymour Chatman, *The Later Style of Henry James* (Oxford, 1972), and David W. Smit, *The Language of a Master: theories of style and the late writing of Henry James* (Carbondale, 1988).

61. *The Ambassadors*, 22:238–9.
62. *The Wings of the Dove*, 19:221, and *The Ambassadors*, 22:247. The cartoon by George du Maurier appeared in *Punch*, 30 October, 1880, the caption based upon a remark attributed to Oscar Wilde; see Richard Ellmann, *Oscar Wilde* (New York, 1988), p. 45.
63. *The Tragic Muse*, 8:117–18.
64. Torgovnick, pp. 75–6. Brooke K. Horvath, 'The Life of Art, the Art of Life', *Modern Fiction Studies*, 28 (1982), 93, discusses the artists and writers in James's fiction. James's shorter tales devoted to that theme were gathered by Matthiessen in the collection *Stories of Writers and Artists* (New York, 1965). Sara S. Chapman, *Henry James's Portrait of the Writer as Hero* (London, 1990) examines only the authors in his fiction.
65. *The Lesson of the Master* is, of course, gentle comedy, mocking at Paul's assumption that Miss Fancourt will wait for him while he travels abroad for two years to mature as a writer, without his having even informed her that he was leaving. But there is a serious side to the story too, as Paul sacrifices wife, home and children to the strict demands of his art. Shlomitt Rimmon, *The Concept of Ambiguity – the Example of James* (Chicago, 1977), pp. 79f., examines this duality. I am indeed aware of the theory that James may have become impotent as a result of a childhood accident, and also that he may have been a homosexual, but both theories are mere conjecture, as Leon Edel and others have pointed out.
66. Oscar Cargill, 'Mr James's Aesthetic Mr Nash', in *Nineteenth Century Fiction*, 12 (1957), 177, first drew attention to the possibility that Gabriel Nash may have been modelled on Oscar Wilde. He notes in his *The Novels of Henry James* (New York, 1971), pp. 190–3, that James seems not to have wished the identification to be too exact. That reservation on James's part accords very closely with the theme of this present chapter, that he admired the basic principles of the movement (Nash's views are accorded considerable respect in the novel), while wishing to dissociate himself from the flamboyance and exhibitionism of Wilde himself.

Index

Index